# IN SEARCH OF PORTLAND

# *In Search of Portland*

EXPLORING A TRANSFORMING CITY

Brian Libby

Oregon State University Press Corvallis

*Oregon State University Press in Corvallis, Oregon, is located within the traditional homelands of the Marys River or Ampinefu Band of Kalapuya. Following the Willamette Valley Treaty of 1855, Kalapuya people were forcibly removed to reservations in Western Oregon. Today, living descendants of these people are a part of the Confederated Tribes of Grand Ronde Community of Oregon (grandronde.org) and the Confederated Tribes of Siletz Indians (ctsi.nsn.us).*

Library of Congress Cataloging-in-Publication Data

Names: Libby, Brian, 1972- author
Title: In search of Portland : exploring a transforming city / Brian Libby.
Description: Corvallis : Oregon State University Press, 2026. | Includes bibliographical references.
Identifiers: LCCN 2026016605 | ISBN 9781962645683 paperback | ISBN 9781962645690 ebook
Subjects: LCSH: Architecture—Oregon—Portland | Walking—Oregon—Portland | Portland (Or.) | Portland (Or.)—History | LCGFT: Guidebooks
Classification: LCC NA735.P55 L53 2026
LC record available at https://lccn.loc.gov/2026016605

∞This paper meets the requirements of ANSI/NISO Z39.48-1992 (Permanence of Paper).


First published in 2026 by Oregon State University Press
Printed in the United States of America

Maps created by Lisa Holmes (pages 7, 49, 85, 125, 181, 221)
Illustrations by Nicolai Kruger (pages 11, 33, 74, 164, 203, 256)
Cover photograph by Brian Libby featuring *Portlandia* statue by Raymond Kaskey, used by permission from the author.

**Oregon State University**
**OSU Press**

Oregon State University Press
121 The Valley Library
Corvallis OR 97331-4501
541-737-3166 • fax 541-737-3170
www.osupress.oregonstate.edu

*To Valarie Smith*

# Contents

*Hold on to the now, the here, through*
*which all future plunges to the past.*

—James Joyce, *Ulysses*

# Introduction

I've fallen in love with this city by the banks of the Willamette River. After living in much smaller and larger places, like Goldilocks, I found the right fit.

Moving to Portland in the spring of 1997, just before my twenty-fifth birthday, I was looking for a fresh start. The previous seven years I'd been crossing the country between my little hometown of McMinnville, Oregon, and New York City, where I attended college. I'd enrolled at New York University in 1990 without ever having been to the city, dreaming of becoming a rich Wall Street stockbroker and living in a skyscraper. Instead, arriving in Manhattan on a sweltering late-August afternoon, I'd been overwhelmed with culture shock. A garbage-workers' strike meant there were piles of trash on the street bigger than cars. Everyone seemed rude and pushy. I cried myself to sleep that first night. But the next morning, the outlook began to improve. Taking an elevator to the top of the old World Trade Center gave me a sense of perspective: looking out across the five boroughs, the Hudson River and New Jersey, and spotting my new home in Greenwich Village marked by the Washington Square Arch, halfway between Wall Street and Central Park. Over the ensuing days and years, I made friends with fellow students from around the country: Chicago, DC, Houston. I sampled world cuisines for the first time: Ukrainian at Veselka, Indian at Panna. I delighted in seeing Branford Marsalis at the Village Vanguard jazz club, Jean-Pierre Melville's *Le Samourai* at Film Forum, and Picasso paintings at the Museum of Modern Art. Dropping my economics major, I embraced the arts and history. Enlightened by classroom and dorm conversations, my politics became more progressive.

And yet I still missed Oregon: its vast evergreen forests, its Pacific coastline, and most of all the Willamette Valley where I grew up. I thought of how, even in downtown Portland, from certain vantage points you could still see Mount Hood. Though I loved the diverse cultures and rich history of New York, I also came to appreciate anew the West Coast's progressive, innovative spirit, and Oregon in particular: a place of dreamers.

After seven years on the East Coast, I decided to make my life in Portland, but thankfully not alone. By 1997, Valarie and I had been together for two years, and though she once had envisioned spending her life in New York, she was now ready to embrace a move west. And we loved it from the start. On weekends, we could easily drive to the Columbia Gorge for a hike or meet my parents at a Willamette Valley winery. Renting a downtown apartment behind the Portland Art Museum, we appreciated how affordable the city was compared to New York. We could work entry-level jobs and still afford to eat in great restaurants and attend symphony concerts. Portland in the nineties was experiencing a kind of beckoning, fertile betweenness, having emerged from its midcentury struggles (suburban flight, heavy-handed urban renewal, and freeway construction) to forge a new identity focused on pedestrians and public spaces, with new civic landmarks like Pioneer Courthouse Square and Waterfront Park, and dense new neighborhoods like the Pearl District reclaimed from former industrial enclaves, yet without the widespread gentrification that would come later.

Back in college, I had found something of myself writing for NYU's student newspaper, the *Washington Square News*, and resolved to make a career in journalism. In Portland, I got my professional start writing movie reviews for *Willamette Week*, while working a succession of office jobs. By 2001, when I took the plunge into full-time freelance journalism, my writing branched into wider directions. While interviewing filmmakers like David Lynch and Sofia Coppola for *Salon*, I also worked on breaking news stories for the *The New York Times*, wrote art gallery reviews for the *The Oregonian*, and profiled chefs for *Northwest Palate*.

Increasingly, though, feeling burned out on reviewing movies, I began transitioning my journalistic focus to architecture, which *Willamette Week*'s editors allowed me to write about, starting with the story of a local Frank Lloyd Wright–designed house threatened with demolition and then, in a compromise, carefully moved to a new site 20 miles away. Soon I was contributing to national design magazines like *Metropolis*, *Architectural Record*, and *Dwell*. Along the way, I realized architecture and cinema were actually alike: each begins with one or two creative authors (architects or screenwriters), yet each is both expensive and elaborate enough to require diverse professional teams to execute, and the greatest success stories of each often involve adapting to changing conditions. While most projects follow formulas and are ultimately forgettable, a few gems become truly memorable.

I also eventually realized cities themselves, not buildings, interest me most: diverse, continually evolving organisms that nurtured the wonder and complexity of creative human endeavor. While our friends began buying their first houses, Valarie and I devoted our resources to seeing great European cities like Paris, London, Amsterdam, Copenhagen, Prague, and Vienna, while I reported from Asian capitals like Tokyo and Beijing. Portland, I came to understand, was unlike most US cities in that it didn't sprawl endlessly with a soul-sucking succession of strip malls. It wasn't dominated by ubiquitous chain stores and eateries. If anything, it resembled the smaller European cities we'd visited and loved most.

Having now lived in Portland for nearly thirty years, I've seen great architecture designed by Allied Works, Kengo Kuma, and ZGF. I've seen the city lauded for its urban-planning success and given increasing attention from the rest of the world for its creative, artisanal-focused culture. Yet I've also witnessed great buildings and places demolished; although real estate development can enliven neighborhoods and districts, it can also threaten historic architecture when the old buildings aren't as big and profitable as zoning regulations allow. Nearly all cities eventually see a majority of their defining local buildings replaced, but here in Portland demolition is also a consequence of an otherwise beneficial institution: the metropolitan area's Urban Growth Boundary, which helps curtail sprawl while preserving forests and farmland, but also makes developable land in the region scarcer. Which is to say nothing of a much bigger lurking threat: an overdue Cascadia Subduction Zone earthquake, which could be far more devastating than those from California's San Andreas Fault. It made me want to document the Portland I know before it's gone.

I recently watched a time-lapse video of house plants growing and moving over several days, belying their apparent stillness from moment to moment. Similarly, learning about the century-plus evolution of so many different city blocks has illuminated for me how much Portland or any city is continuously changing. Buildings and places that I wrote about early in my career have already been demolished or transformed. Ultimately it doesn't take a massive earthquake to wipe most of the architecture away and start anew. It just takes the attrition of weather, changing zoning codes, the chance to make a buck, and one era succeeding another. The buildings that endure over hundreds of years are rare exceptions to the rule.

In recent years, I saw the COVID-19 pandemic bring at least a temporary end to Portland's boom period of the past few decades. Increasingly common since 2020 have been empty storefronts, graffiti-covered surfaces, and a rise in homelessness, fueled in part by a fentanyl epidemic. Today the city has largely rebounded from 2020, which was also made tumultuous by violent police crackdowns on racial-justice protests and catastrophic wildfires across the region. Yet Portland has not, at least in 2026, come all the way back.

I wanted this book to celebrate Portland's remaining great buildings, places, and culture while also commemorating what has been lost. But I needed a way to tie it all together—to make this more than a reference manual or guidebook. I found inspiration in H. V. Morton's 1951 book *In Search of London*, in which a longtime travel writer turned his attention home, traipsing through Britain's capital to celebrate places past and present. Imagining my own such book, I also took inspiration from the architectural walking tours I'd led, winding through the central city to visit well-known landmarks and little-known enclaves, yet never lingering too long. More like cinema than photography, a good walking tour is not just about individual stops but the total experience of moving along a city's streets, taking in a variety of neighborhoods, buildings, shops, parks, public art, and bridges: a chance to be the grand marshal in your own parade.

At the same time, the more I wrote, the more *In Search of Portland* became less about architecture and places and more about the people who have shaped the city and its culture. In some cases, it was those with a decades-long presence: individuals who chose to remain here even when greater fame and fortune might have beckoned elsewhere, or who found an adopted home after immigrating here from other places. In other cases, their time in Portland was relatively short, yet their future accomplishments made beginning here a point of local pride. This city has not given birth to many internationally famous people, and yet writing this book I became a collector of biographies.

Walking Portland's streets today, the fresh eyes with which I saw the city in 1997 may have been replaced by reading glasses. Yet I have been blessed to keep absorbing and learning and, most of all, getting out there to see places and meet people.

Admittedly, for most of my time in Portland, I thought the city's progress was continuous: a line always moving upward on the graph, with the buzz of each new cool restaurant or building opening giving way to the next. In recent years, as the city has struggled and the vacancies piled up, then given way to slow recovery, not unlike what happened in generations past, I've come to realize history is not linear but circular. New York taught me that in its moments of struggle, perhaps paradoxically, its culture and art and opportunity can thrive all the more; I think that's already happening in Portland, as the city has become more affordable again, and not subject to the kind of overspeculation that, say, replaces a beloved food-cart pod with a largely empty Ritz-Carlton Hotel. Besides, there is always the Willamette River flowing past, and Mount Hood in the distance.

*Portland Aerial Tram*

# Prelude

## *Take It From the Top*

I can feel the gondola begin to sway a little as the **Portland Aerial Tram** (2-16 SW Campus Drive) begins its descent from the Upper Tram Terminal on Marquam Hill toward the banks of the Willamette River. Goosebumps appearing on my arms, I'm reminded that in middle age I've developed a fear of heights. Yet there is such an expansive, panoramic view that soon the trepidation gives way to a sense of wonder. From this tram ride, I can take in the immensity of Portland and its diverse landscape. I don't feel dwarfed by the wide view, but part of something greater than myself.

Looking east, where the early-morning sun is blazing, I can see the peak of Mount Hood in silhouette. Local architects will tell you this mountain, even though it's 70 miles away, is the true icon of Portland's skyline. Artists take inspiration from it just as Japan's great nineteenth-century printmakers did from Mount Fuji. To the northeast, I can also see Mount St. Helens, which I watched erupt as an eight-year-old in 1980: a reminder that even mountains are not necessarily permanent, let alone architecture. Portland's incredible setting is defined largely by the way the city sits in the shadow of these peaks and ranges.

Looking down at the Willamette River, I'm grateful to live in a river city. As Portland State University urban studies professor Carl Abbott has noted, while ocean-port cities are often wealthier and more ambitious, building architectural trophies like the Space Needle and the Empire State Building, river cities are more insular yet more comfortable in their own skin. Here in Portland, while there are a few tall towers downtown, the most significant designs are instead egalitarian: small blocks that encourage pedestrian activity and bring more light to the street, plentiful parks sprinkling greenery throughout the central city, and one of the nation's first modern light-rail systems. While most West Coast cities seem designed for automobiles,

*Downtown from the Portland Aerial Tram*

with endless sprawl and strip malls, Portland retains its human scale.

Looking back from the descending tram car toward Marquam Hill and Oregon Health & Science University (OHSU), from which we've come, it occurs to me that it's a strange place for a medical school. OHSU's presence here dates to 1917, when 20 acres were donated by the Oregon-Washington Railroad, which had purchased the land sight unseen, having planned a railroad depot here before the owners realized it was a hilltop. In the late nineties, just after moving to Portland, I worked here as an administrative assistant to a neurosurgeon; a few weeks ago, I took Valarie here for a PET scan, with a view of the tram from the lobby window.

As the tram ride continues, we pass over the Lair Hill neighborhood, one of the city's oldest, where many beautiful Victorian homes remain—but only after a fight. In the 1970s, the City of Portland slated this entire neighborhood for demolition, in an overzealous act of urban renewal. Thankfully citizen opposition in Lair Hill was successful, which became an inspiration to my succeeding generation. Portland's DNA is embedded with activism: a sense that ordinary residents, if well organized, large enough in numbers, and able to make their voices heard, can overcome a powerful few.

As I look down at this tram car's shadow passing over the ground, I'm reminded that in the early 2000s, Lair Hill residents also nearly prevented this marvelous aerial tram from being built, fearful that passengers would look down voyeuristically into their houses. In that case, I'm glad the preservationists lost. A well-composed city balances preserving its treasured spaces with opening up to new possibilities.

Looking north, however, brings the vista I've really come for: a sense of downtown as a collection of buildings nestled into the landscape between the hills and the river. Most notably, there's the Wells Fargo Center, still the city's tallest building after more than fifty years. I can also see Tom McCall Waterfront Park, dedicated in 1978. I can see a succession of Willamette River bridges: the Ross Island, Hawthorne, Morrison, Burnside, Steel, Broadway, Fremont, and, nearest the lower tram terminal we're approaching, **Tilikum Crossing**, the central city's newest span, completed in 2015.

Nearing this ride's conclusion, I get a close look at South Waterfront's cluster of relatively tall buildings, including the sixteen-story Center for Health and Healing by GBD Architects, the first building erected on OHSU's extended campus, and the twenty-three-story Atwater Place condominium tower, a joint venture between GBD and Hacker Architects. Yet as we are about to touch down, I'm reminded that the Portland Aerial Tram (S Moody Avenue at Porter Street) itself is the most remarkable work of design and construction here, and one of the few truly great and timeless works of early twenty-first-century design in Portland. It's only the second urban aerial tram in the United States, after New York City's Roosevelt Island Tram. Its space-age-looking cars are beautiful, and the tram's path, down a steep hillside, over a historic neighborhood, and then over Interstate 5, was not easy to build. A ballooning budget made the tram controversial, and the completed product looked nothing like what the designer, Swiss architecture firm Angélil/Graham/

Pfenninger/Scholl, had originally proposed; yet it's an unmitigated success story: a beautiful, nimble work of engineering.

During this tram ride's final descent, my eye is drawn slightly north, to the abandoned **Zidell Yards** (3121 S Moody Avenue) barge-building facility. The company was founded by Sam Zidell in 1916 as Zidell Machinery and Supply Company. Sam's son, Emery, expanded the business to ship-breaking and

*Tilikum Crossing*

*View from Zidell facility*

rebranded the company in 1946 as the Zidell Ship Dismantling Company, answering a high postwar demand for scrap steel; over the ensuing decade-plus they dismantled more than three hundred World War II vessels. Then, in the 1960s, Zidell began constructing new barges here, completing more than 275 vessels over a half-century period. But, by the late 2010s, the company was ready to sell off its land as the South Waterfront district and the OHSU campus rose around it. In 2017, I toured the facility during its final days of operation, marveling at a massive, nearly completed barge. That day I snapped a photo looking through the barge building's rusty doors south toward the South Waterfront condo towers, as if looking from one era to another.

Zidell's owners had hoped to redevelop their site as an extension of the neighborhood, with several new residential buildings, but their land instead became frozen in time, after reaching an impasse during negotiations with the city over infrastructure costs for the roads and sewers. Now this place feels like a ghost town in the center of our metropolis. Even so, the rusty barge building, though abandoned and lifeless today, has character that the rest of South Waterfront lacks. Yet it could be gone soon as well, for this site has been eyed for a major-league baseball park. But I'll believe that when I see it.

As the tram car touches down at the station and the doors open, I am ready to begin walking. I'll be starting downtown in the West End, then zigzagging into the Pearl District, Old Town, and back into downtown again, slowly making my way east until I've reached the river. Visiting about a hundred buildings and public spaces, and in some cases commemorating long-gone places, I hope to find something greater than the sum of all this brick, mortar, glass, and steel: a remembrance of the past, and a consideration of Portland's future. The city's identity exists somewhere between the offbeat weird-haven fondly satirized on the *Portlandia* TV show, filmed during the height of early twenty-first-century boom times, and the caustic pessimism of the early post-pandemic years from which we're now emerging. To be a Portlander in good times and bad has been my privilege.

# Walk 1

# West End Beginnings

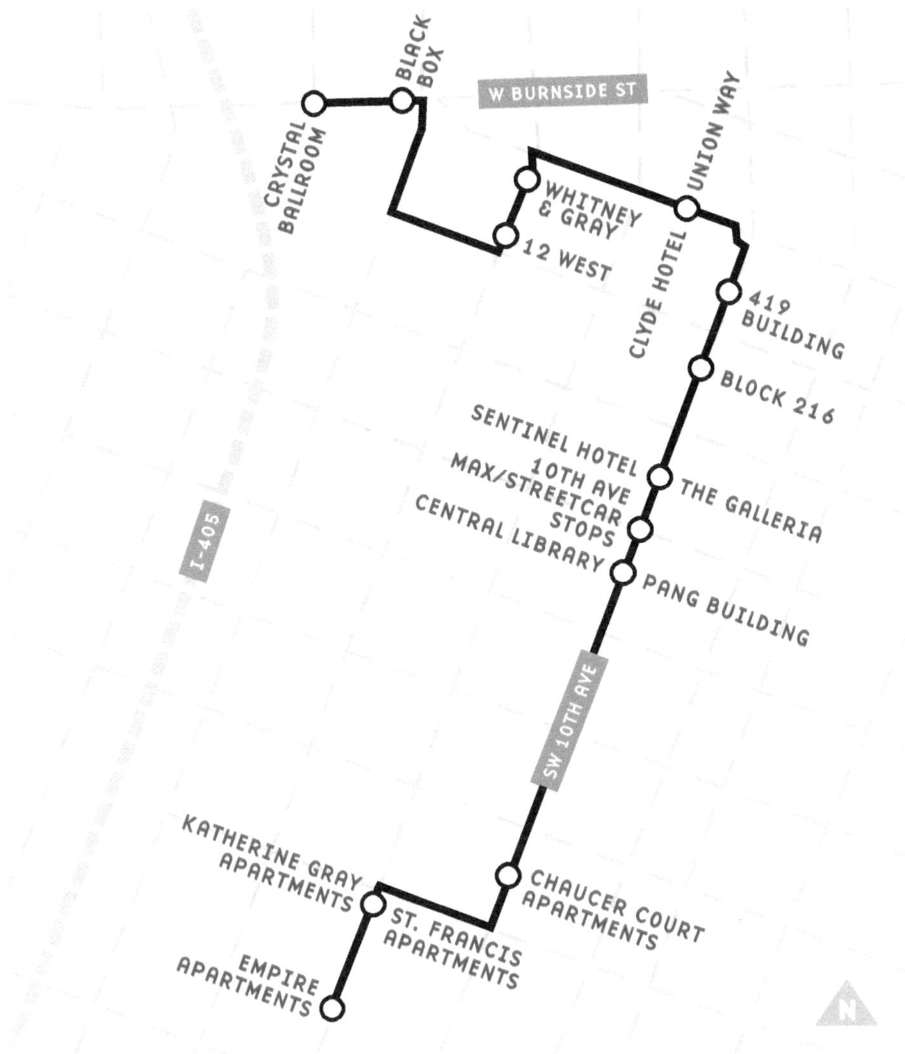

*Empire Apartments*

## *Behind the Brick*

I never expected my first apartment in Portland to be the last one left on the block. The five-story **Empire Apartments** (1217 SW Eleventh Avenue), completed in 1924 near the corner of Eleventh Avenue and Jefferson Street, was where I first lived after returning to Oregon in 1997. But standing here today at the Empire's front door, dodging the rain beneath its small awning, I realize that nearly every other surrounding building that stood here when I moved in has since been torn down.

The corner apartment building next door to the Empire is gone, replaced by a newer, taller structure. The Safeway supermarket that the Empire faced, colloquially known as the "Psycho Safeway" because of the homeless, drug-addicted, and mentally ill people cashing in cans and bottles there regularly, has been replaced by a glass-ensconced condominium tower, the Eliot. The two-story storefront building at Tenth and Jefferson is also long gone, replaced by the Museum Place apartment building. The circa-1905 Portland Korean Church (originally the First German Evangelical Church) at Tenth and Clay, long vacant, is a recent victim of arson. Of all buildings, only the Plaid Pantry convenience store, peddling cigarettes and lottery tickets here since the late seventies, has remained.

From the fourth-floor apartment that Valarie and I shared, I remember watching Princess Diana's funeral on TV. I remember pushing a shopping cart full of groceries from the supermarket across the street, up the elevator and through our front door, laughing at the incongruity and naughtiness before dutifully returning the empty cart to the store. And I remember walking to the nearby Portland Art Museum to see old foreign films at its now-demolished Berg Swan Auditorium. The Empire was a perfect place to land in Portland, until the apartment began to leak rain profusely, so much so that our lovable cool-uncle of a superintendent, Barry, affixed huge plastic sheets along the ceiling and out the window, diverting the water back outside. Barry also treated me with dignity when I was too scared to deal with a persistent mouse infestation, setting traps and disposing of what was caught. We moved out of the Empire within a year, but nearly thirty years and two residences later, Valarie and I are still together. I wish I knew what became of Barry.

The Empire could easily have been first on this block to be demolished, given how early twenty-first-century economic booms had seen taller buildings replace much of the neighborhood's urban fabric. Yet with Portland State University nearby, as well as a host of arts attractions, the Empire is doing well today, even as downtown's office towers have been slow to rebound to pre-pandemic lease rates. As I stand here on a wet gray Tuesday, apartment tenants are continuously coming and going.

My era was not the first to see architecture change here in downtown Portland's West End, which is not an official neighborhood but is located roughly between Broadway and Fourteenth Avenue, south of West Burnside. Beginning in the nineteenth century, there had been an affluent residential enclave of single-family houses here, radiating from the South Park Blocks, rendered in elaborate Italianate and Victorian styles. But after 1905's Lewis and Clark Centennial Exposition, the neighborhood grew and densified. The number of issued building permits increased fourfold, birthing many apartment buildings, fraternal lodges, and commercial structures on these sites. Today, even though much surrounding the Empire Apartments has been replaced, many of the West End's modest brick-clad residential buildings from the early twentieth century remain. That could change, though, because if the large earthquake predicted for the Pacific Northwest were to happen, these seismically unreinforced masonry structures would be the first to collapse. For now, they still have a role to play, offering relatively affordable and centrally located places to live in a time of increased overall housing unaffordability. These buildings have welcomed creative minds past and present, from filmmakers, musicians, and architects to dancers, authors, and restaurateurs. Like the city itself, they share a kind of ideal medium density: at three to six stories (sometimes called "missing middle housing"), they're not too big or too small. You can still see the horizon and maintain eye contact with people on the top floors of most of these buildings. Like in New York's Greenwich Village, where I lived during college, it's an urban setting that doesn't overwhelm.

My first few stops to begin this walk commemorate these older buildings, some still standing and some gone. First, a block north of the Empire is the site of a ramshackle old flophouse, the circa-1927 **St. Francis Hotel** (1024 SW Main Street), a location for the 1989 film *Drugstore Cowboy*, by the great director Gus Van Sant. Valarie and I had been thrilled to encounter it upon moving to the neighborhood, for we had bonded in our very first conversation, back in New York, over a mutual Van Sant fandom.

*Drugstore Cowboy* chronicles a quartet of Portland drug addicts robbing pharmacies to support their dependencies. It also portrays a friendship between Matt Dillon's lead character, Bob, and an aging junkie living at the St. Francis, Tom the Priest, played by famed Beat-era novelist William S. Burroughs. Though *Drugstore* was set in the seventies, it evokes the Portland that Valarie and I encountered in the nineties: a place for dreamers, leavened by overcast skies. "We played a game you couldn't win, to the utmost," Dillon's character says in voice-over narration as the film begins, the camera looking down on his stretcher, in an ambulance leaving the St. Francis. Later in the movie, told in flashback, the camera pans past the building's creamy brick exterior to peer through an open upstairs window, as a newly clean Bob enters his room for the

St. Francis Hotel

first time: a purgatory of varnished wood paneling, hot plates, and resignation.

Van Sant's early trilogy of Portland-set films, including 1985's *Mala Noche* and 1991's *My Own Private Idaho*, have collectively become a time capsule for the central city, when it retained a pre-gentrification, pre-Internet, and pre-smart-phone sense of mystery. Portland had emerged from World War II transformed, its population grown by a third, and become much more racially diverse. But by the mid-twentieth century, the number of people coming into downtown had dropped substantially, and for the first time the suburban population surpassed that of the city proper. Disinvestment spread, leading to dilapidated inner-city homes and boarded-up commercial buildings downtown, while dive bars and porn theaters proliferated. Amid this relative grit, the central city was affordable and accessible, and while many demolitions proliferated in districts like Old Town, much of the built environment in places like the West End and the Alphabet District to the northwest remained intact, from funky Victorian houses to humble little brick apartments. *Drugstore* and the other two trilogy films captured the unpolished beauty of these scruffy years just as they were ending, with great cinematic lyricism.

Itinerant for much of his life, Van Sant had moved to Portland as a teen when his father was hired as president of the White Stag company. After college at the Rhode Island School of Design, then living in Los Angeles and New York while working on TV commercials, he returned to Portland to make his debut feature, *Mala Noche*, based on Walt Curtis's 1977 novella about a gay man's friendship with a straight young Mexican seasonal farm worker living in Old Town. "I think all of my films are about people's relationships to their friends and adopted families," Van Sant told me in 2024. "I think pretty much all of them, you can find the same theme, which I'm not sure was a plan or anything, but was just, I guess, my viewpoint of the world. I moved around a lot, so there were a lot of adopted families."

After *Mala Noche*'s acclaim, Van Sant received offers from Hollywood studios to direct feature films, but not with the final cut he sought. So the director remained in Portland, living in a small apartment that was actually one block away from the Empire Apartments. "It looked out at the Safeway and the art museum. It was a nice little space, a very old building, I think from the turn of the century, and it was kind of going to seed," he said. "I remember the back stairway was falling apart. Eventually, they took it down, but I moved in there about '86 and lived there all the way through *Drugstore* filming."

The movie marked a turning point in the career of actor Matt Dillon, previously known best for teenage roles in 1983's *Rumble Fish* and *The Outsiders*, winning him an Independent Spirit Award. *Drugstore Cowboy* was uncharted territory for Burroughs, who had scarcely ever acted before, but whom Van Sant had first met a decade earlier in New York, hoping to cast the writer in a short film. That role never materialized, but when Van Sant came calling about *Drugstore*, Burroughs remembered him. To get Burroughs to agree to the film, Van Sant let the novelist rewrite his dialogue to sound more like something he would say, and agreed to shoot all of his scenes in one day. But Burroughs took easily to the St. Francis's flophouse milieu. "He was really into the type of city that Portland remained at that time," Van Sant remembered. "He had a cane and he pointed at things while we were walking, which he does in the film. He was pointing and saying to his assistant, 'Are you digging these old hotels? Look at that one there. Look at that one, the Kent, dig that place,' because he remembered living in these kind of rundown hotels."

When I lived just down the block from the St. Francis in 1997 and 1998, its residents would often be sitting in folding chairs out front on the sidewalk, smoking cigarettes and watching the day go by. But just a few years later, as a young journalist in 2001, I reported on the building's demolition. "At one time the white brick building with its antique interior was a stately destination for out-of-town guests and the Portland trolley proudly advertised having a stop there," I wrote in *Willamette Week*. "If there's such a thing as the nobility of poverty, then there's also a quiet grandeur in the neglected buildings of better days, defiantly unencumbered by commercialization . . . [a] hallowed seediness. This is a face of Portland that is, like the St. Francis, rapidly falling away." Today on this site is the St. Francis Apartments, an affordable housing complex completed in 2002.

The St. Francis Hotel was the first demolition of a downtown building I cared about and opened my eyes to the fact that the city was continually regenerating. It was hard to argue that the new St. Francis would give residents better, more updated, and comfortable accommodations, and yet something was being lost along the way: a connection to the past, not just the fictional past of Van Sant's movie but to the 1920s when the building was constructed, as affordable lodging for traveling businesspersons. I didn't do anything to try to stop this building's demolition, save for what I wrote in the paper. In future cases, like the Rosefriend Apartments and Memorial Coliseum, I tried to stop the wrecking ball, either through writing or activism, with a growing sense of historic preservation's importance.

While Van Sant and his crew were filming *Drugstore Cowboy*, the hotel's real residents were still living there and, in some cases, served as extras. A few years ago, curious about their fate after the building's demolition, I tracked down Bobby Weinstock, a housing placement specialist with the nonprofit Northwest Pilot Project, who had helped them relocate. "They were a very diverse group," Weinstock told me in a 2019 podcast interview, three years before his death. "There were refugees, there were low-wage workers, there were folks who were getting disability checks because of various physical and psychological ailments. There were folks who lived there for a few months and folks who were there for decades. For folks who had $75, you could rent a room for a week. It was very low-barrier, so it gave folks who might have some blemishes in their background with bad credit or past evictions or minor criminal history a way to get a place to live." The St. Francis was part of a larger safety net of modest residential hotels that helped keep people of very modest means off the street, most of which have since closed. Particularly as post-pandemic downtown Portland has struggled and homelessness proliferated, it's a reminder of the safety net we need back. Even so, whenever I'm at this corner, I think of Portland's greatest filmmaker and the elation I felt, realizing I lived on the same block as Van Sant's St. Francis.

Across Eleventh Avenue stands another unlikely architectural survivor: the handsome, brick-clad **Katherine Gray Apartments** (1115 SW Eleventh Avenue). Built in 1923 as a residence for single women called the Campbell Court Hotel (and later known as the Martha Washington), today the Georgian-style building offers 108 units of low-income affordable housing. While this portion of my walk commemorates ambitious dreamers behind these buildings' brick walls, I must also recognize misguided ambition, because the Katherine Gray is perhaps best known as the site of a 1983 bombing. It occurred during a brief period when this was known as the Hotel Rajneesh, owned by followers of the Bhagwan Shree Rajneesh, the Indian religious leader who had established a worldwide cult and created headquarters at an 80,000-acre ranch outside the small eastern Oregon town of Antelope. The Bhagwan and his followers dominated local news coverage during my early-eighties childhood.

The Hotel Rajneesh was bombed on the morning of July 29, 1983, and thankfully didn't kill anyone or irrevocably damage the building. Stephen P. Paster, linked to a Muslim fundamentalist group, was later arrested and convicted for the crime. Though in this case the Rajneesh were victims, this incident may have tipped the Bhagwan's disciples into militancy. In 1984, they attempted a bioterror attack on a restaurant in The Dalles, and in 1985 made an assassination attempt on Charles Turner, US attorney for the District of Oregon. The Rajneesh cult was

*Chaucer Court Apartments*

also highly abusive. Women taken as young children to different Rajneesh settlements later recounted having been repeatedly subjected to sexual abuse. When the Bhagwan and his chief followers were convicted of multiple crimes, he fled back to the Indian city of Pune, where the cult had begun its worldwide rise.

Walking one block east on Main Street and turning left onto Tenth Avenue, at Salmon Street is a century-old building I associate with the godmother of contemporary ballet in Portland: the **Chaucer Court Apartments** (1019 SW Tenth Avenue), completed in 1924 as the Odd Fellows Building, for the local International Order of Odd Fellows chapter, one of many such fraternal organizations located downtown in the early twentieth century. As I approach, beneath its terra-cotta entry canopy two elderly wheelchaired residents are sunning themselves, much as St. Francis tenants used to.

Looking upward, Chaucer Court's brick façade gives way to a row of cathedral style windows and a parapet of decorative crowns, in architect Ernst Kroner's blend of Tudor, Gothic Revival, and Chicago Commercial styles. Kroner began his career as a builder, constructing more than a hundred local homes, and designed several buildings throughout Oregon, including the Carnegie Library in my hometown of McMinnville. A German immigrant who was politically active, Kroner was repeatedly harassed during and after World War I but persevered, practicing architecture for more than twenty-five years following this building's completion.

Inside Chaucer Court, there are many original touches, including opalescent stained-glass windows at the entrance, giving way to a marble stairway. But I'm most interested in the former Odd Fellows meeting hall that used to exist on the building's top floor; in a period photo hanging inside Chaucer Court today, I can see the old ballroom as it existed in the 1920s, with American flags hanging from its coffered ceiling and bunting draped over its balcony, which is lined with people, as are both sides of the ballroom's main floor, amid a medal ceremony.

In the mid-twentieth century, this ballroom was the dance studio of Jacqueline Martin Schumacher, a ballerina and longtime dance instructor who became the mother of Oregon Ballet Theater, now a treasured cultural institution. "The studio was two stories, so it had high ceilings," recalls Carol Shults, a historian and former dancer who studied under Schumacher. "The huge gothic windows let in so much light. It was wonderfully conducive to classes and little performances. It was the best studio in Portland."

Raised in Portland as Jacqueline Martin, she was a pupil of Lew Christensen, a former member of revolutionary New York City Ballet choreographer George Balanchine's company, who operated a ballet school in Portland. In 1937, Christensen was hired as a lead dancer for the San Francisco Opera Ballet and named artistic director a year later. In 1940, when Balanchine produced the first full-length US production of *Swan Lake*, he cast Martin and fellow Portland student Janet Reed in the lead roles, as the White Swan and Black Swan. It was an immediate success, which prompted plans for a nationwide tour the following year—but it never happened, because of Japan's attack on Pearl Harbor and the US entry into World War II. Martin married Fred Schumacher, and in 1945 they moved back to Portland. Giving up her career as a dancer, she instead began teaching ballet classes from their home in Southeast Portland. Once established, Schumacher moved to the Odd Fellows Building, creating a studio from its former meeting hall. While her former *Swan Lake* costar Janet Reed went to New York and became a famous ballerina, Schumacher trained generations of young Portland dancers. "She was one of the most regal, elegant, gracious people: just the way she occupied space in the studio teaching," recalls another former pupil, longtime Portland dancer and instructor Linda K. Johnson. "She was so gracious and always looked perfect, her hair in a chignon and wearing a long skirt," Schumacher choreographed more than twenty ballets, and in 1976 founded the Portland Ballet Company, Oregon's first professional ballet organization, which became Oregon Ballet Theater, the city's premier dance company.

It's fitting that I've passed by buildings associated with Gus Van Sant and Jacqueline Schumacher in succession. Each was a unique creative talent who returned to Portland when they could have found greater fame in one of the country's cultural capitals. Maybe if not for World War II Schumacher might have become a famous ballerina; in Van Sant's case, he's left and come back numerous times, and currently resides in Los Angeles. Yet at key moments in their careers, they chose to come back here, and they've made lasting contributions to the city and its cultural fabric. I'm not as talented as these two, yet having moved back to Oregon from New York, forgoing the chance to build a career there or in Los Angeles (where my aspiring-filmmaker friends invited me after college to join them), I saw Van Sant and Schumacher as role models.

Continuing north on Tenth Avenue, my next destination is the **Pang Building** (822 SW Tenth Avenue), completed in 1916 as the single-story Pierce Wright Garage; a second floor was added in 1927 as part of its conversion to commercial and retail use. During the 1940s, a ground-floor storefront space on the building's south side was home to the Clover Club, where Sammy Davis Jr., before he was famous, performed as part of the Will Mastin Trio. After US Army service during World War II, Davis Jr. rejoined this family act in Portland, where his father, Sammy Davis Sr., and Mastin, his godfather, had settled. The younger Sammy quickly attracted attention, receiving glowing reviews in national jazz magazine *Downbeat*. In 1947, he received a telegram in Portland from Frank Sinatra, with an invitation to New York to perform on Sinatra's national radio show, which catapulted Davis to stardom.

From 1994 to 2006 the Pang Building was home to *Willamette Week*, the newspaper where I got my start as a journalist (and where Valarie managed the paper's personals section). For about seven years I reviewed movies, always in a secondary role to other critics, most of whom went on to bigger writing success. Dale Basye, the lead critic when I started, later wrote a series of young-adult novels for Random House first published in 2008 called *Heck*, based on Dante's *Inferno*. Kim Morgan, who took over for Dale, later co-wrote an Academy Award–nominated 2021 remake of *Nightmare Alley* with her husband, multi-Oscar-winning director Guillermo Del Toro. And David Walker, whom I wrote under after Kim, has since written award-winning comics and graphic novels for Marvel and DC Comics. But *Willamette Week*'s most acclaimed writer, who started there like me in 1998, was not a film critic, but he remains on staff today: Nigel Jaquiss, winner of the 2005 Pulitzer Prize for Investigative Reporting.

"It was a wonderful office," recalls Jaquiss of *Willamette Week*'s years in the Pang Building. "I was lucky: I got a desk looking out at Central Library, which provided a nonstop parade of people. I would know when somebody lost their job because they'd be at the library using its resources to look for their next job. Sometimes I'd walk across the street to buttonhole somebody and talk to them. Or they'd come to me; pretty much everybody who thought they had a story would just walk in and want to talk to a reporter. The newsroom was this big wide-open space with exposed rafters and newspapers stacked everywhere, probably a fire hazard. But the scale of the operation was much larger then. We had a massive staff."

Before becoming a journalist, Jaquiss had spent a decade working on Wall Street as a commodities trader, dreaming of becoming a novelist. He completed a manuscript, but failed to attract a publisher. "One of the things I learned as a trader is always have a backup plan," he says. "So I applied to journalism school." At Columbia University, Jaquiss "fell in love with investigative reporting: the nuts and bolts of using public records to build stories. I had an epiphany: that journalism is like carpentry or bricklaying: it's a craft rather than an art. But if you do it well enough, it can become artful. And while writing a novel is a solitary existence, in journalism you're constantly speaking to people, you're engaging with people, you're out in the community, and your work can have an immediate impact."

When Jaquiss and I started at *Willamette Week* amid a late nineties economic boom, the paper was at its apex, with weekly issues often well over 150 pages, and led by charismatic editor Mark Zusman and publisher Richard Meeker, who lent a touch of Woodward and Bernstein panache. Today, after the decimation of US newspapers, *Willamette Week* rarely tops 40 pages and the city's other major paper, *The Oregonian*, is a skeleton of its former self. "The revenue to pay for the kind of investigative reporting and day-to-day beat reporting we used to see twenty years ago, thirty years ago, doesn't exist anymore," he says. "Newspapers don't regularly cover county commission meetings. They don't cover school board meetings. They don't cover routine legislative hearings. That was an amazing resource for people who wanted to know what was going on in their communities and in their state. And that's all been lost. I sound like an old man crying in my beer, but it's a terrible, terrible loss."

In 2005, Jaquiss and *Willamette Week* received the first Pulitzer Prize awarded to a US alternative-weekly newspaper for investigative reporting. Jaquiss had broken the story of former Portland mayor and Oregon governor Neil Goldschmidt's sexual relationship with his children's babysitter (a minor) while in office in the seventies. Jaquiss had plenty of job opportunities after receiving the profession's highest honor, but he has remained at *Willamette Week* for more than twenty-five years, including its 2006 move to a building on Quimby Street in Northwest Portland. I actually visited that office for the first time only recently, at an open house celebrating the paper's fiftieth anniversary, a delightful chance to see many familiar friendly faces, from Zusman, Meeker, and Jaquiss to people like Brian Panganiban and Michael Donhowe from IT and ad sales, respectively, both of whom have been there since the nineties. Even so, every time I walk by this corner at Tenth and Taylor, I look to the Pang's upstairs windows and imagine the paper's offices as if they were still there.

Multnomah County Central Library

## *Cultural Crossroads*

These next six stops on Tenth Avenue all, in different ways, are (or were) places for people: each a kind of crossroads attracting diverse cultures and communities, to learn, shop, eat, and celebrate. Collectively, these are a reminder that great placemaking can occur not only in the city's most prominent and beautiful historic buildings, but also in its smallest, most humble structures. Sometimes the most enticing spots are also the most fleeting; other times they endure for a century or more.

Immediately across from the Pang Building is one of the city's foremost architectural and cultural landmarks, **Multnomah County Central Library** (801 SW Tenth Avenue). The circa-1913 building helped usher in an era of modern libraries, once reserved for only the affluent, as egalitarian places providing books to ordinary citizens.

Central Library was designed by Portland's most celebrated early twentieth-century architect: A. E. Doyle, who also was responsible for the Benson Hotel, Reed College, Civic Stadium (now Providence Park), and the Meier & Frank department store. The son of a humble builder, he apprenticed at age fourteen with the city's most prestigious architectural firm of the time, Whidden & Lewis, designers of City Hall. Doyle opened his own office in 1907, two years after the Lewis and Clark Centennial Exposition, which had prompted a population and economic boom.

Central Library's Georgian style, a version of neoclassicism, expressed the city's ambitions: to be seen as a bastion of culture in the still-wild Northwest. "Architects of Doyle's era used the idiom of historical styles to express the purpose and function of the institution," says Phil Niles, author of the Doyle biography *Beauty of the City*. "It was entirely appropriate that Central Library be Georgian because that was considered to be an American architecture and hearkened back to Thomas Jefferson. It spoke to the ideal of the library, which was to educate the voters of America and strengthen democracy."

Despite a very modest budget, the building's interior was innovative and forward-thinking, overseen by head librarian Mary Frances Isom. She had guided the institution from a subscription-based service occupying one floor of a bank building downtown to construction of its own building, accessible to all free of charge, with an accompanying eightfold growth in library-card holders. Central became one of the first US public libraries to place book stacks at the center of the building, accessible to all.

A regular patron at Central in the 1920s was a young Beverly Cleary, who went on to become an internationally renowned children's author. Cleary was often taken by her mother to the library, in order to overcome her difficulty learning to read. Later, while studying to become a librarian herself, Cleary interned at Central. After the 1950 publication of her first book, *Henry Huggins*, she went on to write more than forty children's novels, selling more than 91 million copies worldwide.

On one of my early visits to Central after moving to Portland, I encountered my aunt, Liz von Behren, working there. In these final years before Internet search engines became commonplace, one of her tasks was to answer the library's reference line, a phone service fielding patrons' questions in a wide range of topics. "We sat in a room surrounded by books, and card files for frequently asked questions, like the names of the Seven

Dwarves from *Snow White*," she recalls. "We would search out-of-town phone books and old city directories to answer certain calls. I remember being amazed by the large number of plastic surgeons in the Los Angeles yellow pages. My very first caller asked if we had passenger lists for ships bringing immigrants to the US in the nineteenth century. And yes, we did." Aunt Liz and other reference line staff also became familiar with repeat callers, like one woman who would repeatedly ask for cooking recipes to be read to her over the phone. "It was often a fun job, and we always cited our source," she adds. "I learned a lot during those years."

Standing outside Central Library today, I notice the famous names inscribed on its balustrades next to the sidewalk and on tablets under the second-floor windows: novelists Cervantes, Dickens, and Austen; scientists Galileo, Darwin, and Copernicus; inventors Pasteur, Morse, and Watt; religious figures from Erasmus to Confucius; and generals Alexander the Great, Tecumseh, and Grant. After passing though the entry foyer, a large open staircase like that in a baronial palace is immediately ahead, illuminated by a large skylight. At the second floor, an ornate circular chandelier hangs over the circulation desk, and the Palladian windows bathe reading rooms in natural light.

Even as downtown Portland has struggled in the initial post-pandemic years, Central has remained busy, reflecting libraries' evolving role as community centers. "Libraries are the most public spaces that exist right now," says Angela Weyrens, Central Library's manager. "That's very important in the climate we have. Things are continually being commodified. It's important for libraries to be able to provide space that's free and open to everyone, no matter who they are. Grand Central Station is a great comparison. We have people who come in all day every day, people that visit us once in a while, and people who come in as a destination from all over the globe." Of all Central's spaces, people particularly love the second-floor reading room, she says, with its large windows. "The light in there in the spring and fall is absolutely amazing. It really makes you feel like you're in a kind of sacred space."

At Tenth Avenue and Yamhill Street are stops for the **MAX** light-rail system and the **Portland Streetcar**. After moving from

New York, I earnestly wanted to believe Portland was becoming a more bustling metropolis: a place that didn't feel empty after five o'clock. These trains told me that, at least to a modest degree, it really was. The truth was more complicated, of course. But the trains continue to stop here. And whenever I pass this stop, I think of one of its designers and his bow tie: Paddy Tillett.

I first met Tillett in 1999 while working at the American Institute of Architects, where I regularly took minutes for the chapter's many committees meetings. My favorite committee was the Fellows, architects who had been inducted into the AIA's College of Fellows, a kind of professional hall of fame. A regular at those meetings was Tillett, who looked especially natty in his trademark bowtie and tweed jacket. Besides being an experienced urban planner and transit designer, Tillett served as president of the Portland City Club, and was enough of a well-known civic presence that a local microbrew beer was named in his honor. Tillett, a native Brit, seemed to possess an outsized affection for his adopted home. "I traveled widely in the US before I came to Oregon, but this is where I felt totally at home," he told me for a 2018 *Portland Architecture* interview. "Maybe it's climatic, but I think it's more than that. Or maybe climate has some influence on values: the liberalism we have in Cascadia is not like most of the rest of the United States, and that fits somehow. I think it's part of what makes this a particular place."

Though Tillett had worked on urban rail projects in Japan and Europe, he wound up in Portland because of a passion for sailing the ocean. In 1980 Tillett quit his job in London and embarked on what became a ten-month, 14,000-mile sailing journey with friends, traveling from the Virgin Islands to Panama, the Galapagos Islands, and French Polynesia. "In that last stretch, we had twenty-three days without seeing land or vessels," he recalled. "It's difficult to explain, but being so completely remote from everybody else was quite something." Tillett's wife joined them in Tahiti, but tired of sailing by the time they reached Hawai'i, so she flew to Portland to stay with a friend. After reaching California and ending the sailing trip, Tillett joined her here, during which time he was introduced to ZGF Architects. As he recalls, former ZGF partner Greg Baldwin said, "'There are no architects here with experience in light-rail. No one in this country has built it for fifty years. Would you like to come work on it?' It was supposed to last eighteen months," Tillett remembered, "and here we are thirty-five years later."

The first MAX line, among the first second-generation light-rail systems in the United States, was a 15-mile east-side connection to suburban Gresham that opened in 1986. Its conception had been a turning point in the city's history and is often associated with the cancellation of the Mount Hood Freeway after years of citizen opposition. But before MAX was built, the design team from ZGF Architects had to overcome substantial skepticism.

"At that time, Oregon was still rattling its saber saying that light-rail was a complete white elephant: 'Why would we spend our money on it?' Nobody really knew what light-rail was," explained Tillett, now retired. "The mental image was an Amtrak train rumbling down the middle of the street, scattering pets and children before it." But MAX was successful enough that the network grew, and was complemented by the return of the Portland Streetcar in 2001, also designed by ZGF. While MAX was about connecting the city to its suburbs, the Portland Streetcar was about connecting the city's densifying, gentrifying neighborhoods. In the 1920s, there had been more than forty different streetcar lines and more than 300 miles of track in Portland, one of the largest urban rail systems in the country. Yet many questioned its need in the nineties, when we'd already established MAX, even though they do different jobs. "We said, 'Why wouldn't we have a real streetcar instead of a suburban train that pretends to be one?'" Tillett recalled. Since then, the Portland Streetcar system has also been expanded numerous times, acting as transit as well as a development tool, as part of new urban districts like the Pearl District and South Waterfront.

Two blocks north on Tenth Avenue is a place I remember visiting when I was six years old: the **Galleria Building** (921 SW Morrison Street). It's also where I learned that a building's soul sometimes comes from its negative space, for when its atrium was demolished, it lost its soul.

Completed in 1910 and designed by Seattle architect Charles R. Aldrich (with interiors by A. E. Doyle), this was one of the city's first department stores, and the first to occupy a full city block: Olds, Wortman & King. The five-story building, centered around a sky-lit atrium, attracted more than 25,000 customers on its opening day. The department store continued to prosper over the next few decades, and in 1947 Olds invested in a renovation supervised by architect Pietro Belluschi designed to increase square footage, which unfortunately meant removing the atrium.

After nearly sixty-five years in business, the department store closed in 1974, amid suburban flight and competition from a new generation of malls like Lloyd Center. The building had sat vacant for two years, then was purchased by developers William and Sam Naito for just $565,000. The building reopened in 1976 as The Galleria, from a redesign by Colburn, Sheldon and Partners (predecessor of SERA Architects) that included a restoration of the atrium and vibrant ground-floor space meant to evoke an outdoor piazza. An assortment of independent shops and restaurants constituted what was called one of the first vertical malls in the United States.

By this time, the Naito brothers, who were of Japanese ancestry and had been displaced from Portland by the US government during World War II, had already spent over a decade as architectural saviors, restoring a succession of gorgeous nineteenth-century buildings in Old Town with distinctive cast-iron façades in the 1960 and 1970s. The Galleria represented a much bigger risk for the Naitos than any of their previous projects, but the project helped revive downtown Portland, attracting thousands upon its opening. During these years, my mom would take me shopping at The Galleria, which along with the Keller Fountain and Keller Auditorium represents my earliest memories in downtown. First we'd visit women's clothing stores and then, if I'd behaved, continue on to the Toy Chest, followed by lunch at Bogart's restaurant, with its menu of sandwiches named after Humphrey Bogart movies. The Galleria was free of chain stores, each a one-off local business. The Paper Parlor offered handmade cards and stationery, Jarring Note sold bottles and jars, Sensuous She offered lingerie, and Chown Showcase sold specialty hardware. But for me that atrium was the planet the shops orbited, and I remember being drawn to the view up and down from its edge.

By the 1990s, The Galleria was in decline, facing new competition from the Pioneer Place mall a few blocks away. In 2011 the Naitos sold the building to the Target chain, which filled The Galleria with an urban version of its big-box retail stores. The deal was hailed for preserving a landmark Portland building, but the original interior, including, crucially, its atrium, was removed and filled in with wall-to-wall floors. Why could it never survive more than a generation? It almost seems to be a barometer of downtown's overall health and prosperity. Today the big skylight is still there, illuminating the top-floor office of SERA Architects. Even so, every time I pass by here, I shake my head over the atrium being gone. It's what made the building special. But at least based on historical precedent, there's reason to hope for its return.

Across from The Galleria is the **Sentinel Hotel** (614 SW Eleventh Avenue), completed in 1909 and perhaps the most architecturally distinctive hotel in Portland. It was designed by William C. Knighton, who went on to serve as Oregon's first state architect from 1911 to 1915 and designed the Oregon Supreme Court Building in Salem. Originally known as the Seward Hotel, its room rates started at $1. The hotel was designed with playfully eclectic exterior decoration, for Knighton was a believer in the Vienna Secessionist school that rejected historical precedents. Some of the terra-cotta gargoyles on its parapet even look like spacemen. I still think of it as the Governor Hotel, its name when I moved here, and when it was immortalized on celluloid.

Today the Sentinel Hotel stretches across two buildings, into the former Portland Elks Temple on Eleventh Avenue, where the entrance was moved (hence its street address). As a result, on Tenth Avenue this building is now emblazoned not with the hotel's name, but that of its ground-floor restaurant, Jake's Grill. But I'm here to see this striking circa-1909 original, which has had more ups and downs than most great works of Portland architecture. During the seventies and continuing into the nineties, the hotel was vacant and its windows boarded up, a victim of middle-class flight from the central city during the midcentury; even as the Galleria Building across Tenth Avenue became revitalized, this hotel remained unoccupied, its windows boarded up. Renovations were eventually completed in 1992 and the hotel reopened.

*Sentinel Hotel*

We've reached another building that served as a location for filmmaker Gus Van Sant: his 1991 masterpiece *My Own Private Idaho*. In the movie, the still-abandoned Governor Hotel is a safe haven for homeless squatters and street hustlers. "People were actually squatting in the hotel when we started filming there," Van Sant remembered in our 2024 interview.

The director had initially planned to make the movie on a shoestring budget using mostly nonprofessional actors, as he'd done for 1985's *Mala Noche*. But Van Sant had the young Hollywood actors River Phoenix and Keanu Reeves in mind for the leads, which attracted backing from one of the era's top independent distributors, New Line Cinema. "It was just the two of them on my wish list. There weren't any other actors we sent the script to," he recalled. "Keanu immediately said, 'Yeah, this is exactly what I want to do.' River was a little more hesitant, but was also interested. I think they were doing bigger films, and looking for something a little more outside the concept of Hollywood."

Filming the movie was a return of sorts for Phoenix, who was born in Madras, Oregon, but whose family had left the state when he was a baby. By the time he agreed to star in *My Own Private Idaho*, the actor had long since become a star, thanks to *Stand by Me* and *Running on Empty*, the latter of which brought him an Academy Award nomination for Best Supporting Actor. But *Idaho*, the third in Van Sant's trilogy of Portland-set films (his follow-up to *Drugstore Cowboy*), a loose interpretation of Shakespeare's *Henry IV, Part I* and *Part II*, would become the role of Phoenix's tragically short life and career. For Reeves, who had already acted in Hollywood hits like *Bill & Ted's Excellent Adventure*, *Dangerous Liaisons*, and *Point Break*, Van Sant's film was an opportunity to show he was capable of leading roles in more challenging art films.

Before *My Own Private Idaho*'s filming commenced, Phoenix and Reeves spent time on the streets of Old Town researching their roles and hanging out with the city's young street denizens. Phoenix plays a hustler named Mike Waters with a handicap: narcolepsy drops him off to sleep in any moment of stress. At the film's outset as well as its conclusion, he collapses on a rural eastern Oregon highway. Reeves plays Scott Favor, the slumming son of Portland's mayor, part friendly companion to Mike, part lover, who agrees to help him find his long-lost mother. Van Sant recalls Phoenix already knew Portland because his family had spent time here. Reeves, less familiar with the city, delved into researching his character even further, hiking through the affluent West Hills, to select a house where he could imagine his character's family lived.

As with the first two films in Van Sant's Portland trilogy, however, *Idaho*'s protagonists are itinerant, coming and going like ships seeking temporary harbor. "The reality for these street kids was they were constantly moving from Vancouver to Seattle to Portland to San Francisco, living in squats and doing what they could to make money," Van Sant explained. It was part of the director's larger interest in Portland's historical identity, as a temporary stop for transients and seasonal workers. When he first lived here as an adult beginning in the late 1970s, after returning from Los Angeles, "I realized Portland is basically a seaport town, and the first one that I lived in. It was amazing, because the streets were so filled with different characters, people that worked out in the ocean or else they worked in the woods, real lumberjacks." To Van Sant, *My Own Private Idaho*'s street hustlers were not just sex workers living rough, but part of a larger population continually drifting in and out of town.

A year after the hotel's 1992 renovation, and two years after *My Own Private Idaho*'s premiere, River Phoenix died of a drug overdose. But his spirit lives on in the film. Now a landmark of gay cinema and a cornerstone of the 1990s US independent film renaissance, for my money, it's also Gus Van Sant's best, the greatest-ever Portland-set movie, and one of my very favorites. In 2017, after some Internet sleuthing, Valarie and I found the stretch of Highway 216 in central Oregon (near the town of Tygh Valley) where the film's opening and closing scenes took place, and we drove there to pay our respects. Valarie collected some dirt from the roadside into a jar as a memento, displayed proudly on a nearby shelf as I write this. Much as I admire *Drugstore Cowboy*, *My Own Private Idaho* hits me even more powerfully for the power of Phoenix's performance, as an *Odyssey*-like quest for home, and for its visual lyricism: shots of a house falling onto the highway, of salmon (the Phoenix character's spirit animal) leaping through rapids upstream, and quick montages of still images portraying moments of sexual intimacy.

After the Governor/Sentinel Hotel's renovation, its ballroom began playing host to a variety of events from weddings to corporate banquets, where I often seemed to wind up in the 2000s. I remember attending a holiday party thrown by Valarie's employer, featuring a performance by rapper DMC of seminal eighties act Run-DMC. Though it was great fun, and DMC was a good sport posing for pictures with us and other employees, there was something slightly absurd about the performance, with DMC performing both parts of the song without his partner, and all these middle-class office workers swinging their arms back and forth to the group's handful of hit songs.

These days, I rarely hear mention of the Sentinel Hotel, as if moving its entrance into the adjacent building took away some of its identity. Thankfully, though, even as downtown has struggled in recent years, the hotel is yet to be abandoned and boarded up again.

One block north is the thirty-five-story tower known as **Block 216** (812 SW Washington Street), completed in 2023. It is the city's fifth-tallest building, and the largest building constructed in Portland since the US Bancorp Tower forty years earlier. Designed by GBD Architects, the tower has an appreciable crystalline quality, its glass façade cut almost like a gem; when viewed from a distance, it often reflects and refracts light differently than any other tall building on the skyline, noticeable even from several miles away. The building holds a Ritz-Carlton Hotel and company-branded condominiums, as well as a day spa, a twentieth-floor restaurant, and a ground-floor food hall.

Before it was even completed, Block 216 became an anachronism, having been conceived in one era and finished in another. Its construction began in 2019, less than a year before the pandemic. Though initially slated for completion in December 2022, it opened roughly a year later. It's arguable that Block 216 gave hope to a post-pandemic economy. But the tower's high-end clientele, particularly given the presence of a Ritz-Carlton, the city's first five-star hotel, also represented a stark dichotomy between the tower and its surrounding neighborhood. Its condos were priced at approximately three times the local average on a per-square-foot basis, and the hotel was charging nearly $500 per night for its smallest double room, even as scores of homeless persons were camped within blocks of the building.

This block is owned by the Goodman family's Downtown Development Group, which for decades operated a surface parking lot on this site. But as anyone who passes its entrance knows, the building was developed by Walter C. Bowen and his company, BPM Real Estate Group. At the front door is a plaque featuring Bowen's picture, identifying Block 216 as "Another world class property" of his and BPM's creation. The plaque doesn't mention that twenty-six affordable housing units, part of the original inclusionary-zoning requirement for Block 216, went unbuilt, nor that in 2025 the building was turned over to its lender.

However, as is the case at the St. Francis and a few other upcoming stops, I'm more interested in what used to be here. The first known structure on this block, constructed in the mid-nineteenth century, was the house of Julius Loewenberg, a Prussian immigrant. After losing his fortune during the Panic

*Block 216*

of 1893, Loewenberg sold the property, and in 1896 a commercial building was erected by business partners Ben Selling and Solomon Hirsch, both members of the Oregon state legislature. The three-story Selling-Hirsch Building, clad in in brick with terracotta and sandstone detailing, included tenants like the Woodmen of the World fraternal organization and, a decade later, the Equal Suffrage League, founded by Hirsch's widow, Josephine, in 1912, the same year Oregon granted women the right to vote. During World War II the Red Cross offered nursing classes here. On the ground floor was the Hazelwood Cream Store, a restaurant, ice cream parlor, and confectionary with its storefront embellished to look like a Swiss farmhouse; it's also where the City Club of Portland was founded.

On this block's southeast corner was the People's Theater, one of Portland's first nickelodeons, completed in 1911 and operated by the People's Amusement Company. It arrived amid a wave of theater building from 1910 to 1913 that also included the Heilig, Baker, Majestic, Pantages, Empress, National, and Orpheum. The People's Theater's design, by Newcomb Engineering, was Classical Revival in style, its arched openings atop an elevated grand staircase modeled after the Paris Opera. Inside, the lobby was trimmed in Mexican onyx and included a custom $10,000 organ. But the theater, which later was called the Music Box and then the Alder, closed in 1952. The building itself, however, remained standing into the early 1990s. Eventually reclad and remodeled to hold storefront retail spaces and offices above, it was where, during high school in the late 1980s, I ate my first pizza by the slice, at Escape From New York, the city's first by-the-slice pizza shop. Though this building was torn down in 1993, Escape From New York and founder Phil Geffner are blessedly still around, having long ago relocated to Twenty-Third Avenue in Northwest Portland.

After the parking garage planned for this block was disallowed, for about thirty years this was a surface parking lot, but what's noteworthy is how the block morphed into something more culturally significant: a culinary hub. Most present-day Portlanders remember the famous Alder Street food-cart pod located here beginning in the late nineties; though cars were still parked in the center of the block, food vendors lined its perimeter

*Alder Street food cart pod*

on four sides. This was the most-visited such pod in an era when Portland food carts began to attract worldwide interest.

"The economy had crashed and people were looking for opportunities," recalls Brett Burmeister, who wrote the Food Carts Portland blog and visited hundreds of these establishments. "It was a launching point for a lot of people's careers. Across Portland, there were 1,500 new vendors jumping into the food-cart scene." At Alder Street, I often visited the People's Pig for its porchetta sandwiches, Spella for espresso shots, or Nong's Khao Man Gai for simple, exquisite Thai chicken and rice. This was a modest but wonderfully diverse community and series of delights. Each cart was a little bit different not only in cuisine but also in its makeshift architecture.

"Early on everything was very do-it-yourself," Burmeister says. "A lot of it was converted old construction trailers. Some of the smaller ones, I think they just got a flat trailer and put up posts, with it all held together by glue and duct tape. Other people would buy old travel trailers. I remember one guy had an Aloha travel trailer and he sold only Frito pie. He used the existing stove in there to cook the chili. It was popular. It was in business for two years, and he sold the cart for about $14,000. Great location, perfect timing."

I have a soft spot for small dining establishments because when I was four years old, my dad purchased a small, year-old restaurant on McMinnville's main street called The Sage in an old department store building. I spent most of the next twenty years there: hanging out with my dad, learning to cook and bake, and working my first job. Like these food carts, its kitchen was cramped, for The Sage occupied just a small mezzanine within the larger storefront. But while the restaurant had struggled under its previous owner, my dad made The Sage a destination, with customers lined up for tables at lunchtime. I think of the tenuous and against-the-odds nature of the restaurant business when I see Portland's food carts, which don't even have buildings to call home. Food carts are itinerant by nature, so maybe it's misguided to be outraged by the Alder Street pod's demise. But I still miss it, not just for the food but for the gritty entrepreneurial spirit of its operators, and the vibrant sense of place that existed here. There are still food-cart clusters scattered around Portland, and they remain popular, but they have become less of a phenomenon downtown, given how the number of office workers here has substantially declined. Even so, I don't want to forget how food-cart pods like this one at Tenth and Alder made a substantial contribution to world cuisine. And I think they say something about Portland's unhurried pace, for this is not exactly fast food. You're likely to have to wait a while at a food cart, first in line and then for your meal to be prepared. Yet particularly where several carts are joined together, with shared seating, there is a lovely communal vibe.

This five-block stretch of SW Tenth Avenue concludes with one of my favorite works of downtown architecture, known as the **419 Building** (419 SW Tenth Avenue). Completed in 1962,

*419 Building*

the 419 Building's interior is unremarkable, but I adore its exterior façade of multicolored panels, recalling a Rubik's Cube. For many years in the 2000s this building was home to the Portland Institute for Contemporary Art, producer of the popular annual Time-Based Art Festival (the organization has since relocated to Northeast Portland).

I once attended the retirement party for a former boss, Saundra Stevens, who in 2001 had fired me from my job at the American Institute of Architects. She had repeatedly caught me writing *Willamette Week* movie reviews instead of doing the tasks I'd been given, and at the time, in my late twenties, I was arrogant enough to sometimes argue with her when reprimanded. But it was a benevolent firing. Saundra knew I wanted to become a full-time journalist, and offered me enough freelance work to be able to take the plunge. "I think in time you're going to thank me," Saundra said. At that retirement party, about twenty years later, I finally did so.

Decades before the 419 Building's construction, on this site was the Music Hall, a nightclub opened by Paul Schneiderman in 1937. Its name referenced the old English musical hall tradition, but its feature attraction was more risqué. After World War II, when Schneiderman's son Leonard took over booking, the club became known for female impersonators, as well as touring bands and singers. In 1950, the younger Schneiderman booked a nationally renowned act: The Mills Brothers, the Ohio singing group that had twenty years earlier become the first Black artists to have their own show broadcast on nationwide radio. Instead of giving the Music Hall's resident cross-dressing performers the night off, the club incorporated them into the Mills Brothers' show. A member of the city council attended one of the performances and was offended, prompting an investigation later revealing that the Music Hall was serving alcohol without a license. The businesses closed and never reopened.

### *Pink Triangle*

Turning left from Tenth Avenue, I come to a cluster of blocks south of Burnside that for much of the twentieth century was called the Pink Triangle, the Burnside Triangle, or Vaseline Alley. A group of traditionally LGBT-friendly businesses and entertainment destinations had been located here as far back as the 1940s, where gay and lesbian citizens could meet each other, escape from the conformity and persecution of mainstream American life, and be entertained. More recently, in the 2000s, this area gentrified into a hot spot of independent shops and restaurants surrounding the Ace Hotel. But, like the Pink Triangle, it too has faded.

At the center of this neighborhood within a neighborhood is Harvey Milk Street, renamed in 2007 in honor of the San Francisco gay rights leader assassinated in 1978. The street had long been named for Benjamin Stark, one of Portland's earliest landholders (it retains the Stark Street moniker outside downtown). After arriving in 1845, Stark purchased Asa Lovejoy's half-interest in the original townsite and was later elected to the territorial and (after 1859) state legislatures. When the Republican US Senator Edward Baker died in office in 1861, Stark, a Democrat and supporter of slavery, was appointed as Baker's replacement. But he lost the subsequent 1862 election, and after leaving Congress, Stark also left Oregon for Connecticut. Though Harvey Milk had less of a connection to Oregon, the Pink Triangle's history made renaming this street in his honor fitting.

In 2014, I wrote a *New York Times* travel article spotlighting a new generation of shops and eateries located on and near Harvey Milk Street: Petunia's Pies & Pastries for vegan sweets, Solestruck for exotic shoes, Tender Loving Empire record store and gift shop, Clyde Common restaurant, and the Jewish deli Kenny & Zuke's. They were like satellites surrounding the Ace Hotel, which seemed to be ground zero for hip Portland. Indeed, I remember running into Pink Martini bandleader Thomas Lauderdale at a Stumptown Coffee adjacent in the hotel's lobby. I later interviewed local indie rock bandleader Sam Coomes of Quasi there.

Today the hotel has returned to its original name, the **Clyde Hotel** (1022 SW Harvey Milk Street). Built in 1912, this was one of more than twenty-five lodgings established in this neighborhood during the 1910s, amid the emergence of nearby Broadway as an entertainment district. The hotel was built for the estate of Charles Friendly, who had previously established a homestead with his wife Clara on this site. The design by local architects MacNaughton and Raymond added classical ornament to an otherwise fairly utilitarian brick structure. For many decades a modest residential hotel, the place came alive in the mid-2000s as only the second outpost in the Ace Hotel chain, the country's hottest boutique hospitality brand of its time. Each Ace Hotel renovated an old building, with an eclectic interior style blending high and low culture, conceived by company founder Alex Calderwood. He chose the hotel's name from the playing card, as both the high and low point of the deck, representing a similarly desired mix of high and low culture.

In the wake of the pandemic, the energy of this block collapsed, with numerous vacant storefronts. A moment in late 2023 has particularly stuck with me: peering into the closed Kenny & Zuke's, where its chalkboard with handwritten daily specials was still sitting on the otherwise-empty floor. But Petunia's, Solestruck, and others remain, including one of the most creative adaptive-reuse projects I've encountered, **Union Way** (1025 SW Harvey Milk Street). A circa-1920 automobile garage, in the late nineties it housed a gay-friendly club called the Red Cap Garage. In 2013, however, the building was renovated for developer Tom Cody into a micro-retail complex with a focus on local businesses like Danner boots, Self Edge boutique, Quinn artisan candy, and Boxer Ramen (today only Danner remains).

The Union Way design, by Lever Architecture, essentially inverted what you might expect for such a retail project. They

*Union Way*

turned the original structure inside-out, cutting a central spine down the center of the building, with tiny storefronts arranged on either side. It seemed quintessentially Portland, a quirky little anti-chain mall, a successor of sorts to The Galleria with its local focus. Union Way also took inspiration from similarly narrow shop-lined alleys in dense cities like Paris and Tokyo. Though its tenants took a risk by eschewing street frontage, Union Way's sky-lit central pathway acts as a shortcut from Harvey Milk Street to Burnside. Light from a succession of skylights reflects off the poplar-clad walls to make the space glow even on the most overcast days.

Lever Architecture went on to become one of Portland's best twenty-first-century firms. Founder Thomas Robinson is a California native who came to Portland in 2003 to join the city's most-acclaimed firm of the time, Allied Works (featured in the next walk), after working for the world's most prestigious firm, Switzerland's Herzog & de Meuron. Established in 2009, Lever became a pioneer in using mass timber, as part of a worldwide trend. (Mass timber is stronger structurally than traditional wood construction, more fire resistant, and is prized for its carbon sequestration.) And Robinson has always seemed passionate about the craft of architecture and the search for novel solutions, like Union Way represented.

"I like the beginning of the projects, when you don't know what you are really doing and everything is out there," the architect told me for a 2013 *Portland Architecture* interview, upon Union Way's opening. "You have the opportunity to free associate and visit the site and think about what is possible." In conversation over the years, we have bonded over the idea of buildings as pieces of a larger whole. "There are definitely a few buildings in Portland that I admire, but the structure of the entire city is what I find special," he added. "The way that all of the buildings, large and small, work together with the river, the hills, and the neighborhoods to create a fabric is powerful. For me, that fabric is what is absolutely unique about Portland especially since it is such a young city." In the past decade, Lever has gone on to design large-scale projects including the US headquarters for Adidas in Portland and NBCUniversal in Los Angeles. Yet tiny little Union Way may still be my favorite.

Continuing west on Harvey Milk Street, I come to a humble work of historic architecture with an outsized cultural presence: the **Whitney & Gray Building** (409 SW Twelfth Avenue). It was completed in 1910 from a design by William Knighton, whose Seward Hotel had opened a year earlier. The Whitney & Gray's façade of cream-colored brick and galvanized iron is certainly the more modest of the two, but the cultural history associated with it is just as significant. This building too was originally a hotel, and went by many different names—the Kingwood Hotel, the Van Gorder, the Iroquois, the Belmont—before being converted to apartments in 1968.

The Whitney & Gray has long been known for its ground-floor tenant, Jake's Famous Crawfish. With its interior of polished brass, parquet floors, white tablecloths, and oil paintings depicting Pacific Northwest landmarks, it is Portland's second-oldest continuously operating restaurant and actually pre-dates the building itself. Originating as a saloon at Eighteenth Avenue and Washington Street in 1892 called Mueller and Meier, the restaurant moved here in 1911 and initially went by several other names: the Frieman & Hackman Restaurant, Jacob Mueller Soda Drinks, Mueller & Meier Café. When prohibition began in 1919, the founders sold it to waiters J. Rometsch and Jacob Frieman, the latter of whom, an expert crawfish chef, lent a shortened version of his first name to the new moniker: Jake's Famous Crawfish.

When Valarie and I moved to Portland, Jake's became our go-to special occasion restaurant: anniversaries, visiting parents. By this time, there were certainly hipper and more luxurious options, but Jake's had atmosphere and deeper roots. Then there was the taste of the baked-brie-in-filo-dough appetizer. The restaurant was packed the night of our first visit, just before Christmas in 1997, and the succession of dining rooms seemed to go on forever; Jake's actually stretches into an adjacent building. Initially and for several years, the restaurant stayed open until 4:00 in the morning. It was where local power brokers congregated, as well as visiting celebrities like comedian Jack Benny, singer Bing Crosby, and comedian Buster Keaton. Jake's best-known customer was actor Humphrey Bogart. From 1938 to 1946, the same years he rose to become Hollywood's biggest star, Bogart was married to Portland-raised actress Mayo Methot. Near the restaurant's entrance, a small plaque denotes what had been the couple's favorite table.

Though she's far from a household name today, Methot is arguably still the most accomplished movie actor from Portland. Her family moved here when Methot, named for County Mayo in Ireland and born in Chicago, was a young child. She began acting in local theatrical productions soon after, and left for New York in 1922 at age eighteen. Within a year Methot was discovered by Broadway impresario George M. Cohan, who wrote a character in his play *The Song and Dance Man* especially for her; they were also rumored to be lovers. Moving to Hollywood in 1930, Methot acted in eighteen films over the ensuing fifteen years, including collaborations with famed directors like William Wyler and Frank Capra. "Hollywood in the 1930s was crying out for an actress like Methot, who talked tough and embodied world-weariness with ease," wrote film historian Pamela Hutchinson in a 2024 tribute published by *Sight and Sound* magazine called "So Good at Being Bad."

Methot and Bogart fell in love while filming 1937's *Marked Woman*, and married within a year. During regular visits to see Methot's mother in Portland, they often spent time at Jake's. But domestic bliss it wasn't. The couple became known in the press as the "Battling Bogarts," and Methot even allegedly attempted to stab her husband one drunken night (which was kept out of the press by Bogart's studio, Warner Brothers). When Bogie divorced Methot in 1944 for Lauren Bacall, Methot returned to Portland and died seven years later, in 1951, from complications related to alcoholism. In the years between her death and Bogart's 1957 passing, he sent flowers each month to Methot's final resting place, at Portland Memorial Mausoleum.

Though several Portland restaurants closed during the COVID-19 pandemic, Jake's Famous Crawfish remains. "Jake's is kind of a magical place," general manager Brian McConnell told me in a 2019 podcast interview. "I still remember the first time I walked in, for my job interview. I remember thinking to myself, 'Wow. Can I work at this place?' You walk in and right away your jaw kind of drops." In a normally high-turnover job, many of the bowtie-clad waiters at Jake's have worked there for decades. "I've got servers who have been there fifty-plus years,"

*Twelve West*

McConnell added. "I've got a dozen who have been there thirty years. I've got a couple servers who are over seventy years old. It makes for a different level of service because we'll serve twenty-five to thirty species a day, and they know where the trout came from, they know where the ahi came from, they know about the salmon, the crab, the mussels." And while it's been eighty years since Bogart and Methot frequented Jake's, the restaurant's deep and continuing presence helps preserve the city's soul.

Next door to the Whitney & Gray building is **Twelve West** (1223 SW Washington Street), a handsome twenty-two-story glass tower designed by ZGF Architects, completed in 2009. In the 1940s, on this site had been the Buick Café, a popular meeting spot for the city's growing lesbian community. That building was torn down in the 1960s, and for several decades there was a surface parking lot here, one of many in downtown owned by the Goodman family. Twelve West was among the first redevelopments of their parking lots.

Though Twelve West was the nation's first urban tower topped with wind turbines (which provide a modest fraction of total power), what I like on its exterior is the way its glass façade can seem almost like liquid, able to reflect and refract light. Inside, the first few floors at Twelve West are occupied by the firm that designed the building, ZGF; its second-floor office is reached by ascending a stairway hanging from the ceiling on thin wires that reminds me of a stairway in one of my all-time favorite movies, 1946's *A Matter of Life and Death* by Michael Powell and Emeric Pressburger, leading to the celestial realm.

ZGF has existed since 1942, and for much of my time in Portland, the firm's lead architect was Robert Frasca. Since 2023, Sharron van der Meulen has been the firm's managing partner, and like many at ZGF, she's spent much of her career there, going back to the late eighties. And, to the firm's credit, its design prowess has never really been about any singular architect so much as a kind of collective authorship. Yet it's longtime ZGF partner Eugene Sandoval whom I associate with Twelve West and its façade. I remember coming here many times beginning in the early 2010s to interview Sandoval, mostly about a succession of projects for the Nike World Headquarters in Beaverton and the University of Oregon's athletic department in Eugene. Knowing our shared passion for Oregon Ducks football, Sandoval always had insider stories to share about the team's coaches and players. Although today the architect's best-known work for ZGF is the stunning new Portland International Airport terminal, with its massive timber roof and forty-nine skylights, as Twelve West exemplifies, Sandoval is especially gifted as a conjurer of glass architecture.

Sandoval was born on the island of Palawan in the Philippines, and his family practically lived on the water, which influenced his future career. "I grew up in this landscape where there's almost no boundaries: just the horizon of the water," he says. "When you're in water there's this fluidity. It's almost like suspended animation. But it's also the effect of the light at different times of day. I grew up free-diving down to 50, 60 feet. That's when you experience how light shifts with the depth of the water. My favorite thing was to turn around and look at the sky and see how the light is refracted. And that's the way I view glass. You have to understand that glass is liquid. Glass is not a solid form. It's really like water. The buildings I work on, even though it's gloomy here in the Pacific Northwest, they find a way to harvest and reflect light."

### *Making Music*

I've almost reached the West End's end, but the walk would be incomplete without two final stops significant to music history. At Thirteenth and Burnside is an unassuming two-story brick building built in 1916, today known as **Blackbox** (413 SW Thirteenth Avenue) after being renovated from a design by its owner, Skylab Architecture. But I think of it as the "Louie Louie" building. On April 6, 1963, five members of Portland rock band The Kingsmen assembled at the Northwestern Studio upstairs to record the definitive version of an iconic pop song.

The Kingsmen weren't the first to record "Louie Louie," but their version made the song famous. It had been written and first recorded by Richard Berry in 1955 and released in 1957, as an interpretation of an earlier song, "El Loco Cha Cha" by Cuban-born American composer René Touzet, which itself had rearranged Cuban bandleader Rosendo Ruiz Jr.'s "Amarren El Loco" ("Tie Up the Madman"). One day before The Kingsmen recorded "Louie Louie," another version of the song was recorded at the same studio by another local band, Paul Revere & The Raiders. That version reached the airwaves first and was slightly more polished, yet it became only a regional hit. The Kingsmen's version, however, reached No. 2 on the Billboard singles chart, and it's the version known around the world. It also proved controversial.

During the recording, the only available vocal microphone was hanging from the ceiling, several feet above lead singer Jack Ely, which made the lyrics difficult to discern. The FBI, suspecting indecency, investigated the song and reached no conclusion. But the lyrics were actually clean: "A fine little girl / She wait for me / Me catch a ship across the sea / I sailed the ship all alone / I never think I'll make it home / Three nights and days we sailed the sea. Me think of girl constantly." Ely quit the band soon after the recording, and The Kingsmen never duplicated its success. Even so, "Louie Louie" lived on, covered by a succession of acts over the next two decades including the Beach Boys and the Kinks. I associate it most with renditions by the Oregon Ducks marching band at Autzen Stadium, where I regularly watched football games with my dad throughout the 1980s. In 2018 the song was also inducted into the Rock and Roll Hall of Fame in the singles category.

The Blackbox building where "Louie Louie" was recorded limped along for decades. In the seventies, one ground-floor tenant was Oregon's chapter of the American Atheists. There also was a gay-friendly bar known as The Eagle. Both establishments were still there in 1995 when David Cress and Craig Henderson rented offices on the building's second floor for their production company, Food Chain Films. "It was close in and it was super cheap," Cress recalls. "But about once a week we'd be sitting at our desks and hear a crash. Drivers were always rear-ending each other on Burnside because they were gawking at the scantily clad prostitutes. It was like clockwork." Food Chain went on to produce music videos for bands like the Dandy Warhols and the Red Hot Chili Peppers.

In 2008 Cress and Henderson sold the building to Skylab Architecture, which by then had become acclaimed for projects including the Hoke Residence, featured prominently in the Twilight movie franchise, and the popular Doug Fir retro-style diner and rock club. When founder Jeff Kovel and his partners bought this building, their intent was to tear it down in order to construct a twenty-seven-story tower called the Weave. But the Great Recession prompted investors to back out, so Kovel and his team pivoted to renovating the existing building, adding its now namesake paint color. "I do like the building quite a bit," Kovel says. "It's just that there is that long-term earthquake concern." His heart remains with the unbuilt Weave. "I guess that I'm reluctant to give up," he adds. This has become a common refrain in Portland, as newly stringent seismic codes for old buildings have been enacted: the upgrades make their renovations and expansions prohibitively expensive. In 2023, Skylab Architecture decamped for another location, and another renovation, of an old Quonset hut. In the meantime, I like that the DNA of the "Louie Louie" studio lives on here.

One block west at Fourteenth and Burnside is one of the city's most unique performance spaces, featuring a vibrating dance floor: the **Crystal Ballroom** (1332 W Burnside Street) or, as it was originally known, Cotillion Hall. Before the building was constructed in 1914, there was a home on this site, built by Dutch German immigrant and businessman Prosper van Fridagh in 1869. Following his 1902 death, van Fridagh's children developed Cotillion Hall in partnership with local dance impresario Michael "Montrose" Ringler, for whom a bar in the venue is still named. After coming to Portland in 1897, Ringler had opened a gym and dance studio on Morrison Street. An enthusiastic athlete, he was credited for bringing basketball to the city after learning the game from Dr. James Naismith in Springfield, Massachusetts. Heavy streetcar traffic outside Ringler's Morrison studio caused the dance floor to tremble every few minutes, which led Ringler to seek backing for new studio elsewhere.

The three-story Cotillion Hall was designed by German-born local architect Robert F. Tegan in a Renaissance Revival style, with pilasters and arched panels over its brick façade. Although today the Crystal is known for the novelty of its vibrating floor, Tegan's design is actually meant to do the opposite: insulate the dance floor from outside vibrations. Under the maple surface are hundreds of curved wood cradles, attached to ball-bearing rockers that support a moving wood strip parallel with the cradles. Cotillion Hall opened with a formal dress ball hosted by Ringler, and quickly became one of the city's most popular dance halls. It also was a target for police who, reportedly egged on by Ringler's well-connected competitors, would raid the hall if it stayed open a moment past midnight. Ringler was also criticized for playing jazz, which was discouraged by conservatives who feared racial mingling. But the music and dancing continued, including a 1923 dance contest judged by movie star Rudolph Valentino.

The venue was renamed the Crystal Ballroom in the 1950s under new owners, who over the next two decades welcomed several blues and R&B stars, including James Brown, Marvin Gaye, Ike and Tina Turner, and B. B. King. Brown's 1965 Crystal Ballroom performance concluded memorably. The custom was to end each show with his song "Please, Please, Please," during which Brown would kneel and shake, as if every last ounce of energy had been used up. A cape would then be draped over Brown, which he would suddenly tear off and resume singing one more verse. For this show, Brown's management recruited two Portland police officers, including future city council member Dick Bogle, who dragged Brown off the stage as part of the act. That same year, rock pioneer Little Richard performed at the Crystal, supported on guitar by a future superstar, Jimi

*Crystal Ballroom*

Hendrix. Legend has it that the singer actually stopped mid-song to admonish Hendrix's playing, and fired him from the stage. Just three years later, the Jimi Hendrix Experience would be headlining at Memorial Coliseum. In the late sixties, the Crystal's focus turned to psychedelic and protest rock acts: the Grateful Dead, Frank Zappa, and Buffalo Springfield, as well as a performance by Beat poet Allen Ginsberg during an anti–Vietnam War event called "Peace Rites."

By this time, the Crystal Ballroom had fallen into disrepair. During B. B. King's 1968 performance, drops of leaking water fell onto his head. The business closed later that year. In the 1970s its dance hall floor was filled with artist studios. Then, in 1997, the venue was reborn under new owners: Brian and Mike McMenamin, who had been part of the city's microbrewery explosion in the 1980s when it became legal to sell alcohol made on premises. Today McMenamin's operates establishments across the Pacific Northwest and has become locally celebrated for renovating a host of old buildings, from movie theaters to schools to even a former funeral home.

Since its 1997 reopening, the Crystal Ballroom has hosted renowned local rock acts like Sleater-Kinney, The Shins, Everclear, Modest Mouse, Elliott Smith, and the Dandy Warhols, as well as touring acts like George Clinton, Billy Idol, Nick Cave, and Arcade Fire. I saw jazz legend Herbie Hancock perform there in 1998, reunited with his popular seventies fusion band, Headhunters, after twenty-five years. My friend Paul Wolff, who had introduced me to Hancock's music, insisted we get there early, in order to secure a spot on the dance floor near the front of the stage. I could see the band's facial expressions—how happy they seemed to be reunited—which also came out in the funky music's energetic, flowing groove.

Having reached the northwest corner of downtown Portland's West End at the Crystal Ballroom, next to the Interstate 405 trench and the white noise of cars zooming by, makes a natural stopping point for this walk. Yet I'm eager to continue the journey, into a reborn former industrial enclave. There too, artists and creative minds led the way.

# *Walk 2*

# Finding the Pearl

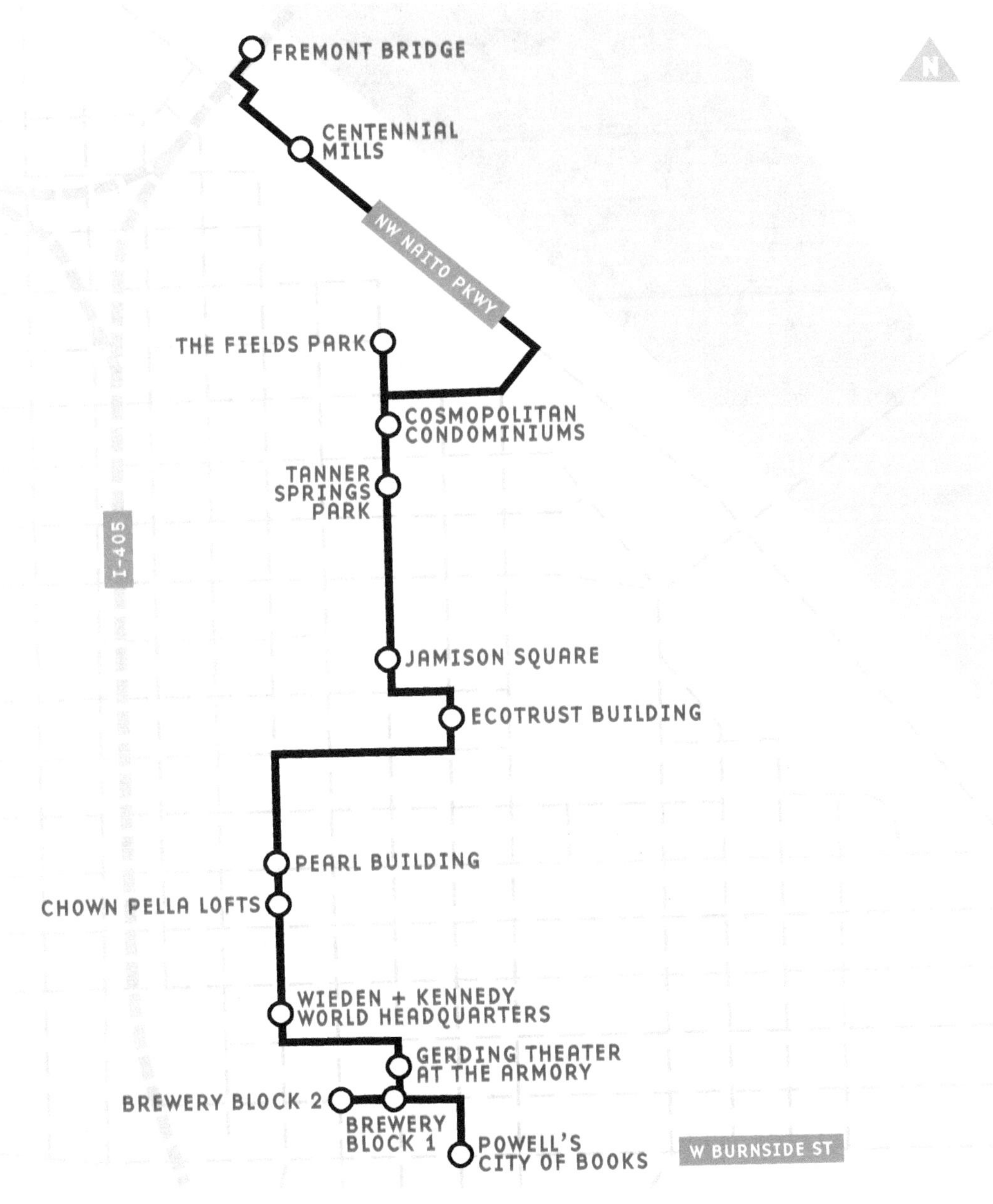

Powell's City of Books

## *Books and Brew*

The northward trajectory I began in the first walk continues as I cross Burnside Street and enter the Pearl District, which over the past forty years has been transformed more than anywhere in the central city. When I first came here as a child with my parents in the seventies, this was not the Pearl District but an enclave of early twentieth-century warehouses known as the Northwest Industrial District or the Northwest Triangle. To a child, it seemed a foreboding place, often with a ghostly emptiness on weekends, though the smell of brewing beer (which I remember comparing to stewed tomatoes) still emanated from the massive Blitz-Weinhard brewery along Burnside.

In those days, our family was going to **Powell's City of Books** (1005 W Burnside Street): a full city block occupying a renovated cluster of old American Motors automobile showrooms and repair shops. Our car would make a nerve-racking climb into the bookstore's narrow, steep, in-house parking garage, avoiding the walls and other cars seemingly by millimeters. Once inside Powell's, though, a whole world unfolded, where my dad could stock up on J. R. R. Tolkien and Carlos Castañeda paperbacks or copies of *Omni* magazine.

Today Powell's is the country's largest independent bookstore and is arguably the cultural heart of Portland as much as any museum or auditorium. With its concrete floors and exposed wood rafters, one can feel the bones of its old buildings. Inside, although there are often hundreds of people, the store's size allows a kind of relaxed ambling. I consider Powell's City of Books one of my two ultimate happy places in the greater downtown: each a kind of secular church. At the Keller Fountain I get an almost sublime sense of wonder from its cascading water; at Powell's I feel part of a congregation, my mind awakened to possibility.

After Valarie and I moved here in the nineties, by which time the surrounding Pearl District had begun transforming into a place of art galleries, restaurants, and condos, including a massive redevelopment of the brewery next door, Powell's was our weekly Friday evening destination. Valarie had worked at a literary agency in New York, and seemed to have found in Powell's a Mecca, reassuring her that she hadn't left the world of books behind. After walking here from the Empire Apartments, we'd fill our shopping baskets with novels and filmmaker biographies, then we'd meet in the corner Anne Hughes Coffee Room to compare titles over a mocha and a vanilla latte.

Standing at the Tenth and Burnside front entrance today, I'm reminded that only a few years ago Powell's was in trouble. In 2020, amid the COVID-19 lockdowns, the company closed all of its stores for a time. Company president Emily Powell warned that the City of Books could actually shutter permanently. But in time it recovered, and today it's hard to imagine Portlanders would ever allow this beloved cultural institution to fail.

The Powell's story actually began in Chicago. Michael Powell, a Portland native, had grown up on the east side of the city near Sandy Boulevard, and as a child spent summers working alongside his commercial-fisherman grandfather on the Columbia River. "I think I may be one of the last people alive in Oregon who could build a net from scratch," he told me in a 2017 interview. But Powell had bigger fish to fry, finding his way to the University of Chicago in the late sixties for a master's degree in political science. Between classes, he began selling used textbooks and paperbacks on consignment at a local co-op. Sales were brisker than he expected, and Powell soon quit school to open his first brick-and-mortar establishment, Powell's Bookstore in Chicago. His down payment came via a loan from three professors interested in bringing a bookstore to the neighborhood: sociologists Morris Janowitz and Edward Shils, and novelist Saul Bellow. Michael Powell was successful enough to quickly pay back the loan, and even inspired his father Walter, a retiring realtor, to open a separate bookstore back in Portland in 1971. Powell's Books, as the father's store was known, is actually the business that lives on today, because Michael moved home and joined him a few years later.

That first Portland Powell's was located at Burnside and Twelfth Avenue, two blocks west of the current site. But then Walter Powell learned the former American Motors dealership on Tenth was for sale. "When he told me it was a full block, I took a deep breath," Michael Powell remembered. "But I figured we could lease out some of it, which we did. My dad's real estate experience helped give us that confidence, and it was critical to our future success. Otherwise somebody would have flipped it and we'd have been gone." The buildings had been constructed in 1912, as a one-stop shop for automobile purchase, maintenance, and painting, including the aforementioned three-story parking garage. The original structure remains intact along Burnside, but the northern side of the block was torn down and rebuilt in the late nineties, from a design by Portland architect Ernest Munch.

Powell's found success with the then-uncommon practice of mixing new and used books. "It gave the store a kind of special tone: that people could get a cheap book, yet we were as up to date as any bookstore. It was the best of both worlds," Powell said. "That was my dad's idea, and I didn't think much of it, but he was right. It was counterintuitive for most people in the book biz, but not for our customers." Today Michael Powell is officially retired, and his daughter Emily has long run the company, but when I last met with him in 2017, he was still coming to work every day as a book-buyer. "It keeps the wheels turning," he explained. "I always liked to say I learned a lot being a commercial fisherman. My dad watched me at a trade fair once and said, 'I get it: your net's always in the water.'"

The store is vast enough that it's possible to have a whole aisle to yourself. Some of my best Powell's memories are of sitting on a stool meant to reach upper shelves, to instead read a few pages of a potential book purchase. Powell's is also a destination for author readings and signings. Valarie and I got books signed by the likes of Allen Ginsberg, Will Self, and Paul Theroux. I remember a fan just ahead of me in line asking Ginsberg if he was wearing Gap khakis, since their TV commercials were popular at the time; the poet lifted his leg above the table and replied, "No, I'm wearing Salvation Army khakis." In those years, my *Willamette Week* colleague Steffen Silvis, the paper's theater critic, moonlighted at Powell's as a liaison to visiting authors. He recalled to me recently, "Kaye Gibbons is drugged, Anne Perry is certifiably mad; and Harlan Ellison, who I loved, truly sent Michael Powell packing after his reading. Then there was the time that William T. Vollman perched a loaded revolver on top of the podium as he read."

As I come out of Powell's on its northwest corner at Couch Street, the light rain is continuing, although the forecast calls for plenty of sun breaks. Though this walk will continue north for a while yet, first I'm diverting a block west of Powell's, to the former Blitz-Weinhard brewery building, now known as **Brewery Block 2** (1120 NW Couch Street). In 2006 it was converted into offices and retail, from a design by GBD Architects for developer Gerding-Edlen. With its historic red brick smokestack still soaring upward, the circa-1907 brewery is part of the five-building Brewery Blocks complex of commercial and residential buildings on the extended Blitz-Weinhard site, some new and some renovated, with ground-floor retail storefronts. The Brewery Blocks were a pioneering example of early twenty-first-century sustainable design in Portland, among the city's first to achieve the US Green Building Council's LEED (Leadership in Energy and Environmental Design) certification.

This area also became a local hot spot in the early 2000s, with the increased population of office workers and condo residents combining with the immensely popular Powell's next door and a new streetcar line with a stop on Tenth Avenue to give this stretch of blocks surrounding Couch Street more foot traffic than anywhere else in the Pearl. The Brewery Blocks' success helped accelerate the pace of industrial to mixed-use redevelopment in the broader neighborhood and exemplified a nationwide trend of middle-class residents and shoppers returning from the suburbs to high-density, pedestrian, and mass-transit-oriented city centers.

"These developments are really about creating a framework for social interaction and accidental collisions," Gerding Edlen president Mark Edlen told me in a 2008 *Metropolis* magazine interview. "How do you create great places that people want to come to live, work, and play in? It's one person bumping into another and having the opportunity to talk about their work, their kids' soccer game, or the play they saw last night." Edlen and his partner, Bob Gerding, also found that successful place-making tied to historic preservation can be more resilient: that generally people prefer renovated old buildings with character, when given a choice, and will return there time after time. "The natural inclination for a developer is, 'How can I build the least costly product?' But we really learned from the Brewery Blocks experience," Edlen added. "We were digging a hole for this five-building project right when 9/11 hit. The office market went way down. But occupancy rates in the office buildings we did were higher than the rest of the city. I think it's because we were able to highly differentiate our product and create a great place for people to come."

The original Blitz-Weinhard brewery was designed by Whidden & Lewis, the city's most esteemed firm of the era, in a Romanesque style, with brick cladding embellished by limestone windowsills and corbel cornices, giving way to a prominent cylindrical brick smokestack. German immigrant Henry Weinhard had opened the brewery in 1856, partnering with the aptly named George Bottler. By 1875, Henry Weinhard's beer was being shipped to locations across the United States and even Asia. As his wealth grew, Weinhard became an active citizen. When the Skidmore Fountain was unveiled in 1887, he famously offered to connect it via hoses with his largest beer tank to have the fountain spout free beer. The brewery continued to make beer on this site for a century. When I was growing up, Henry Weinhard's TV commercials portraying the Old West were beloved. But after the company was sold to Stroh's, the last bottle was capped on August 27, 1999, and the building put up for sale the following month. Thankfully it quickly took on new life, and a quarter-century later, the Brewery Blocks remain a popular place.

As it happens, the old brewery building today known as Brewery Block 2 isn't the only historic building that was renovated. One block west is its sister property, **Brewery Block 1** (1225 W Burnside Street), a compelling hybrid of old and new by GBD Architects. At its base is the original façade of a circa-1929 Chevrolet dealership. Burnside Street was once lined with automobile dealers, and while most of that history is long gone, this building

*Brewery Blocks*

and some of the remaining Powell's structures provide a link to that century-old past. The southeast corner and the upper floors of the building are all a contemporary steel and glass structure with noticeably large exterior columns, almost like a new tree growing from an old stump. The added structural bracing helps carry the extra weight of a rooftop high-efficiency chilled-water plant. A Whole Foods market occupies the ground floor, and an 80,000-square-foot telecommunications and data center upstairs.

Traffic on Eleventh Avenue at Couch Street, waiting for the light at Burnside, is backed up to Davis Street as I walk a block north to the Pearl District's foremost arts institution: the **Gerding Theater at the Armory** (128 NW Eleventh Avenue). Named for developer Bob Gerding and considered an extension of the Brewery Blocks redevelopment, today the theater is home to the Portland Center Stage theater company. Constructed in 1891, this was originally known as the First Regiment Armory Annex because a small adjacent structure (now long gone) had been completed three years earlier. The first true armory in the state, it was built for the newly organized Oregon National Guard and came amid a wave of armory building across the west, prompted in response to a wave of anti-Chinese violence and fears of labor militancy. Designed by McCaw and Martin, the Armory Annex is a rare local example of the Castellated architectural style, a fortress-like structure of stone and brick. Almost like a Postmodern caricature, its recessed arched entrance is flanked by turrets above and its roofline punctuated with vertical slots in the façade to fire guns through. The First Regiment of the building's name, about 1,600 troops commanded by Colonel C. F. Beebe, took part in the invasion of Manila during the 1898 Spanish-American War.

The Armory interior was a single large open space, enabled by massive bowstring roof trusses made from old-growth timber and iron, still visible today from the Gerding Theater lobby. More than a century before the Gerding Theater was built, when not used for military purposes, the Armory often served as a spectator venue, with six thousand removable seats. In 1897, audiences received an early glimpse of moving-picture technology, with a program of short films made with an electrograph, a forerunner of the movie camera. There was a 1902 performance by opera singer Mary Garden (said to be Claude Debussy's mistress), and

*The Armory*

later that decade a series of concerts led by legendary military-march composer and conductor John Philip Sousa (of "Stars and Stripes Forever" and "Semper Fidelis" fame). In 1911, former president Theodore Roosevelt, President William Howard Taft, and then-New Jersey governor Woodrow Wilson each spoke there at separate events, before running against each other the following year (an election Wilson won). The Blitz-Weinhard brewery purchased the Armory in 1968 for warehouse space. Once in a while in the 1990s, I would happen upon the building's massive sliding doors open, while kegs or other cargo were moved in or out, pausing to marvel at its wide-open vastness and those massive bowstring trusses.

In the late nineties, the Armory was nearly torn down when a host of would-be tenants backed out of leases, but then Gerding Edlen learned the city's largest theater company, Portland Center Stage, was looking for a new home. "We had a set of demolition plans, and I was just dying at the thought of it," Stephen Domreis of GBD Architects told me in a 2007 *Metropolis* article. "Then I thought, 'How are we going to get a theater in here?'" To create what became the first historic-building renovation to earn a LEED Platinum rating from the US Green Building Council, the key was to treat the interior theater like a self-contained building within the Armory's aging brick walls—what Domreis describes as "a ship in a bottle"—a complete building within a historic shell.

Along the way, the architects formed a bond with their client, regularly attending Portland Center Stage performances. "I've seen *Cabaret* seven or eight times. We could just go in and the floor managers knew us," Domreis remembered. "We could come in to the back with our dates and sit in the docents' chairs—no tickets. We could watch a few parts of the performance, or the whole thing. And we ended up making friends with a lot of the actors, because we'd go out with them afterwards." However, the architects discovered there were limits, as Domreis noted with mock indignation. "We asked [then-artistic director] Chris Coleman, 'Okay, Halloween's coming. We need Halloween costumes.' But he wouldn't loan them to us. And then some other people, board members, ended up at a Halloween party wearing their costumes. We were not happy," he added with a laugh. "I would have liked something from Shakespeare."

Portland Center Stage's current artistic director, Marissa Wolf, visited the Armory building for the first time in 2018 while interviewing for the job. "I was completely floored," she says. "When you've got a history that is complicated like the Armory, you can feel that, when you walk in. I love that a space built for military activities can now find a greater and bolder purpose in the arts. I am very interested in excavating the Armory's past, and thinking about that for future commissions: going towards the complicated, violent and racist past that it lived at one point. That feels important to acknowledge and to hold and look at." Today, like many arts organizations, Portland Center Stage has struggled to remain afloat financially, given deep cuts in federal arts funding since early 2025. But the company's matchless content, and the special old building that plays host, will hopefully see them through.

### *Warehouse Row*

The rain has let up, and clouds are beginning to roll through as I continue north into the Northwest Thirteenth Avenue Historic District, following the path of an industrial railroad spur line, erected to easily move goods between waterfront ships and these warehouses. Originally residential, this area developed as an industrial distribution center following the 1905 Lewis and Clark Centennial Exposition. These buildings are not simply utilitarian industrial structures, but have a special timeless elegance nevertheless rooted in function, which inspired early Modernist architecture. Made official in 1987, the historic district includes twenty contributing buildings.

Between Davis Street and Everett Street is the most imaginatively restored of these warehouses, and the most celebrated work of twenty-first-century Portland architecture: the **Wieden + Kennedy World Headquarters** (224 NW Thirteenth Avenue), renovated in 2000. The building was originally constructed in 1908 for the Fuller Paint company, which was described in an advertisement of that time as "Importers and Wholesale Dealers in Paints, Oils, French Window Glass, Brushes, Varnishes, Turpentine, Glue, Gold Leaf, and Artists' Materials." In the 1940s, under new ownership, the building was converted to a refrigeration warehouse and its windows covered, remaining in that state until the late 1990s, when it was put up for sale.

That's when architect Brad Cloepfil came across the structure, just after his firm, Allied Works, had been commissioned by Wieden + Kennedy to design a new headquarters. "I was driving by and they were just starting to tear the brick off the

*Wieden + Kennedy World Headquarters*

window openings," Cloepfil recalls. When the architect showed the building to agency co-founder Dan Wieden, "Dan literally said, 'There's no way in hell we're moving into this building. Are you crazy?' I said, 'Just let me show you what's possible.' I wasn't talking about office space or anything but just a kind of beautiful place, with amazing light. I think that got to him." It's a testament to Cloepfil's imagination that he foresaw in a windowless building a future space teeming with sunlight.

Cloepfil, Portland's most acclaimed architect since mid-century modern maestro Pietro Belluschi, was relatively unknown before interviewing for the Wieden + Kennedy commission. A Portland-area native and University of Oregon graduate, he had spent his early career working for two prestigious firms: in Los Angeles at Skidmore, Owings and Merrill, then in Europe under famed Swiss architect Mario Botta. After returning home and founding Allied Works, and subsequently gaining momentum with commissions such as downtown's Saucebox restaurant and the *Maryhill Overlook* sculptural installation in the Columbia Gorge, he approached the Wieden + Kennedy interview with gusto. "Brad was the final presenter of the day," recalls the agency's former executive creative director, John C. Jay. "His confidence, clarity, and vision came across so clearly. He spoke with a folksy eloquence. He drew on rolls of tissue paper to express his thoughts. With almost no architectural models to show us—he hadn't built much yet—almost no props, he spoke and spoke about the power of space and how creativity could grow in a new space. Experience aside, he appeared to be a supreme problem solver."

At the time, Wieden + Kennedy was perhaps the nation's most celebrated advertising agency, with clients including Nike, Microsoft, ESPN, and Coca-Cola. The agency had been founded in 1982 by Dan Wieden and David Kennedy, who had worked together at another Portland agency and formed their own company at the suggestion of their most prominent client, Nike co-founder Phil Knight. Wieden + Kennedy gained notoriety with a series of celebrated TV commercials for the athletic company, perhaps most notably those starring Michael Jordan (the "Mars Blackmon" series, with movie director Spike Lee) and two-sport star Bo Jackson (the "Bo Knows" campaign). It was Dan Wieden who came up with Nike's enduring "Just Do It" slogan, first appearing in a 1988 commercial; it was said to be inspired by the last words of convicted murderer Gary Gilmore before his execution: "Let's do it!"

Cloepfil's design for Wieden + Kennedy cut a sky-lit atrium into the center of the building, around which offices were arranged. This also helped unite the agency's workers, who were often divided into different client accounts and, in Dan Wieden's eyes, lacked unity. The atrium configuration was one of several different options. "We must have studied that building a hundred different ways," Cloepfil says. "My favorite had a kind of pinwheel of openings that interlocked. It was more spatially complex, but it wouldn't have served them at all. Dan chose the atrium design instead, because he wanted everybody to be in one room. Once we got into it, we saw the potential, and it was pretty exciting."

I once described the Wieden + Kennedy headquarters to Cloepfil as a kind of secular cathedral, and he laughed. "One of the high points when the building was done," he explained, "came as I was walking through it with a Presbyterian minister, who said to me, 'You made a church.' I think in a way all my spaces aspire to be spiritual—spaces that move you, that give you a sense of wonder, a quality that you just can't quite describe. That's what you hope."

Occupying the base of the Wieden + Kennedy Building for just over twenty years was Bluehour restaurant, arguably Portland's most popular fine-dining destination of its time. Founded by restaurateur Bruce Carey with interiors also by Allied Works, its dramatic two-story space was lined with tall curtains and coffered wall panels. Chef Kenny Giambalvo's menu ranged from seared foie gras to roasted suckling pig, and Bluehour was a place to be seen. When Valarie and I would dine there on birthdays or other special occasions, Bluehour felt like a giant stage set. The restaurant went out of business in the summer of 2020, amid pandemic lockdowns, in a wave of high-end restaurant closures. The Pearl, however, has been quicker to recover than the rest of downtown, because while Wieden + Kennedy remains anchored here, it's mostly a residential rather than a commercial district. Meanwhile, the agency continues to thrive; the most recent Super Bowl, US advertising's most celebrated moment, featured the agency's commercials for McDonald's, Fan Duel, TurboTax, and Michelob.

Continuing north through the Thirteenth Avenue Historic District, crossing Flanders Street makes me smile. This is one of several Portland street names that were used for the names of characters on long-running TV show *The Simpsons*—in this case, Ned Flanders, the next-door neighbor of Homer Simpson. The show's creator, Matt Groening, was born and raised in Portland and graduated from Lincoln High School in Goose

Hollow, less than a mile from here. Three more streets here in Northwest Portland are associated with *Simpsons* characters: Kearney Street (Kearney Zzyzwicz), Lovejoy Street (Reverend Lovejoy), and Quimby Street (Mayor "Diamond" Joe Quimby). The series debuted in 1989, when I was a senior in high school, and I vividly remember watching its first episode, a Christmas special called "Simpsons Roasting on an Open Fire." Now I'm in my fifties and, incredibly, *The Simpsons* is still going.

I next come to the **Chown Pella Lofts** (416 NW Thirteenth Avenue), one of the first Pearl warehouses to be converted to nonindustrial purposes. Completed in 1910, it was originally known as the Oregon Transfer Building, a four-story warehouse designed by Edward T. Root. One year later, a six-story addition was added on the northwest corner, and the two structures, though architecturally distinct, have operated as a single building ever since. The Oregon Transfer and Storage Company had been the Pacific Northwest's largest freight transport company, and the first to utilize horse-drawn carriages and ferry boats. Later, in the twentieth century, a succession of products were

*Chown Pella Lofts*

warehoused here: bottles of Coca-Cola, Wrigley chewing gum, Pond's cold cream, and Sheepskin of Oregon car-seat covers.

In 1979, the building was purchased by local architectural hardware company Chown, in partnership with Iowa-based window and door manufacturer Pella. By that time, many of the warehouse businesses were moving to industrial enclaves outside the central city like Swan Island. The companies didn't need all the upstairs spaces, so they were rented out to artists for studios, including Tad Savinar. "It was a nice big space on the fourth floor, about 3,000 square feet with huge old-growth timbers," recalls Savinar, a venerable local visual artist and urban designer. "I stored all my work there, and I had an expansive space to create. It was the first time I could do everything in one space."

Sometimes while Savinar worked late into the night, he heard thieves breaking into other portions of the warehouse. "It was really scary," he remembers. "I went to my dad and said, 'I'm not safe in my studio. Do you have a gun?' He gave me this little lady's Derringer and I thought, 'Fuck! That's not going to protect me.' Then I went and made a toy shotgun out of wood. The barrels were 6 feet long. Just the act of making the gun somehow made me feel better, even though it wasn't real." Savinar kept his Chown Pella studio for over a decade, but toward the end he remembers visiting with developer Al Solheim and seeing a glimpse of this industrial district's future. "Al pulled me into his office and said, 'I want to show you what we're doing.' It was what would become the whole Pearl," Savinar recalls. The idea was to create an arts district, but the master plan renderings showed block after block of condominium and apartment buildings. "I said, 'Where's the ballet school? Where's the tavern?' Al said, 'What do you mean?' I said, 'It's not an arts district if you only have residences.' It was a marketing plan."

Developer John Carroll commissioned the Chown Pella building's conversion to condos, from a design by Portland firm Ankrom Moisan Associated Architects. "We essentially rebuilt that building from the ground up," architect and longtime Ankrom Moisan principal Jeff Hamilton recalls. At one point, while new interior bracing was being constructed, a portion of the exterior brick wall collapsed onto the sidewalk, just missing a mother pushing a baby carriage and flattening a parked car.

Once the building team recovered and completed the residential spaces, they proved immediately popular. "To come into this neighborhood when it was just starting to revitalize was an amazing chance, and not just for us as the architects," Hamilton says. "It was completely sold out before it opened."

### *Rail Trail*

Heading east on Hoyt Street for three blocks and then turning left onto Tenth Avenue, just after a Portland Streetcar passes by, I'm walking into the northernmost portion of the Pearl District. From about 1905 to 1998, some 40 acres here along the Willamette River made up the Hoyt Street Yards, a railroad switching and fueling yard. In 1994, developer Homer Williams and his company, Hoyt Street Properties, contracted with the City of Portland to build 5,500 units of housing for 15,000 residents, interspersed with open space. Over the ensuing thirty years, a succession of condominium buildings have been constructed, giving this northern portion of the Pearl a more contemporary feel than the southern half, where so many old warehouses remain.

That said, my first stop in this neighborhood-within-a-neighborhood is one of the few remaining historic structures: the **Ecotrust Building** (721 NW Ninth Avenue), headquarters for the eponymous nonprofit devoted to sustainable forests, farms, and fisheries. Completed in 1895, the building was originally known as the McCracken Warehouse, its original architect unknown. In historic photos, the building is the lone piece of architecture in a sea of railcars and tracks. The McCracken was where building supplies transferred from incoming ships to outgoing trains. Still discernible inside are stenciled destination names of cities and counties across the region.

Renovated in 2001 from a design by Holst Architecture, this was the first historic building in the United States to receive a Gold-level LEED certification from the US Green Building Council. Ecotrust founder Spencer Beebe (an ancestor of the aforementioned C. F. Beebe) insisted on renovating the McCracken despite skepticism. "Everyone said, 'It's unreinforced masonry right on top of a fault line. It's basically just sheer madness,'" Beebe recalls. "Bricks had fallen off the cornice and blackberries were growing off the roof. Admittedly it was

*Ecotrust Building*

a mess. The board said I was betting the organization on it." But Beebe was adamant that renovating the McCracken was a greener choice than constructing a new building. And just as the McCracken had been a fulcrum for industry, he reasoned, so too could Ecotrust be a crossroads for a burgeoning green economy. "On the river where the salmon are jumping upstream, that's where the seagulls and the bears concentrate. It's an ecosystem for interaction," he says. "We wanted to create that model in a building. We had to make the numbers work, but we were trying to create an ecosystem."

Holst's design seismically reinforced the building by erecting steel bracing towers on the northwest and southwest corners, which double as exterior stairways. The original Douglas-fir planks and ceiling beams were preserved, and the timber ceiling rafters and brick walls were left exposed; even an original stuffed moose head on the wall was kept. "At one point somebody asked me, 'What color do you want to paint the walls?' I said, 'Why waste the paint? There is history in that paint falling down," Beebe recalls. "I said, 'Do the seismic reinforcement and make sure it doesn't fall down, and that's all." Beebe's instincts proved right. Purchased for $2.5 million, the Ecotrust Building is now worth more than ten times that amount, he says. And here in the northern Pearl, the Ecotrust headquarters is particularly significant: a modest old brick building amid the shiny glass and steel condos.

Now my focus turns to the open spaces created as part of Hoyt Street Properties' development deal with the city: the neighborhood's imaginatively designed single-block parks. As is the case in downtown Portland's South Auditorium district, with the magnificent Open Space Sequence by Lawrence Halprin, which I'll be visiting later, these beautiful Pearl District gathering spaces are the best designs in the neighborhood, not the buildings. But whenever I visit here, I think of a more ambitious plan that never came to fruition. Early on in the Hoyt Street Yards master-planning process, ZGF Architects partner Greg Baldwin suggested a canal, which would have restored a portion of Tanner Creek that once flowed here, and has long been diverted via underground pipes. "We said, 'Forget what the zoning code says. What could we do to really make it something special?'" recalls retired ZGF principal Paddy Tillett. "It was going to be logistically difficult, but we could do it." After opposition from railroad companies, however, the proposal was scrapped. That's when the design team decided on what Tillett calls "three discrete parks that would complement each other."

In 1999, Berkeley, California, landscape architecture firm Peter Walker & Partners, one of the nation's most acclaimed firms of the era, was hired to provide concepts for these open spaces. Walker & Partners also designed the first park to be completed, which today remains the most popular: **Jamison Square** (between NW Tenth and Eleventh Avenues and Johnson and Kearney Streets). Opened in 2000, its focal point is its fountain, which emulates a shallow tidal pool. From thin cuts in a low-slung wall of stacked granite blocks, water streams into low pools, then drains like a bathtub and is recirculated. "The idea of this was a natural spring," explains landscape architect David Walker, Peter's son and firm partner. "I think this is important to Portland. You see these water fountains going all the time, around the city—the Halprin [Open Space Sequence] parks and even those Benson Bubbler drinking fountains just running continuously. From here in California, it seems like a wonder that you've got that resource, that abundance."

Jamison Square is named for gallerist William Jamison, who coined the Pearl District's name. In 1985, the Jamison/Thomas Gallery became one of the first of a succession of art galleries that ultimately moved to the Pearl from downtown. Jamison had come to Portland from his native Ohio in 1974. His William Jamison Gallery, as it was originally known, dealt in folk art before Jamison brought on as his partner curator Jeffrey

*Kenny Scharff's Tikitotmoniki Totems at Jamison Square*

Thomas, son of former Metropolitan Museum of Art curator Michael Thomas and Hollywood actress Brooke Hayward (and stepson of Hayward's second husband, actor Dennis Hopper). But as Jamison/Thomas Gallery struggled to break even, they needed more affordable space. "The whole Pearl thing didn't exist. It was just all derelict train tracks," recalls Thomas. "But that's what galleries do: they look for cheap space. That's how we ended up at 1313 NW Glisan." The new storefront space, on the ground floor of what's now called the Pearl Building, was small, only about 15 feet deep, but it had large windows, in front of which the gallerists hung sculptures to attract passers-by. "At the time, William and Brad [Rogers, Jamison's longtime partner] were squatting behind that fake wall," Thomas remembers. After the new Jamison/Thomas Gallery shifted to contemporary art, they were successful enough that the partners decided to open a satellite gallery in New York City helmed by Thomas, while Jamison oversaw the original location.

While Jamison/Thomas wasn't literally the neighborhood's first gallery, Jamison helped cement its reputation as an art destination. Jamison and fellow dealer Bob Kochs of Augen Gallery came up with the idea for the First Thursday art walk, with all Pearl galleries open into the evening once a month as a way of drawing potential new middle-class buyers. "We had great parties. That's what people remember maybe more than anything," Thomas says with a laugh. But Jamison's goodness and charisma, he adds, was also part of what made the gallery memorable. "William had this extraordinary ability to gain the artist's trust and respect. It was a real gift. He put people at ease. There are wonderful stories of him going to meet artists. This is what made William such a great man. He wanted to see people succeed." In the late 1980s, Jamison contracted the HIV virus, in a time when the AIDS epidemic was ravaging the country. Jamison died in 1995, five years before Jamison Square was completed, and named after him.

At Jamison Square's west edge is one of my favorite works of public art in Portland, Kenny Scharff's *Tikitotmoniki Totems*, a quartet of colorful Pop Art sculptures inspired by Native American art. The totems have a functional purpose: covering electrical poles for the Portland Streetcar, the tracks of which run along the square's east and west sides. Although Scharff

*Tanner Springs Park*

originally designed the totems for a site in New Orleans, "I love the way they relate to the Pacific Northwest culture as well as the universal Tiki culture, which extends from the South Pacific through the Northwest and up to Alaska," he said when the artworks were dedicated. "Art should, above all, be fun, and these huge 3D forms translate that perfectly."

Although we're not far from the end of this second walk, I'm stepping into Lovejoy Bakers for an espresso before continuing on to **Tanner Springs Park** (between NW Tenth and Eleventh Avenues, Marshall and Northrup Streets), kid-friendly Jamison Square's quieter, more contemplative companion piece, which is actually an ideal spot to sit on a park bench for a moment and drink my coffee.

Tanner's design, by German landscape architect Herbert Dreiseitl, features a small grove of native oak trees giving way to tall grass and reeds before sloping downward to a marsh and pond, into which a small dock-like metal path extends. Although it's not literally restoring Tanner Creek, as ZGF had proposed, it appears to do so and certainly pays symbolic homage, while providing a chance to sit by the water. "It's a key idea for the park," Dreiseitl told me for a 2006 *Metropolis* story, "going from dry to wet, from hill to valley or forest to open fields." Forming the edge of the pond beside the boardwalk is an undulating wall fashioned from locally reclaimed railroad ties, which create the implied effect of the landscape being pulled back to reveal the creek. It's a lot to squeeze into a 200-by-200-foot block. But it's "not a question of scale," Dreiseitl argued. "You find the same systems and patterns on a large scale in the landscape as you do in one little seed."

Continuing north, I come to the Pearl District's tallest structure and the tallest residential building in Portland, the twenty-eight-story **Cosmopolitan Condominiums** (1075 NW Northrup Street). Designed by Bora Architects and completed in 2016 for Hoyt Street Properties, it essentially marks the architectural northern edge of the Pearl, and the end of the former Hoyt Street Yards. The Cosmopolitan appears from afar to be of a pair with the US Bancorp tower at the edge of downtown, like architectural bookends. I like it better than most Pearl condo buildings because its greater height adds a sense of slenderness. Honestly there are some real stinkers in this portion of the neighborhood: aesthetic failures that even in their short lives haven't aged well. There's an apartment building just north of here, for example, called the NV, which is pronounced just like the word "envy," but with its mirrored stainless-steel tiles, gaudy would seem to be the more appropriate choice. Nor am I fond of The Encore, a block northeast of here at NW Ninth and Overton, which looks like a suburban office building. The Cosmo isn't a masterpiece per se, but it's a lot easier on the eyes.

By the time the Cosmopolitan was completed, Hoyt Street Properties had developed a succession of condo buildings, growing in height as one moves north, and increasingly taking inspiration from the Vancouver, British Columbia, signature building form, slender "point towers" above wider residential bases. Hoyt Street Properties president Tiffany Sweitzer had told me ten years earlier, in a 2006 *Portland Architecture* interview, "We really have an opportunity to make this anything we want. It does not have to follow the grid. We could put the streets in the way we want to. But there's a learning curve of not only the architecture and how something sits on a block, but everything that has to fall into place to make it work—which none of us knew at first." Ultimately they *did* follow the street grid, and because of how these building and blocks are interspersed with parks, it's a nice neighborhood at a distinctive spot. When the Cosmopolitan was completed in 2016, I remember touring the building with architect Brad Demby of Bora, and being awed by the vantage point, looking past the Fremont Bridge down the Willamette toward the shipyards, or back toward the downtown skyline.

Stanley Penkin, a Cosmopolitan Condominiums resident and former president of the Pearl District Neighborhood

*Cosmopolitan Condominiums*

Association, believes cultivating neighborhood vitality has been a challenge. "I think the Pearl has evolved into almost two different Pearls," he told me for a 2018 story in *The New York Times*. "If you look from maybe Lovejoy [Street] south or north, it's almost a demarcation line. I lived initially on Couch Street at The Henry [Condominiums, part of the Brewery Blocks], and I really loved that part of the Pearl because it was a little more organic down there. There were some old and new buildings and there was a mix. You've got these smaller buildings that have resisted the pressure and survived as property values have gone up. You still had machine shops, auto-repair shops, the Armory that was rehabbed. As you go farther north it's much newer. We moved up to this end of the Pearl and it feels very, very different. I used to refer to this upper Pearl as a Disneyland. It lacked the genuineness I felt in the lower part of the Pearl. But now that we live up here almost as far north as you can go, it's kind of nice because it's much more peaceful."

The Cosmopolitan looks out at **The Fields Park** (between NW Overton Street, NW Eleventh Avenue and NW Naito Parkway), which at 3.35 acres is the largest of the three northern Pearl District greenspaces (along with Jamison Square and Tanner Springs Park) constructed as part of the 2001 River District plan. That plan actually called for four parks, including a waterfront park on the Centennial Mills site. So The Fields, designed by the San Francisco landscape architect Cheryl Barton, was meant as part of a procession to a final park that never came. Even so, while lacking the compelling concepts of Jamison and Tanner, this park is a versatile gathering space, with playground equipment, an oval walking path, and a large grassy open space in the middle, surrounded by an earthen berm of constructed wetlands that provide stormwater-management infrastructure.

Walking across The Fields Park, I am already looking past it, across Naito Parkway, where that riverside fourth park was supposed to be, but instead today is the fenced-off site of a crumbling industrial ruin, or what's left of it: the **Centennial Mills** complex (1362 NW Naito Parkway). It's a missed opportunity twice over in that neither the culminating Pearl District riverfront park nor the community-driven historic preservation effort succeeded. In fact, "missed opportunity" is letting the City of Portland, which

Centennial Mills

owns this land and failed multiple times to redevelop it, off easy. It's a tragedy and a comedy of errors. (But this could be my double-espresso talking.) For the time being, even as only a fraction of the complex remains, and even though it's now covered by graffiti, I'm thankful that even it is still standing.

Centennial Mills was designed by San Francisco engineer Leland S. Rosener, the first of what would become a multi-building structure completed in 1910 as Crown Mills. As it expanded, the mills formed a nexus for the city and region's thriving wheat trade, along with Albers Mill just east of here. And, more than most locals realize, this was actually Oregon's most important crop, not timber. "It was through the wheat trade that Portland, in a sense, became Portland," explains Portland State University historian and former Oregon Historical Society director Chet Orloff, noting that almost one-third of US wheat exports were once distributed through this city. "Once Portland had established itself in the 1840s, wheat was already being brought by wagon down to the wharfs there, loaded onto ships, and then taken down to San Francisco, to Europe, and especially to Asia—Japan and China." Oregon wheat did especially well in China, which Orloff believes actually influenced the history of Chinese cuisine. "Oregon's rich topsoil was deposited by volcanoes thousands of years ago, and it produces this great soft wheat," he explains. "At some point in the 1860s, as the story goes, some trader took it home, ground it up, and made it into noodles, and discovered that Oregon soft white wheat made great noodles. It sounds silly, but I think there's a lot of truth to it. Within the next ten years, China became the major market for Oregon wheat."

"By the 1880s, there were three wealthy cities in the US: New York first, Philadelphia second, and Portland third," Orloff adds. "We were the third-wealthiest city in the nation based on the wheat trade. We were able to build buildings like the Pioneer Courthouse and the Portland Hotel in the 1890s. It led to an elegant collection of historic buildings downtown and along the park blocks, most of which were funded through the wheat trade."

A second six-story concrete flour mill and the first grain elevator were completed in early 1911, after which flour was shipped from Crown Mills for the first time. Barely a year after it opened, the flour mill caught fire and, because its upper floors were beyond the reach of fireboats, the interior was gutted. Yet the structure survived, and the mill was quickly rebuilt with a large water tank atop the roof for built-in protection from future fires. By the end of World War I, Crown Mills was operating around the clock, with 120 workers onsite. Its name was changed in 1949, after the original owner, British firm Balfour-Guthrie and Company, sold the facility to Centennial Flouring Mills of Tacoma. It was expanded in 1962, about the same time Orloff worked there as a young man. "It was quite loud, a noisy place," Orloff recalls. "The milling machines were grinding wheat into flour, moving it along conveyor belts and into these large bins that then were loaded onto ships. There were a lot of moving parts: big, dangerous moving parts. You really had to be careful if you were working in a technical aspect; I wasn't, fortunately. They wouldn't let me close to the machinery. I would have been ground up or something. But it was a noisy place, and dusty from the flour. Only later did I realize that kind of flour can explode."

In 2016 I attended a public forum to explore whether Centennial Mills might still be saved, in which the Pearl District Neighborhood Association's chair, architect Patricia Gardner, described the past fifteen years succinctly. "In 2000 the city bought the site. It was a working flour mill all the way through the nineties. The city wanted to tear it down and build a park. We went through a public involvement process as part of the Pearl District Development plan. It talked about a different vision: not tearing it all down, and having some sort of public, civic use to that site along with park land," she said. "We started lobbying the city hard to keep the buildings. In 2005 they decided to keep them. That took a lot of effort. They voted to move forward with a framework plan and come up with a different vision that involved keeping some parts of the site for historical purposes." A developer was chosen with public input, but before any reconstruction began, "the recession hit, PDC kind of changed the rules on them, and that deal fell apart," she added. "A new development agreement was made with another developer, And that deal fell apart." Just a few months after this hopeful meeting, the City of Portland began tearing down much of the complex.

Two years before the partial demolition, I toured the largest of two remaining mill buildings when developer Jordan Schnitzer was considering purchasing the complex. It was a precarious setting, where swaths of water-damaged upstairs floors were marked with spray paint to warn of potential cave-ins. The wharf buildings sitting precariously along the riverfront seemed like the Big Bad Wolf could blow them down with one exhalation. Raccoon tracks were among the subtler examples of animal intrusion, and we had to wear facemasks to avoid inhaling various noxious chemicals. "I guess I'm wearing my civic hat first on this," Schnitzer told me for a 2014 *CityLab* article. "Certainly, if we wanted more real estate projects, there would be easier ways to do it. But it's one of the few sites left on the waterfront that tells of a time and place in the past that was a critical building block of this community. That's why I think there was a human cry when the city was going to tear it all down."

I used to be indignant about the loss of Centennial Mills, writing a succession of blog posts and opinion pieces arguing for its retention, if not by renovating its remaining structures than at least as an architectural ruin, around which the city could build a park (as many other cities have done with industrial relics). Even now I have my moments of anger. Today there is scarcely any visible history of Centennial Mills left. Yet I'm thankful to see the flour mill and its water tower remain. They may not be there much longer, however, for there is talk of leveling the site for affordable housing. Even so, I retain hope that the park originally called for can take its place.

Meanwhile, a little older now, I've largely come to accept the fate of Centennial Mills as another reminder that cities are ephemeral: that on nearly every building site, what's there will eventually be replaced, and when there are exceptions, they are to be celebrated. In these first two walks, I've been able to visit and pay homage to numerous historic structures still standing, while also commemorating those that have been lost. Maybe keeping Centennial Mills was always naïve folly, yet it's also a point of pride that people tried. And, as it happens, just down Naito Parkway is another old mill building, more modest in scale yet successfully repurposed and still standing.

The Pearl District's northern terminus, and my final stop on this walk is the **Fremont Bridge** (NW Naito Parkway near Fifteenth Avenue), downtown Portland's most recognizable span with its postcard-worthy arched form. Together the circa-1973 Fremont and its sibling, 1966's Marquam Bridge, bookend downtown with two interstate-highway river crossings, as part of one loop joining I-405 and I-5. They arrived amid a wave of mid-twentieth-century automobile infrastructure development that carved wide paths through this and almost every major US city. But because the Marquam, a tall and flat double-level truss

Fremont Bridge

bridge, had been widely panned by the public for its utilitarian ugliness, the government invested more in the lyrical arch-shaped Fremont design, by New York–based Parsons Brinckerhoff (today WSP USA), one of the country's pioneering transit engineers, responsible for subway systems in New York City, San Francisco, and several other cities around the world.

Standing at the Fremont Bridge's west end today, beside Naito Parkway, I'm reminded that, unlike any other bridge in the city, this one spans clear across the river, without any piers in the water. The Fremont has always been a captivating work of engineering: a year before the bridge's completion, thousands watched as the bridge's 6,000-ton central arched span was hoisted into place by a group of barge-based hydraulic jacks—the largest such lift ever attempted. At the top of the Fremont Bridge, 381 feet above the water at the center of the rainbow span, are US and Oregon flags erected in 1976 as temporary decorations for the United States Bicentennial but made permanent at the public's behest.

The Fremont is even more compelling as an experience. Traveling west across the Willamette at the top of the bridge, its steel arch rising over the highway as a panoramic view of river and city unfolds, is one of my favorite ways of seeing the city. At 55 miles an hour (or more), it's all over quickly, yet with downtown to the west, the industrial waterfront to the east, and the forested ridge of the West Hills in the background, it's a visceral thrill.

The man for whom the Fremont Bridge was named, John Charles Frémont, was nicknamed The Pathfinder for a series of expeditions in the 1840s to document and map the country's new western states; he later became one of California's first two United States Senate members and, in 1856, ran for president. But, by 1973, the biggest paths America built were freeways that cut through its most populated urban settings, with little regard for those in the way: usually neighborhoods populated by immigrants and people of color. Perhaps it's symbolically fitting, therefore, that however much the Fremont Bridge seems to embody strength, its opening was delayed by months because of a crack discovered on the bridge's west side. Even today, it's inspected more often than any other local bridge. For decades now, Portland's urban core has been encircled by interstate highways, arguably a design flaw of its own. Yet there's no denying that the Fremont Bridge is one of the city's most identifiable landmarks.

# Interlude

## *A Bridge with a View*

*Broadway Bridge*

Let's pause for a moment to take in the view. Over the past two walks, I've made my way from the West End of downtown through the Pearl District to the Fremont Bridge. I am about to trek through more of the Pearl and dip into Old Town on my way back into downtown. But first I'm doing something I couldn't do at the automobile-only Fremont. I'm walking onto the **Broadway Bridge** (NW Naito Parkway at Broadway). That way, like on the Portland Aerial Tram, the wider view gives me a sense of not just buildings one-by-one but together, as a composition.

Being here also brings a thrilling sense of the Willamette River itself. This isn't the book's only time reaching the river, but it's the moment I'm able to get truly out over the water and sense its flow. There's an inherent duality to the Willamette's presence: both permanent and always changing. No matter how much Portland's built environment is continually remade, the river is a constant presence. At the same time, its water is continually moving past, beginning as mountain snowfall hundreds of miles away and passing here on its way to the Pacific Ocean.

Today from the Broadway Bridge's southwest walkway, I can see a river barge slowly making its way north, but it doesn't trigger any drawbridge openings like visiting navy vessels during Rose Festival, the citywide celebration held each June, when thousands of people line the waterfront to greet the massive military ships as they reach port, with the central-city bridges opening in succession. I can also see the Portland Streetcar going across this bridge, as part of its central-city loop, making this bridge a nexus for five different travel modes: watercraft, cars, trains, bikes, and pedestrians.

The Broadway Bridge was built at a kind of pivot point, a bend in the river, which also gives me a special perspective. I can look upriver from here, where the Willamette heads in a northwesterly direction, past the Fremont Bridge to the shipyards beyond. I can look south to the downtown skyline. Looking west I see the Pearl District and, beyond that, the West Hills.

Bookending the Broadway Bridge are beautiful buildings restored after being threatened with demolition. Here on the west side is the brick-clad **Albers Brothers Milling Company Building** (1200 NW Naito Parkway), completed in 1911, just one year after its larger neighbor, Centennial Mills. Converted to

*Veterans Memorial Coliseum from Broadway Bridge*

offices in 1989, it's one of many adaptive reuse projects commissioned by Bill and Sam Naito's company, Norcrest.

At the east end of the bridge is **Veterans Memorial Coliseum** (300 N Ramsay Way), the Modernist masterpiece by Skidmore, Owings and Merrill, its glass façade gleaming. Opened in 1960, the Coliseum is where our beloved Trail Blazers basketball team won the 1977 NBA championship, and where my mom saw the Beatles perform in 1965. When the arena was threatened with demolition in 2009, I co-founded the Friends of Memorial Coliseum with architect Stuart Emmons to try to save the arena, not just for its cultural history but also for the masterful design: a building equivalent to over two city blocks in size but standing on just four columns, and offering a 360-degree view from the arena seats to the outside. I once watched the sun set over the entire downtown Portland skyline from my seat during a Trail Blazers exhibition game. It took more than fifteen years of advocacy, but finally, in 2025, a renovation was completed. Behind the Coliseum stands the larger, less beautiful Moda Center, the Blazers' home since 1996, which I've always joked was designed by Fred Flintstone. Just beyond it along the river is the massive Dreyfus grain elevator, a hulking row of concrete cylinders,

*Broadway Bridge*

usually with a massive barge docked in front. The waterfront on that east side is vacant, a continual missed opportunity, but there are plans to build a public park here as part of the broader Albina Vision, rebuilding this historically Black neighborhood.

To the south, there is also the **Steel Bridge** (NW Naito Parkway near Glisan Street), completed in 1912 and perhaps the city's most robust-looking span, as well as maybe the most hardworking. A through-truss, double-decker vertical lift span designed by Kansas City Waddell & Harrington (also responsible for Portland's Hawthorne Bridge and Interstate Bridge), it carries Amtrak passenger and freight trains as well as MAX light-rail trains across the river on its upper deck, with a pathway for pedestrians and bicyclists on its lower span, connected to the Eastbank Esplanade and acting as the northern terminus of Tom McCall Waterfront Park. Beyond the Steel, I can see the rest of the downtown bridge collection: the Burnside, Morrison, Hawthorne, Tilikum. and Ross Island Bridges.

Up close, I love the Broadway Bridge's muscular steel supports and the decorative lanterns. This remains the longest Rall-type bascule bridge (a drawbridge moved by a counterweight) in the world. Designed by Polish-born Chicago engineer Ralph

Modjeski, its two cage-like center pieces pivot on steel wheels connected to a pair of 1,250-ton counterweights in order to make way for passing ships. Modjeski (1861–1940) was known as the country's greatest bridge builder of his era, having been among the first to design suspension bridges, including the Manhattan Bridge in New York City and the Bay Bridge between San Francisco and Oakland; one of his protegees, Joseph B. Strauss, designed the Golden Gate Bridge.

The year the Broadway Bridge was completed, 1913, was transformative for the city. This was the year women's suffrage leader Abigail Scott Duniway died, and popular two-term governor Tom McCall was born. It's when future legendary artist Mark Rothko emigrated here with his family from Latvia, and Portland's beloved Central Library was completed. The bridge's opening also coincided with the renaming of Seventh Street as Broadway, beginning a new era for downtown Portland as an entertainment district. This came amid exponential nationwide growth in automobile ownership, for 1913 was the year that the Ford Motor Company began producing the Model T on an assembly line for the first time. Over the ensuing decade, car ownership grew more than tenfold.

A few months ago, at Nine Gallery in the Pearl District, I saw an installation by the late John Montague called *Willamette Greenway*, featuring hundreds of video clips and still photos taken over several years at the base of the Broadway Bridge, but focusing on just a few square feet of the riverbank. The other side of the river was not visible, nor was the bridge or any building. Yet Montague captured an incredible amount of change: in light and shadow, in weather, in wildlife and shipping traffic, in the river's currents and water level. It was a moving reminder to stop and appreciate the spirit of place, not only because Montague passed away before his work was ever exhibited.

The Broadway Bridge isn't my only opportunity to pull back and enjoy the wider view, but while taking in so many sites at street level I'm thankful for these moments to stop: to take a deep breath, to marvel, and to be reminded that, from two and a half million people and what was originally a cluster of small towns, we have conjured one city. But, like this river, it is continually changing and flowing.

# *Walk 3*

# On and Off Broadway

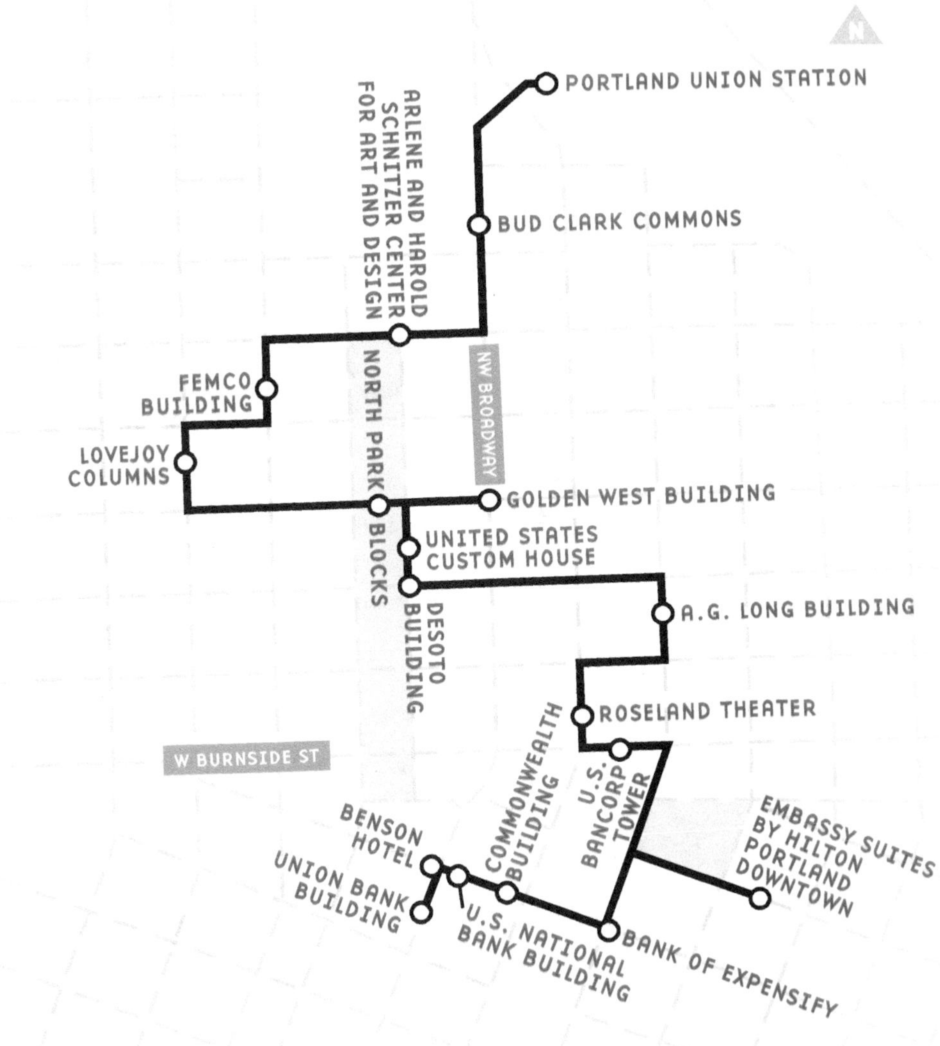

*Arrival and Transition*

Now it's time to explore both sides of Broadway, passing south through the Pearl and Old Town on the way back to downtown. My first stop is one of the city's most venerable architectural landmarks, **Portland Union Station** (800 NW Sixth Avenue), a busy train depot since the nineteenth century yet perhaps best-known for its signature clock tower.

On this site before the station had been Couch Lake, which was more like a swampy wetland edge of the Willamette River

*Portland Union Station*

than an actual lake. At its edge had stood the home of Captain John Couch, a commercial ship captain from Massachusetts who arrived here in 1845 and became one of Portland's founding fathers. Couch convinced Asa Lovejoy and Francis Pettygrove that their land claim, several miles north of the more populous Oregon City, was a better-positioned port. (Lovejoy and Pettygrove famously flipped a coin to determine which of their hometowns, Boston or Portland, Maine, to name the new city after.) Couch's claim, immediately north of theirs, was made one year before the Oregon Treaty of 1846, which made the Oregon Country below the 49th parallel a permanent part of the United States. Four years later, the Donation Land Claim Act's 1850 passage allowed Couch (as a white male) to take full possession of 256 acres, which became known as Couch's Addition and comprised most of present-day Old Town and the Pearl District.

The impetus for a major train station in Portland began in the early 1880s, as the country's transcontinental railroad neared completion. A few blocks west of this present-day Union Station site, a much larger station called Grand Union Depot was planned at the northern edge of the North Park Blocks. Financier Henry Villard, who had come to Portland from Germany to oversee German investments in the Oregon and California Railroad, commissioned New York's McKim, Meade and White (the nation's most prestigious architecture firm) to design what would have been the largest train station in the world. But constructing the railroad had cost more than expected, causing financial collapse for Villard and his investors. In 1884, construction of the grand Portland Hotel was halted, and the Grand Union Depot was abandoned before it could begin. The smaller Union Station, opened in 1896, was designed by Kansas City architecture firm Van Brunt & Howe. Lead architect Henry Van Brunt had previously co-designed several buildings at Harvard University before relocating the firm to Missouri, where he and partner Frank M. Howe designed a series of stations for Union Pacific Railroad.

Union Station is oriented toward the railroad tracks, which angle northwest–southeast in parallel with this stretch of the river, putting the building on a diagonal with the surrounding street grid. The Romanesque-style station is defined by a dramatic series of hipped-roof forms and a large covered awning. Inside, the main space is resplendent with travertine floors, marble walls, and a decorative coffered ceiling, all added during a 1930 renovation overseen by architect Pietro Belluschi; the original interior had been clad in wood. Because commercial offices above Union Station's main lobby prevent the possibility of skylights, the lobby has a relative lack of natural light. Union Station's interior seems romantically melancholy, a kind of Edward Hopper painting waiting to happen. The building's low-slung horizontality is contrasted by the verticality of its clock tower, which recalls a medieval Italian bell tower. Or at least it did before 1948, when neon signs were added at the top, reading GO BY TRAIN on the northeast and southwest sides and UNION STATION on the northwest and southeast sides.

I'll never forget the wonder I felt in 2023 climbing to the top of Union Station's clock tower, at the invitation of a friend, Aaron Choate, who was renting an office above the main lobby. It was one of those rare moments that, ironically, given that it involved a timepiece, seemed timeless. Overcoming my fear of heights was not easy, especially climbing a multistory portion in the middle of the tower where the stairs and their meager banister hang precariously against the old brick. Near the top floor, I actually resorted to crawling up the stairs, my hands and knees covered in dust, while Aaron waited, graciously withholding ridicule. But I correctly sensed that something magical was up there, worth persevering for.

When I reached the top, I half-expected *The Wizard of Oz*'s namesake Wizard to be waiting there, operating the tower's four frosted-glass clock faces. Instead, within the already-small top floor space there was a kind of room within a room: a wood-paneled enclosure protecting the clock mechanism itself. Sized like a robust grandfather clock, it was emitting a wonderfully muscular ticking sound. Four metal rods protruded from the clock mechanism upward and outward, about 10 feet off the floor, turning the hands of the four clocks. There wasn't much room to move around the clock and its wood enclosure; Aaron and I were right up against the brick walls and the glass clock faces. I noticed the cracks in their glass, as fragile and decayed as the old brick itself, as well as how the glass subtly glowed with absorbed sunlight. And because we were behind the clocks, their hands were turning counterclockwise, as if reversing time.

As I leave Union Station and begin walking in Old Town, I notice a tent on the sidewalk at Irving Street and Broadway. Indeed, the neighborhood has always had more people living on the streets than anywhere else in the city. That's partly because Old Town has long been associated with poverty, and partly because of the concentration of nonprofits serving the needy here. One prominent example is the **Bud Clark Commons** (665 NW Hoyt Street), a homeless-services center and residential building completed in 2011 as part of a larger initiative begun by the City of Portland in 2005 to end homelessness within ten years. At the time, an estimated 4,000 people were on the streets each night, putting Portland in the top ten US cities per capita for homelessness, and first nationally for homeless youth. Despite the ten-year plan, which from the start seemed unlikely to succeed, those numbers have continued to increase. Yet this only makes the Bud Clark Commons more necessary.

The mayor for whom this building was named, John Elwood "Bud" Clark Jr., was among the era's most popular, and certainly City Hall's most colorful, personality. Before winning the 1984 mayoral election in an upset of incumbent Frank Ivancie, Clark was proprietor of the Goose Hollow Inn tavern and had never previously run for office. In a sense, he was best known as a flasher. Clark had been the model in a popular circa-1978 poster sold in many local shops, with the phrase "Expose Yourself To Art" accompanying a photo taken by his friend Mike Ryerson, featuring Clark in a long raincoat (taken from behind), revealing to a statue his presumably naked body. With a handlebar moustache and knickerbocker pants, Clark was a quirky and refreshing alternative to the conservative and dour Ivancie, who had become especially unpopular after trying to halt construction of Pioneer Courthouse Square. Clark even had his own signature catch phrase—"Whoop, Whoop!"—with which he greeted Johnny Carson while a guest on the *Tonight Show* in October 1984, just before taking office.

Yet Bud Clark was no buffoon. As mayor he created a nationally recognized strategy for curbing homelessness, supported the nascent MAX light-rail line's growth, and led the campaign to build the Oregon Convention Center. Clark also lent his name to the Mayor's Ball, an annual charity concert at Memorial Coliseum featuring bands from the Pacific Northwest. He was reelected in 1988 and would likely have won a third term had he chosen to run in 1992, but Clark instead retired from politics and went back to running the Goose Hollow Inn. That's where I met him in 2004, as a freelance photographer assigned to take his picture. I remember Clark sitting patiently for me in a tavern booth, casually dressed in shorts, suspenders, and a campaign button for then-presidential candidate Howard Dean.

Designed by Holst Architecture, the Bud Clark Commons provides a range of services at one site to help homeless people transition off the streets. On the eight-story building's north side is a day center offering medical and mental health treatment, showers, and laundry facilities, as well as a ninety-bed temporary shelter. On the south side are 130 studio apartments reserved for those with very low incomes. Before beginning the design process, architects from Holst traveled to several other cities to see how other agencies and nonprofits addressed homelessness. "We didn't find any projects that combined all three of these elements—the day center, the temporary shelter, and the permanent housing—and condense that onto a half-block," Holst partner Dave Otte told me for a 2011 *Portland Architecture* blog post. "It took a lot of creative geometry."

The Bud Clark Commons' multicolored brick façade makes the building seem unexpectedly whimsical, which is perhaps appropriate given the late mayor's persona. "The aspirations for the building were pretty high," Holst co-founder John Holmes recalled in that same post. "One of the ways to get around the stickiness of putting more homeless people in this neighborhood was to do a good strong building. And with its proximity to the Broadway Bridge, this building needed a kind of gateway quality. You needed to have a sense of arrival. But the big challenge when you're dealing with 130 units, all exactly the same, was how you get away from the uniformity. How do we give this building a kind of presence? The color and the details helped de-institutionalize it."

Operated by nonprofit agencies Home Forward and Transition Projects, Bud Clark Commons has functioned well. "Any time you bring together large groups of people—we have ninety in that shelter—that's a challenging thing to do, to create spaces where folks are comfortable," explains Transition Projects senior public policy director Tony Bernal. "In the old location, this used to be our most frenetic shelter. There was not a lot of privacy; people were on top of each other. It just did not function well. All of that went away when we went into the Bud Clark Commons."

## *Art on the Park*

Just south of Bud Clark Commons on Broadway is a former federal building that in 2015 was renovated as a new home for the Pacific Northwest College of Art (PNCA): the **Arlene and Harold Schnitzer Center for Art and Design** (511 NW Broadway). Completed in 1918, the original design by San Francisco architect Louis Hobart blended the Classical Revival and Chicago Commercial styles, with two monolithic stone columns with Ionic capitals at its entrance. Originally this building housed a post office, but over the ensuing century before PNCA's purchase, a variety of federal agencies were located here, including the Immigration and Naturalization Service.

PNCA was founded in 1909 as the Museum Art School within the Portland Art Museum, before going independent in

*Arlene and Harold Schnitzer Center for Art and Design*

1991. In 1998 the school relocated to a renovated Pearl District warehouse known as the Feldman Building (near present-day Jamison Square). I loved the Feldman, where classrooms surrounded a two-story open space lit by a large skylight, and the building's industrial origin provided a gritty ambiance. As PNCA grew, however, what became the Schnitzer Center offered a more spacious setting, and its historic architecture a grander locale. The building's redesign, by Allied Works, filled the building with natural light, uncovering old skylights, removing drop ceilings and fluorescent light fixtures, and creating a new multistory atrium. "It's like surgery," architect Brad Cloepfil told me in a 2015 *Portland Architecture* interview, as we toured the project. "Where can you touch it and have the most impact? We knew we wanted a gathering space, so we opened up this atrium. But what's the identity? This is a very proper old institutional building that's going to be occupied by these irreverent, irascible, inventive kids. There needs to be an energy of the old and new, and something a little bit raw, a little unexpected."

The new locale didn't impress everyone. Before the Schnitzer Center's renovation, artist Stephen Slappe, then a PNCA professor, received permission to film inside the old building. "There were all these creepy spaces," he remembers. "I'd been in the building before, because my wife is an immigrant and we went there to get her citizenship paperwork. When I started filming, I remember going first into what had been the detention center. It was this really bad energy." While Slappe acknowledges the renovated space is beautiful, "As a teacher, it was a difficult adaptation," he says. "It's a really bureaucratic space, because that's what it's designed for. It's siloed rooms and walls made of marble, so you can't put push pins in it. And it's historic, so you can't change it. It's huge, but it's broken up in weird ways that aren't necessarily conducive to how artists work. I don't think I was the only one that was sensitive to that. It's something we talked to the architects about. When the artists are crammed into small rooms, that atrium starts to seem ostentatious."

In 2020, PNCA ceased to be an independent institution, acquired by Salem-based Willamette University. That same year, Slappe lost his teaching gig. Recent times had seen two other local small colleges close for good during the pandemic,

*FEMCO Building*

including the city's other art school, the Oregon College of Art and Craft. And it seems more than likely that the financial impact of taking on the 511 Broadway renovation was a factor in PNCA's loss of independence. Even so, hopefully the art school is here to stay, because like the larger Portland State University at the southern edge of downtown, PNCA's student body infuses its Pearl District neighborhood with youthful energy.

I notice there are more people on the streets as I move west, closer to Powell's Books and a variety of restaurants, but I'm on my way to another visual art destination, at the **FEMCO Building** (417 NW Ninth Avenue), home since 2004 to Elizabeth Leach Gallery. The building was completed in 1930, its name an acronym for the Fouch Electrical Manufacturing Company, founded in 1904 by W. O. Fouch. Early in its history, the company outfitted transport ships for the Spanish-American war. The FEMCO name is still visible at the top of the building, just below the parapet.

When Leach opened the gallery in 1981 with her then-husband, artist Richard Gruetter, the city had few commercial art spaces, but local institutions like the Portland Center for the Visual Arts convinced the couple that there was an interested audience here. Initially intending to exhibit art by out-of-town artists from the gallery's original location downtown, Leach instead began representing some of the Northwest's most acclaimed artists, such as landscape painter James Lavadour and installation artist MK Guth. As a visual art critic for *The Oregonian* in the mid-2000s, I came to regard Elizabeth Leach Gallery as the best in town, evidenced not only by these locals but also by artists like Vietnam's Dinh Q. Lê, who created magnificent large-scale weavings from multiple photographs, and by California's Hap Tivey, a pioneering member of the Light and Space movement, who made vibrant multicolored light sculptures.

The gallery's design by Randy Higgins casts a subtle spell. The three exhibit spaces are staggered so one has a view of the whole gallery, diagonally, from the back room or the front door, even as the individual spaces remain intimate and distinct. "The open plan just gives away too much," Higgins says. "I liken moving through spaces to reading a book. You tell the stories of buildings the same way, so that if someone wants to pay attention, it's able to reward that." Higgins also designed the Lumber Room upstairs, founded by philanthropist Sarah Miller Meigs as a space for artist residencies and private exhibit space, in a similar way.

My next destination, one block away, is not a building or even an architectural ruin, but a kind of preserved infrastructural relic. In the small plaza of the Elizabeth Lofts condominium building stand the two remaining **Lovejoy Columns** (316 NW Tenth Avenue). These concrete columns for the original Broadway Bridge viaduct were salvaged from its 1999 demolition, in order to preserve the murals painted on their surfaces. Whimsical images of doves, owls, lions, anthropomorphic trees, Greek mythical gods, and Bible figures were created by Athanasios "Tom" Stefopoulos, a night watchman for the rail yards between 1948 and 1952.

When I moved to Portland in the nineties, the Lovejoy Columns were a kind of known secret place, which the Stefopoulos-painted columns made a destination for street-art connoisseurs. Beneath the viaduct, the combination of vast empty space and the rhythmic sound of cars passing overhead created a unique ambiance. Gus Van Sant utilized the columns for a flashback scene in his 1989 movie *Drugstore Cowboy*, including for its official poster. When the ramp was about to be demolished,

*Lovejoy Columns*

artist James Harrison led a grassroots effort to save and relocate the columns, ten of which were hoisted away.

"What spoke to me was how much Tom transformed a derelict space into a temple," Harrison recalls. "He saw the beauty in the underside of the ramp. I think he really quickly got excited by the possibility, and started painting the columns as a collection." Harrison had hoped all ten columns could eventually be displayed, but only these two at the Elizabeth Condos survived long-term. The rest, kept in storage for a decade, were eventually destroyed in a fire. Harrison was racked with guilt, taking the loss personally. "Looking back, I realized the connection I felt to Tom and his work was my way of attempting to connect with my grandfathers, whom I didn't know," he says. "But it's not my battle anymore. And the columns have inspired enough people that they keep telling the story themselves."

Much as I appreciate these remaining Lovejoy Columns, I think their power has been lessened by removal from their original location, which Harrison acknowledges. Yet I still like coming to this plaza, to pay homage not only to Stefopoulos but also to Harrison, who was an inspiration as I later fought my own historic-preservation battles. And Harrison has continued to move forward, in recent years leaving his art career behind and pursuing clinical hypnosis. "Practically speaking, I'm a guide who can help you recover treasure from dark places," Harrison writes on his website. It strikes me that this could easily describe his efforts a quarter-century ago to save the Lovejoy Columns.

Backtracking one block east, my attention turns to one of the central city's primary greenspaces: the **North Park Blocks** (between NW Park and Eighth Avenues, Ankeny and Glisan Streets). Commissioned by Captain John Couch and bequeathed to the city in 1869, just before his death, these blocks were inspired by the South Park Blocks downtown (which I visit in the next walk) and were meant to be connected to them, as one continuous green strip. But Benjamin Stark, who owned the blocks in between the North and South Park Blocks, refused to go along with the plan.

After the North Park Blocks' completion, this became a thriving neighborhood, occupied in the nineteenth century largely by European immigrants. By the turn of the twentieth century, this became a largely Black and multi-ethnic neighborhood centered around two houses of worship: the Bethel AME Church and the Mount Olivet Baptist Church. By the early 1920s, automobile dealerships and garages began appearing along Broadway.

Though it is lined with the same big-leaf maples as the South Park Blocks, the North Park Blocks formed its own identity. In 1904, an ordinance was passed setting aside one block specifically for women and children. Two years later, the city's first playground was built there, attracting children by the hundreds;

a perimeter fence had to be quickly added to keep out men, who were goading boys into boxing matches and taking bets. During the 1960s, the North Park Blocks fell into decline, beginning with the loss of several mature trees during the 1962 Columbus Day Storm. But as the Pearl District gentrified in the 1990s, so too did the area around this green space, as art galleries and the Pacific Northwest College of Art arrived. In recent years, the struggles of nearby Old Town have extended here, as the Park Blocks became a kind of liminal space mixing affluent condo residents and tourists with the drug addicted and houseless. In that way, the park is a kind of bellwether for central-city Portland.

The North Park Blocks are set for expansion from NW Glisan to NW Johnson Street, as part of the massive, multiblock Broadway Corridor project on the former site of the US Postal Service's downtown distribution center. There is not yet a timeline for completion, for the Park Blocks' expansion is tied to numerous affordable-housing projects on the same site, as managed by Prosper Portland, the City of Portland's development agency. But the design, by local landscape design firm PLACE Studio, promises a compelling mix of plazas and gathering spaces. The North Park Blocks expansion is also tied to a much larger initiative, the Green Loop, creating a constellation of greenspaces around the central city.

The rain has ended and the sun is out. With my pale complexion, I instinctually seek the shade of this park's tall trees. But it's worth diverting east again to Broadway for one stop: the **Golden West Building** (707 NW Everett Street), a Black history landmark that, like the Bud Clark Commons, provides social services and affordable housing. From 1906 this was the Golden West Hotel, one of the largest Black-owned lodgings west of the Mississippi River. Founded by William D. Allen, the Golden West served many Black railroad workers coming through nearby Union Station, who were turned away from other local hotels because of their race. In 1914, its basement bar hosted the first known jazz performance in Portland, by Freddie Keppard's Original Creole Orchestra. The building also came with quirks. One whole wing, constructed last, was framed with recently cut green wood that hadn't been properly dried, causing floorboards to bounce and buckle, so much that walking its floors felt like being on a ship. The manager's office was located in a converted walk-in safe that extended underground past the property line, beneath the sidewalk. Though the Golden West Hotel prospered for over a quarter-century, the Great Depression prompted its closure in 1931. After being sold, the hotel returned and continued for another four years, but then shuttered for good in 1935.

Today the Golden West is owned and operated by the nonprofit Central City Concern, with seventy-three units of affordable housing, part of a dwindling network of single-room-occupancy residential hotels. "One of the reasons homelessness increased in this country is that SROs like this, as they faded or were condemned or flipped into condos, were not replaced," explains Sean Hubert, Central City Concern's chief housing and strategy officer. "Residential hotels like this provided the lowest-barrier housing in the nation, and we've lost about 2 million units nationwide. Even when modern low-income housing started in the 1980s under Reagan, that was for-profit and actually screened out people with the most need."

The Golden West Hotel's architecture gives residents an opportunity to connect. Off the lobby is an open staircase that

*Golden West Building*

winds up into the building. "The elevator is old and tiny, so that stairwell is kind of the center-hub of the building," Hubert explains. "There's a great skylight over the space. All this sunlight just sort of pours down as you're walking up the staircase. It's just a very resonating space, warm and inviting. Particularly with affordable housing, as people are making transitions and meeting other people on a similar trajectory, it just becomes a wonderful feature that serves them well."

Crossing Everett Street and taking a few steps west back toward the North Park Blocks, I arrive at the circa-1901 **United States Custom House** (220 NW Eighth Avenue), with its Italian Renaissance Revival details including ornamental scrolls, quoins, arches, dentils, and keystones. The Custom House's construction reflected Portland's late nineteenth-century growth, which necessitated the creation of a regional custom house to regulate trade and impose fees. Though officially credited to James Knox Taylor, supervising architect of the US Treasury from 1897 to 1912, the Custom House's lead designer was local architect Edgar Lazarus, who is best known for Vista House at Crown Point in the Columbia Gorge. On the Custom House's entry side facing the Park Blocks is a long arcade-like wall with arched openings and iron fencing, creating an enclosed courtyard but also acting as a barrier. A trio of arched doorways leads into the marble-clad lobby and its wide-open stairway, with marble treads, acanthus-ornamented balusters, and molded oak handrails. I note many interior stairways in this book, but the Custom House's is my favorite. There is a kind of otherworldly spell cast that's greater than the sum of its parts, reminding me of Dutch artist M. C. Escher's illustrations depicting infinitely rising and falling stairs.

Following the federal government's 2004 departure, the Custom House sat vacant for a decade before being renovated in 2015 from a design by GBD Architects and architect Peter Meijer, for national shared-office chain WeWork. "It's my favorite building in the city," Meijer told me for a *Portland Architecture* post that year. "It just strikes me as the height of the Italian Renaissance building style. It's so extremely well done and just very highly ornamented, both inside and outside. I'm always finding new stories about it."

WeWork brought the building alive with a mix of temporary office spaces at different scales, from closed-door private suites leased for months at a time to individual "hot" desks rented by the hour. The latter I particularly remember because of how the desks were separated into cubicles with glass partitions, simultaneously seeming maze-like and open, recalling the hall-of-mirrors climax to Orson Welles's 1947 classic *The Lady from Shanghai*. The Custom House's original interior was left largely untouched, as well as the large walk-in safes on each floor.

*United States Custom House*

"It was such a pleasure every day coming to that building," recalls Maigen Thomas, a software designer who worked at the Custom House from 2017 to 2019, "because you'd get to walk up these big wide steps and you open the doors and here's this gorgeous staircase." The office suite her company rented had previously been a location for the NBC television show *Grimm*, and the door to her office was still marked with a fictional Portland Police sign. "Every time I found some kind of architectural detail, like the bank vault or some other little alcove, it made me wonder, 'What did this do?' It ties you to a history in a way you can't get any other way," Thomas adds. "I always wanted to go see a new part of the building, and I'd take my laptop with me as an excuse. Then I'd get there and after a while realize I hadn't opened the laptop once, but I'd visited with six dogs, talked to four people, and tried a new kind of espresso. You were in a space where you knew you could talk to people. It was the little central hub, kind of a third place *and* a workplace."

Devastated by mismanagement and the COVID-19 pandemic, WeWork closed the Custom House office space and all its Portland properties. Reopened by another shared-office provider, Industrious, its tenancy proved even more short-lived. As of this writing, the building has been foreclosed and is headed for auction. Hopefully the next owner will see it not as a tear-down but as their chance to be the next steward of a building that has so far evolved with the times and possesses a sense of atmosphere that transcends its public and private-sector purposes.

One block south of the Custom House is perhaps the North Park Blocks destination I've visited most often, thanks to the galleries located there: the **DeSoto Building** (720 NW Davis Street), a pair of adjoining early twentieth-century structures adapted in 2006 into an arts hub for developer Jim Winkler by LRS Architects. Because zoning would have allowed a new building of up to twenty stories here, "a rational economic person would knock down this turkey," Winkler joked to *Portland Tribune* reporter Joseph Gallivan when the building opened. But Winkler, a longtime arts patron, wanted to provide stability to the tenants, giving them ownership of the individual spaces, explaining, "They can be more gutsy, more innovative, take on more artists, show young artists."

Winkler was always an imaginative developer. I'd met and interviewed him five years earlier for my first-ever national architecture magazine feature, about his redeveloping the former Bess Kaiser Hospital into a new US headquarters for athletic-apparel giant Adidas. Soon after, Valarie went to work for the company, her office in the former maternity ward (where two of my cousins had been born). So an arts hub on the site of a century-old car dealership was no surprise.

Originally called the Lombard Automobile Buildings, the structure included the three-story, brick-clad Overland Automobile Showroom facing Broadway, completed in 1915, and the adjoining two-story, stucco-walled Oregon Motor Company Showroom along the North Park Blocks, added a year later. The buildings' architect, Joseph Jacobberger, went on to design many acclaimed houses as well as the original University of Portland campus. Both Lombard Automobile Buildings were constructed with double-height ground floors and enclosed with glass, to display Willys and Studebaker vehicles for sale. Following the auto dealers' departure in the 1950s, a succession of light-industrial and wholesale businesses occupied the buildings: an electrical supplier, a printer, and, for over three decades beginning in the 1970s, the millinery-pattern company Daisy Kingdom. Today the DeSoto's corner space facing Broadway is occupied by Augen Gallery and, upstairs, LRS Architects. Next door, on the Park Blocks side, the ground-floor spaces are home to nonprofit museums, Blue Sky Gallery and the Oregon Jewish Museum and Center for Holocaust Education.

Perhaps the local art space I've frequented the most, along with Elizabeth Leach Gallery, Blue Sky was founded in 1974 by photographers Christopher Rauschenberg, Ann Hughes, Robert DiFranco, Craig Hickman, and Terry Toedtemeier. Rauschenberg, the son of legendary artist Robert Rauschenberg, had come from New York City to attend Reed College, and describes 1970s Portland as "noticeably whiter than what I was used to. If you got on the bus, everybody was speaking English—not Chinese in this row and French in that row." But Rauschenberg loved Oregon's natural wonders and warmed to the city. "Portland has a very distinctive collaborative culture, and it was cheap in those days to live here. You could try things," he says. At first, an

*DeSoto Building*

entire day might go by without a visitor entering Blue Sky. Yet the gallery gained acclaim exhibiting photographers from around the world. Blue Sky's founders all went on to significant careers. Toedtemeier, for example, served as the Portland Art Museum's photography curator until his death in 2008, and took striking black-and-white pictures of Oregon's landscape and geology. And Rauschenberg has become known for his meticulous travel photos as well as for curating more than a thousand Blue Sky Gallery exhibits. "For me, photography is part of this active struggle to pay attention," Rauschenberg explains. "What I wanted my work to be about is this idea that the ordinary world around you is not ordinary if you pay attention to it."

The Oregon Jewish Museum and Center for Holocaust Education was founded in 1989 as the Oregon Jewish Museum. In 2014, it merged with the Oregon Holocaust Resource Center, afterward taking on a pivotal role in educating hundreds of schoolchildren about bigotry. A 2020 survey found 63 percent of Americans born in the 1980s and 1990s did not know that 6 million Jews were murdered in the Holocaust, and 20 percent of respondents erroneously believed that Jews *caused* the Holocaust. Particularly since the 2016 election, bigotry has seemingly been on the rise. "I think of the urgency of our work, particularly now," Judy Margles, the OJMCHE's then-director, told me in a 2020 interview (she retired at the end of 2023). In 2019, the State of Oregon passed new legislation requiring school districts to begin teaching about the Holocaust and genocide, with the OJMCHE helping write the curriculum.

Margles also acknowledged the suffering outside the museum. She recalled once preparing to welcome a donor and finding a homeless person sleeping in the doorway. Old Town, just across Broadway, is where numerous social service agencies are located, and where many are living on the street. "It's like the most bifurcated neighborhood imaginable," she says. "You can go to a fancy store two blocks away and you can go to Union Gospel Mission two blocks away." Rather than turn away from the problem, Margles said she chose to engage head-on. "We had always understood we would have a core exhibit about the Holocaust, about Oregon Jews. But then we started head-scratching and saying, 'How do we give notice? How do we pay attention to the neighborhood we're in?' Clearly, it meant we were going to be in the Park Blocks feeding the houseless." Being a good citizen, she reasoned, meant not just understanding history but living compassionately in the moment.

Now I'm leaving the North Park Blocks and crossing the multilane traffic on Broadway, from the Pearl District into Old Town. Yet the focus is still on the arts, starting with the **A.G. Long Building** (117 NW Fifth Avenue). Completed in 1904 to house Alexander Gotwald Long's firefighting-supply business, the building's double-height third floor originally provided room for long firehoses to be dried. The red brick façade and arched Venetian windows give the building a touch of Richardsonian

Romanesque style. Today on the ground floor is retro video arcade Ground Kontrol, where games like *Galaxian*, *Super Punch-Out*, and *Pole Position* still occasionally cause me to surrender my quarters. I want to point out the A.G. Long Building, however, because the Portland Center for the Visual Arts was located here from 1972 to 1987.

The city has never had a contemporary art museum, but the PCVA felt like one, exhibiting renowned US contemporary artists including Donald Judd, Robert Rauschenberg, Agnes Martin, Richard Serra, Dan Flavin, James Turrell, and Ed Ruscha. It was founded by local artists Mel Katz, Michele Russo, and Jay Backstrand, the latter of whom had, on a Fulbright fellowship in London, been inspired by the nonprofit Whitechapel Gallery. Katz, who at the time was married to future Portland mayor Vera Katz, secured the vacant third floor of the A.G. Long, recognizing that its 5,000 square feet of open space would be ideal for exhibitions.

PCVA provided visiting artists a chance to road-test their work before showing in New York or London, while offering access to the Northwest's bountiful nature. Artist Carl Andre collected rocks along the Clackamas River for an installation called *144 Blocks and Stones*. Donald Judd went whitewater rafting on the Rogue River after completing an installation that wrapped PCVA's 5,000-square-foot exhibit space in plywood; the artist's later renovations of several buildings in Marfa, Texas, also resembled the A.G. Long Building—sensitive to the craftsmanship of the original brick-and-wood structure while stripping down the interiors to expose the rafters and internal volumes.

Other artists created installations that challenged and surprised. For a 1975 show, performance artist Chris Burden built a replica of his apartment, living there with his girlfriend for a week. The couple kept a small chain across the bedroom doorway to prevent the public from entering at will, but on opening night, a local art writer removed the chain and walked into the room. "Burden went nuts," recalls art writer Paul Sutinen, who saw the artist "dragging the guy by his hair across the floor." Artist James Turrell, the Light and Space movement pioneer, created a simple illusion at PCVA, cutting a hole into one of the walls without viewers even noticing. "I took four students to see that piece, and one at a time I said to them, 'Tell me what you saw,'"

Sutinen remembers. "They each said, 'That's a gray rectangle painted on the wall.' I said, 'Go back and look at it again.' That piece was just mind-boggling in its simplicity."

Portland artist Tad Savinar curated a 1982 PCVA exhibit that changed his career. *A Few Good Men* featured photographs by Robert Mapplethorpe, wall drawings by Mike Glier (one featuring Ronald Reagan as a Medusa), and a monologue from Eric Bogosian featuring thirteen different characters. "Eric was trained as an actor, which was a huge difference from performance art. It wasn't rubbing chocolate on your body," Savinar recalls. "He understood how to work an audience." The following year, Bogosian and Savinar co-authored a play staged at PCVA, *Talk Radio*, which was later adapted into a movie of the same name by Academy Award–winning director Oliver Stone. Instead of embracing a theatrical career, however, Savinar spent the ensuing decades in an uncommon dual role as visual artist and urban designer, including many years as a member of the City of Portland's powerful Design Commission. "Artists are amazing problem solvers," he says.

By 1987, despite its unprecedented success, PCVA ceased operations. Founded by artists and possessing a plucky independent streak, it had become a victim of its own success: more substantial than a gallery, yet not quite well-funded and organized enough to graduate into a full-fledged contemporary art museum. It's a typical Portland story: a community of creative people finding a way to build something unique and memorable despite limited funds, yet ultimately unable or perhaps unwilling to establish a lasting institutionalized successor. Even so, I like walking by this former firehose warehouse where some of the greatest artists of the late twentieth century came to experiment and hold court.

Approaching Fifth and Couch, I pause for a moment to commemorate a corner I used to visit often. On the north side was Just Be, a Japanese toy store with an art gallery upstairs, where I once reviewed a show of excellent graffiti-inspired paintings and, on another occasion, attended an autograph signing for Trail Blazers basketball players Nicolas Batum and Patty Mills. As I stand here now, a MAX train is departing from the Fifth and Couch station, headed south from Old Town into downtown.

But the show must go on, so I'm headed to the **Roseland Theater** (8 NW Sixth Avenue), one of Portland's most venerable performance venues, and the site of my first concert. In 1985, my dad took me here (to what was then known as Starry Night) to see rock and roll pioneer Chuck Berry. Though I was just thirteen, Berry was nearly sixty and past his prime, as evidenced by his playing only a half-hour medley of "Johnny B. Good" and his other hits, after letting the opening band, Johnny Limbo and the Lugnuts, play for more than ninety minutes. Even so, the night is a cherished memory because Berry's presence, however brief, was electric.

Long before the venue was built, the first known occupant of this block was Aaron Meier, founder of the Meier & Frank department store in 1857, who built a house here. Later, there was a single-story saloon on this site, which was demolished to make way for the Apostolic Faith Mission in 1922, which still stands. An eye-catching architectural detail of this building was the white striping painted onto its otherwise red-brick façade, but its most dominant feature was an electric sign on the roof that until 1981 read "JESUS THE LIGHT OF THE WORLD" and could be seen from across the city. On the ground floor were the

*Roseland Theater*

church's offices and printing presses, while upstairs was the large meeting hall, able to accommodate more than 1,100 people. But originally the building was also about 20 feet longer than it is today. When Burnside Street was widened in 1933, the façade was cut open, a middle section removed, and the two remaining halves knitted together, set farther back from the street. The church sold the building in 1981, but is still headquartered locally, with branches all over the world.

The Starry Night club opened in the former Apostolic Faith Mission in 1982, and was for many years the city's only midsized venue for touring rock acts. David Leiken, whose Double Tee Promotions has owned the venue since 1991, believes the acoustics are, "especially for certain kinds of music, as good as it gets." He cites the numerous times performers like Bob Dylan have rehearsed here, before performing at larger venues.

I learned from Leiken why Chuck Berry was late taking the stage for the 1985 show my dad and I attended. He was waiting to get paid. Leiken remembers Berry sitting in a car outside the venue before the show, refusing to go inside until his fee was delivered in dollar bills. "We didn't have enough cash. It was a lot," Leiken recalls. "We ended up raiding all the beer-stand money, merch money, and any we could put together. I think we had ten grand on hand and came up with another twenty before we were done. Chuck Berry and his son sat in the town car we rented for them and were counting the money. Finally Chuck says, 'I think there's enough here.'"

Leiken had been booking shows for Starry Night in the 1980s before purchasing the club. He particularly remembers an energetic, sweaty 1987 Miles Davis performance. "In those days there wasn't any AC. It had been about 100 degrees that day, and during the performance there was condensation coming down the walls," he says. "But Miles was kicking ass. He had come out of retirement and was playing with a group of young musicians. You heard all the rumors about him playing with his back to the audience. But he was having a ball."

Starry Night's era came to a violent close in 1990 when, after a John Lee Hooker concert, then-owner Larry Hurwitz and an employee, George Castagnola, killed the club's twenty-one-year-old publicity agent, Timothy Moreau, who had discovered their counterfeit-ticket operation. Hurwitz sold Starry Night and left the country, at which time the Roseland Theater name took effect. In 1997 he was extradited to the United States. Convicted of Moreau's murder, he was sentenced to ten years in prison and served eight.

"Tim Moreau was in my store delivering tickets on that Friday. I presume he got murdered on that Saturday, the next day," remembers Terry Currier, owner of local record store Music Millennium and a longtime promoter of Starry Night/Roseland Theater shows. "Larry definitely had this conniving quality about him. I had been in the Key Largo club one night when Larry had come back into the States from Korea. I remember my friend Chris [Carlson] from the Duffy Bishop Band saying to Larry, 'Would you do that?' Larry said, 'No, I'd never murder someone like that.' Two weeks later they arrested him."

Besides the Chuck Berry concert, I visited Starry Night on one other memorable occasion, just a few months before Moreau was murdered. My friends and I were there to see a popular local band of the time, Dan Reed Network, who arrived onstage by climbing down a rope from the attic, passing through a ceiling tile that had been removed. It's this little moment of delight, and the earlier thrill of Berry's presence, that stay with me.

## *Banking on a Legacy*

Crossing Burnside Street back into downtown on Broadway, as the sun once again disappears behind the clouds and a throng of traffic waits at a stoplight, I'm headed to a succession of bank buildings and hotels. They offer examples of both traditional and modern architecture, while communicating the wealth, power, and ambition of their clients. Though Portland generally avoids ostentatious displays, these buildings tell the story of a twentieth-century city gaining wealth and increasingly seeking the world's attention.

I'm beginning with one of the skyline's most recognizable buildings: the forty-two-story **US Bancorp Tower** (111 SW Fifth Avenue), better known as "Big Pink." Although it's a few feet shorter than the city's tallest building, the forty-story Wells Fargo Center, the US Bancorp has two more floors and it actually stands out more prominently, because there are no comparably tall adjacent structures. I think Big Pink is particularly handsome, with its parallelogram shape, zigzagging upper-façade glass pattern, and the pastel-toned Spanish granite cladding that inspired its nickname. This tower has long offered one of the city's best views, from the popular Portland City Grill on the thirtieth floor and, before that, Atwater's Restaurant, the latter of which Valarie and I dined at soon after moving to Portland, tourists in our new city.

For its first nine years, beginning in 1974, Big Pink was not big at all, comprising only a seven-story podium, which is technically a separate adjoining structure. The tower's 1983 completion marked the end of an era in local architecture, as the last completed project from the Portland office of Chicago architecture firm Skidmore, Owings and Merrill. Known best for skyscrapers like New York's One World Trade Center and Chicago's Willis Tower (originally the Sears Tower), SOM was America's premier twentieth-century office building designer. The local branch is perhaps best remembered for two enduring spectator venues, Memorial Coliseum and Eugene's Autzen Stadium, as well as

*US Bancorp Tower*

several downtown Portland offices. The US Bancorp Tower was a collaboration with the city's most celebrated architect, Pietro Belluschi, and a full-circle moment, because SOM's Portland office was started when Belluschi had sold his firm to SOM in 1951, after becoming dean of the Massachusetts Institute of Technology's School of Architecture and Planning. By the mid-1970s, Belluschi was back in Portland and, though no longer running his own firm, would collaborate with others, as he did with Yost Grube Hall Architecture on numerous exceptional late-career churches.

SOM and Belluschi's client for Big Pink, US Bancorp, is today the fifth-largest financial institution in the United States, with more than three thousand branches. The original company, United States National Bank, was established in Portland in 1891. Three years after its 1997 acquisition by Minnesota's First Bank System, US Bancorp sold its namesake tower and moved its headquarters to Minneapolis. The building's ownership has since changed hands numerous times.

Big Pink's 1983 opening came amid the Postmodern architectural movement's brief flourish. One year earlier, the Portland Building by architect Michael Graves, the nation's first major work of Postmodern architecture, had been completed, while Pioneer Courthouse Square, a Postmodern design by Will Martin, arrived just one year later. Unlike those designs, with their oversized historical references, Big Pink was designed in a clean-lined Modernist style, yet its zigzagging upper-facade patterning hints at Postmodern flair. SOM principal George Crandall won an in-house design competition to determine how Big Pink would be placed on its irregularly shaped site. The block was cropped by the street-grid change between downtown and Old Town, and combined a block-long stretch of Ankeny Street with the adjoining parcel to make a superblock. Though completed nine years apart, the podium and tower were conceived together.

"I knew the bank wanted their front door on Oak Street [facing south], because Burnside to the north was in bad shape at the time," Crandall recalled in a 2016 *Portland Architecture* interview. Although placing the tower at the south end of the site along Oak near other fairly tall buildings was the most intuitive move, his scheme instead placed the tower to the north along Burnside, where it stood alone. That way, Crandall explained, "it would be prominent forever: this narrow needle." Where Ankeny Street had been, before creation of the superblock, Crandall conceived a glass-ceilinged galleria between the two structures, ceremonially continuing the public right-of-way.

Crandall's scheme won his SOM colleagues' support, but he still had to convince Belluschi. "I knew that Pietro, being Italian, would know about gallerias," Crandall recalled. "He looked at the scheme and said, 'George, that is the right thing to do. I will talk to the bank about that.'"

Belluschi contributed the idea for the pink-hued façade material that gave Big Pink its nickname. "We were looking for a stone to use for the exterior cladding. Pietro said he'd come across this Spanish pink granite," Crandall said. "It had a warm tone and in Portland we had a lot of cold buildings." Belluschi favored the granite for its ephemeral quality, appearing lighter or darker depending on the time of day. The windows, glazed in a semitransparent coating of copper and silver that looks pink from the outside, also changed in different conditions, absorbing or reflecting sunlight.

SOM, which closed its Portland office in 1990, "was highly specialized in two things: office buildings and hospitals. We had a downturn in the economy and the office market just dried up," Crandall recalled. "They weren't diverse enough to survive here." Its principals went on to found several enduring local firms such as GBD Architects and Fletcher Farr Ayotte.

Coincidentally, today downtown Portland is again facing a collapsed market for office space, as the COVID-19 pandemic has changed the nature of working, with a large swath of employees staying home to do their jobs instead of commuting to the central city. Even at the five-year mark from the pandemic, downtown Portland's foot traffic was down 40 percent compared to what it was before 2020. Tall office buildings like Big Pink and the Wells Fargo are unlikely to be supplanted in height anytime soon. Yet city centers are not meant to be monocultures of commercial space. That's what my time in New York taught me: that the best urban places have a mix of places to work and live and hang out. Big Pink will always have its place, but its neighborhood will be more vibrant if some of its workers happen to live in apartment and condo buildings nearby.

My next destination, today known as the **Embassy Suites by Hilton Portland Downtown** (319 SW Pine Street) and originally called the Multnomah Hotel, is a place I've visited many times over the years, be it for pre-event drinks or to attend a conference. Yet I associate the hotel with a publicity stunt generations ago, four months after its 1912 opening. On June 10, pilot Silas Christofferson took off in his biplane from a makeshift wood-plank runway atop the building, witnessed by over 45,000 spectators, landing in Vancouver, Washington, twelve minutes later. Unfortunately, Christofferson lived only another four years, dying in an airplane crash when the engine of an experimental new plane he was flying gave out over Redwood City, California.

The nine-story Multnomah Hotel, designed in an American Renaissance style by Frank Gibson and Bernard J. S. Cahill, was immediately popular. Celebrity guests included pilot Charles Lindberg in 1927 (in Portland to dedicate the new Swan Island airport), Bob Hope and Bing Crosby in 1948 (here for a charity dinner), and Elvis Presley while on tour in 1957. In the latter case, overzealous fans climbed an exterior trellis trying to reach The King's second-floor room. John F. Kennedy, staying at the hotel in 1960 while campaigning for the presidency, gave an impromptu speech from his balcony. As a jazz fan, I also note the Dave Brubeck Quartet's concerts at the Multnomah Hotel on April 3 and 4, 1959, just four months before their seminal album *Time Out* was recorded.

In 1965 the Multnomah Hotel closed, amid competition with other luxury hotels like the Benson and a new downtown Hilton. The building was converted to government offices, which remained until 1992. It reopened as a hotel in 1995, part of the Embassy Suites chain, and has been a steady presence ever since. Standing outside the hotel today, I'm tempted to stop for a late breakfast at its ground-floor restaurant, Mother's Bistro, which does an excellent corned beef hash. But alas, I might need a nap afterward, so it's better to continue.

A few blocks to the southwest is the **Bank of Expensify** (401 SW Fifth Avenue), which I love for its wondrously wide-open atrium; it took me only two decades to discover it. Completed in 1916 as First National Bank, the building was part of a generation of architecturally ambitious structures constructed in the early twentieth century. Its architect, Boston firm Coolidge and Shattuck, a successor to the legendary Henry Hobson Richardson's architectural practice, had previously designed the Art Institute of Chicago and (with Frederick Law Olmsted) the original Stanford University campus. The First National Bank, marble-clad and Greek Revival in style, was modeled after the Parthenon in Athens and resembles the Lincoln Memorial in Washington, completed just three years earlier by another Boston architect, Henry Bacon. In 1921 the First National was expanded by a quarter-block, stretching to Sixth Avenue, and its large skylight added.

*Bank of Expensify*

This building was nearly demolished the year I was born, 1972, after the bank decamped for the forty-story tower First National Bank Tower (today known as the Wells Fargo Center). *The New York Times* architecture critic Ada Louise Huxtable accused the bank of "pulling off a double whammy involving two kinds of destruction—the erection of a monstrous new building and the demolition of a beautiful old one. Three kinds, really, because the fine old one will come down for a parking lot." She called the demolition plan "demonic," "cultural vandalism," and "a perfect doomsday package." But the building was saved, in a turning point for local historic preservation. The Portland City Council designated the structure a historic landmark for a six-month period ending in June 1972, which gave the building just enough time to find a new owner, Oregon Pioneer Savings and Loan Association. This later became a Bank of California branch, before being sold to Expensify, which commissioned a 2018 renovation by ZGF Architects.

When I finally entered this building for the first time that same year and walked up the staircase from the foyer, I gasped at the three-story atrium, which resembled a grand Victorian railway station, perhaps not surprising considering that Coolidge and Shattuck had designed many. In fact, the Expensify interior is more architecturally dramatic than Portland's own Union Station. ZGF Architects' renovation added two conference rooms cantilevering off the back wall, with usable space underneath; on my visit, a children's swing had been hung there.

It feels like there should be a drumroll as I approach the city's most historically significant and innovative work of Modernist architecture: the **Commonwealth Building** (421 SW Sixth Avenue), completed in 1947 from a design by Pietro Belluschi. I've mentioned his name several times before now, yet only now am I coming to one of his great architectural works. Originally known as the Equitable Building, a headquarters for the Equitable Savings and Loan Association, it was the country's first commercial building with a glass curtain wall (where the façade is nonstructural and can be made from a lightweight material). The Equitable Building was also the first commercial structure with double-pane windows, and the first air-conditioned office tower. Yet because such Modernist office buildings became ubiquitous after World War II, it's easy for the fourteen-story Commonwealth to today hide in plain sight.

Belluschi was born in Ancona, Italy, and served in the Italian army during World War I. After earning an engineering degree from the University of Rome, he came to the United States to study at Cornell University and, after graduation in 1925, decided to extend his stay for a few months in order to visit the west before returning home. He took a temporary job with an Idaho mining operation as a helper-electrician before continuing on to Portland. By this time, however, Benito Mussolini's Fascist government had taken power, and the young architect's family cautioned him to remain in the United States. Belluschi secured a job in the office of A. E. Doyle, and rose rapidly, soon becoming chief designer. In 1932 came the first major project of Belluschi's career as lead architect: the landmark Portland Art Museum (which I'll be visiting on the next walk), an early work of Modernist architecture. Over the ensuing two decades, Belluschi won acclaim for a variety of projects, from single-family houses and churches to libraries and office buildings.

The architect had first designed a headquarters for Equitable back in 1929, in an Art Deco style, which was never built because of the onset of the Great Depression. The timing was unlucky again a decade later, when Equitable purchased a half-block at Sixth Avenue and Stark Street to build a new headquarters, but construction was delayed indefinitely because of building material restrictions caused by World War II's onset in Europe. But, in 1943, an opportunity emerged. The Portland area had become one of the nation's largest shipbuilding centers, employing 97,000 workers. That same year, *Architectural Forum* magazine had published Belluschi's design for a future office tower utilizing aluminum framing and exterior cladding. Equitable Savings and Loan president Ralph Cake, eager to start building and also intrigued by aluminum's possibility, used his connections at the War Production Board to win approval for nonmilitary use of construction materials before the national wartime ban was lifted. This is what allowed the Equitable to become the first office building in the United States completed after the war.

The meticulous Belluschi insisted that no bolt, rivet, or other fastener extend more than seven-eighths of an inch from

*Commonwealth Building*

the façade, ensuring a flat surface. His design also featured the largest expanses of double-pane glass ever constructed. The first manufacturer that Belluschi approached, Libbey-Owens-Ford, said it could not meet the architect's specifications. At first Pittsburgh Plate Glass declined too, but agreed after Belluschi persisted. Although several panes wound up cracking, they turned out to be defective; the rest of the installed glass has continued to perform well.

Inside, the building's lobby includes a distinctive mural, which Belluschi conceived himself, albeit reluctantly. Originally the architect had secured a commitment from the great Alexander Calder to create a mobile for the lobby, but the client balked, perhaps because of the $4,000 price tag (equivalent to just over $72,000 in 2025). Also distinctive is the corner storefront, a two-story space where originally an Equitable Savings branch was located and which was occupied, during my early years as a journalist, by Sienna Architecture Company; while passing by on the sidewalk, I remember stopping to look at their architectural models placed near those floor-to-ceiling windows. This building's success launched Pietro Belluschi to new levels of notoriety, having prefigured landmark Modernist office towers in New York City such as Oscar Niemeyer's United Nations Headquarters and Skidmore, Owings and Merrill's Lever House. Today, the Commonwealth Building's aluminum exterior has developed a weathered patina, but it and the green-tinted glass remain exceptionally responsive to fluctuations in light and atmosphere. On certain days, the whole façade glows.

Belluschi died in 1994, three years before I moved to Portland and seven years before I began writing about architecture. Sometimes it feels like I've spent my entire career chasing him, or at least visiting and celebrating his architectural legacy, mostly in Portland but also landmarks like San Francisco's sublime Cathedral of Saint Mary of the Assumption, or New York's Julliard School. I've been fortunate to know and befriend members of Belluschi's family, first his late grandson Jeff, then his widow, Marjorie, and, later, Belluschi's son Anthony and his wife Marti; the latter couple have become important caretakers of his father's legacy. And although Pietro Belluschi wasn't born here, his love for Oregon came through not just in his architecture, but in his humble reverence for nature, exemplified in one of his best-known quotes: "We never could design a building as beautiful as the trees."

A few steps down Harvey Milk Street is a very different style of bank headquarters, designed by Belluschi's former employer: the great A. E. Doyle. Resembling a Roman temple, the **US National Bank Building** (321 SW Sixth Avenue) was completed in 1917, three decades before the Equitable, yet the gap in time seems considerably longer. Maybe that's not just due to the building's neoclassical architecture but because this once prominent headquarters has in its current emptiness taken on a ghostly quality, almost like a ruin. Yet from its marble floors and mezzanine balustrade to its bronze ornament and 30-foot-high coffered ceiling, this is an exceptional space.

Inspired by the Knickerbocker Trust Bank in New York by McKim, Meade and White, the four-story US National Bank was completed in stages, beginning with a quarter-block building at Sixth and Stark in 1917. This was a kind of apex for the city of Portland, the final years when it was bigger and more financially powerful than West Coast neighbors like Los Angeles and Seattle. US National Bank was a crucial commission for Doyle; in the years before this project, his firm was struggling. By 1919, however, the Oregon chapter of the American Institute of Architects selected this bank as one of the ten most noteworthy works of architecture in Portland, along with three other Doyle buildings.

The US National Bank was expanded to the west in 1923, reaching Broadway to occupy the full block and taking the place of the Elks Building. Plans originally called for a twenty-one-story tower here, which would have been Portland's tallest building until the 1960s. But the client abandoned the idea because of the estimated million-dollar cost, and because the steel bracing for such a tower would have taken up much of the existing building's lobby. Nevertheless, the expanded US National Bank became

*US National Bank Building*

the most prominent in an emerging financial center, and helped solidify the realignment of downtown farther west, away from the river.

In late 2023, US Bank closed this branch for good, after just over a century of service. Yet the bank had moved on in a broader sense many years earlier, having first relocated its headquarters to the massive US Bancorp tower in the 1980s, and then to Minneapolis in the early 2000s. Chances are a new tenant will make use of this grandiose space, just as the online bank Expensify did with the First National Bank just down the street. Yet the US National's current emptiness actually feels fitting, maybe because of how it evokes Greco-Roman architectural antiquity. I wouldn't mind if this building was bequeathed to the public and made permanently empty, allowed to decay naturally, its marble floors taking on a weathered patina and its columns slowly becoming pockmarked with further age.

Across Broadway is another Doyle-designed landmark (among the trio on the 1919 list), one still thankfully full of life: the **Benson Hotel** (309 SW Broadway). Completed in 1912, it's where many presidents have stayed, beginning with William Howard Taft in the hotel's first year. Franklin Roosevelt was a guest while attending the 1937 opening of Timberline Lodge at Mount Hood. Aviator Amelia Earhart visited the Benson in 1933, four years before she disappeared with navigator Fred Noonan over the Pacific while attempting to make a circumnavigational flight around the globe. My grandfather, Donald M. Libby, then a young US Navy enlistee, was part of the official search party. On my wall is a certificate commemorating his crossing the equator for the first time during that voyage.

Before the Benson, on this site was the Hotel Oregon, completed seven years earlier, originally as an office building for businessmen Moy Back Yin and Goon Dip. Its conversion to a hotel was immediately successful, and its manager considered an expansion that would have included a pair of ten-story structures. Instead, a deal was reached with Simon Benson, the self-made timber baron turned real estate developer, who bought the hotel, commissioned an expansion, and changed the name.

Benson had emigrated from his native Norway in 1868 at seventeen years old, initially settling in Wisconsin and learning

Benson Hotel

the lumber business there. In 1879, seeing that the Pacific Northwest was overtaking the Midwest in lumber production, Benson moved to Oregon and began acquiring forest land along the lower Columbia River. Over the next two decades, he amassed over 45,000 acres and proved to be a technical innovator. Benson replaced the ox teams towing felled trees to the river with steam-powered railcars; he used unprecedently large convoys of logs carrying up to 6 million board feet of timber down the Columbia, through open ocean to Benson's sawmill in California, where wood sold for higher prices. In the early twentieth century, Benson, then in his fifties, became a real estate investor.

The Benson Hotel was designed by A. E. Doyle in a Baroque style that was more opulent than any heretofore seen in Portland. The lobby was paneled in rare, now-extinct Circassian walnut imported from Russia, its staircase clad in marble, and the coffered ceilings hung with crystal chandeliers imported from Austria. Guests were initially given a complimentary cup of hot clam nectar every morning, before the hotel switched to coffee.

I've been to the Benson Hotel several times, including for a 2002 interview with movie director Stephen Frears in an upstairs suite. When we took the elevator downstairs together afterward, fellow director Gus Van Sant was waiting for Frears, his lunch date. There was also an embarrassing moment here in 2004, when I reluctantly accepted a *People* magazine assignment to investigate sexual-assault allegations made against Los Angeles Lakers basketball star Kobe Bryant by a Benson Hotel employee. The case was later dropped, but I remember being paid to have dinner at the Benson's basement restaurant, London Grill, just so at the end of the meal I could ask the waiter whether he'd heard anything about the alleged incident (he said he hadn't). In 2008, British drummer Mitch Mitchell of the Jimi Hendrix Experience died at the hotel.

As enduring a landmark as the Benson Hotel may be, I sometimes smile thinking that the most beloved work of Portland design associated with Simon Benson is actually much more modest. Around the same time his namesake hotel was completed, Benson hired Doyle to design downtown Portland's decorative water fountains, known as the Benson Bubblers and still in service. The first was erected nearby at Fifth and Washington, and ultimately fifty-two were built across downtown, each fountain featuring four copper bowls from which water bubbles upward. I've never seen drinking fountains in another city like these, and I think the Benson Bubblers speak to Portland's egalitarian nature.

Although Broadway begins at the bridge of the same name several blocks north of here, I think of this downtown stretch, particularly after the Benson Hotel, as the best for strolling. The street narrows, making it more conducive to pedestrians without so much automobile exhaust, and a succession of beautiful early twentieth century commercial buildings emerges. Yet my next stop, the **Union Bank Building** (707 SW Washington Street), is an outlier, in both style and scale. Although it's a striking fusion of Brutalist and International styles, designed by San Francisco firm Anshen & Allen, I've always thought of the Bank of California Building (as it was originally known) as a work of trophy architecture in a city that's not about trophies. Occupying the full block, it's set back from the streets it faces on three sides, and yet, rather than seeming to be a generous provision of public space, the effect instead seems standoffish. Yet its simple, monumental forms are compelling.

Union Bank Building

Seen from above, the fifteen-story Union Bank Building has a cross-shaped footprint. Its concrete service core, which gives the building its primary structural support, is left exposed and clad in gray-green slate that was quarried from the same area in Wales as the stone used to build Stonehenge. Largely windowless, it recalls the alien monolith in the movie *2001: A Space Odyssey*, which premiered the year before this building was completed. Perpendicular to the slate service core is the main office tower, a curtain wall of glass and white precast concrete panels. At the entrance, the precast concrete extends like a drape over the stairway to form entry columns; though not load-bearing, they make a nice reference to the neoclassical US National Bank. I particularly like the Union Bank Building's single-story annex on the northern half of the block, where the precast panels become wider apertures for tall, thin windows.

Two of Portland's earliest movie theaters were located here: the Majestic and the Liberty. Opened in 1911 at Washington and Broadway, the Majestic was the first of Portland's grand movie palaces ("palace" denoting a venue with more than a thousand seats), part of a wave of theaters built in this era on Washington Street and Broadway. Shortly after opening, the Majestic became the first Portland movie house to show a feature-length silent film: Italian import *The Fall of Troy*. In 1929 the venue was sold and rebranded as the United Artist Theater, continuing under that moniker until the building was demolished in 1957. The Liberty Theatre was completed in 1914 as the Broadway Theatre but changed its name just three years in. At 2,200 seats, it was one of the city's largest movie and vaudeville houses. Among its interior flourishes was a large statue and fountain in the lobby with water descending into a goldfish pond. In a 1921 photo, a sign for the Liberty extends over Broadway, and a four-story sign is erected above its entry canopy advertising Charles Chaplin's film of that year, *The Kid*. The theater was demolished in 1959.

The Majestic and Liberty theaters were pre-dated on this site by the Portland Library Association Building, completed on the north side of the block in 1890. It was designed by architect William Whidden, who co-designed the landmark Portland Hotel that same year and City Hall five years later. The Library Association's Romanesque style featured semicircular arched windows and a somewhat imposing brick façade, yet the overall composition was an undeniable influence on A. E. Doyle's masterful Central Library of 1913. In addition to being a literary storehouse, the Library Association Building was also the original location of the Portland Art Museum.

From here, I'll be continuing south down Broadway, eventually to the edge of downtown at the Portland State University campus and, beyond that, the South Auditorium District. At this point I'm getting hungry, and I wish my old favorite burger spot, the Red Coach Restaurant, was still located on the next block, in the Charles Berg Building; but alas, its red-vinyl booths and wonderfully greasy cheeseburgers are no more. But there is at Broadway and Washington (in the storefront where I used to get my pre-digital camera photos developed at The Shutterbug) now an outpost of the local St. Honoré Boulangerie chain, and one of their baguette sandwiches will do nicely. As I continue from here, increasingly the focus will be not on Broadway itself but on the public gathering spaces nearby, from squares and plazas to parks and fountains.

# *Walk 4*

## Park to Park

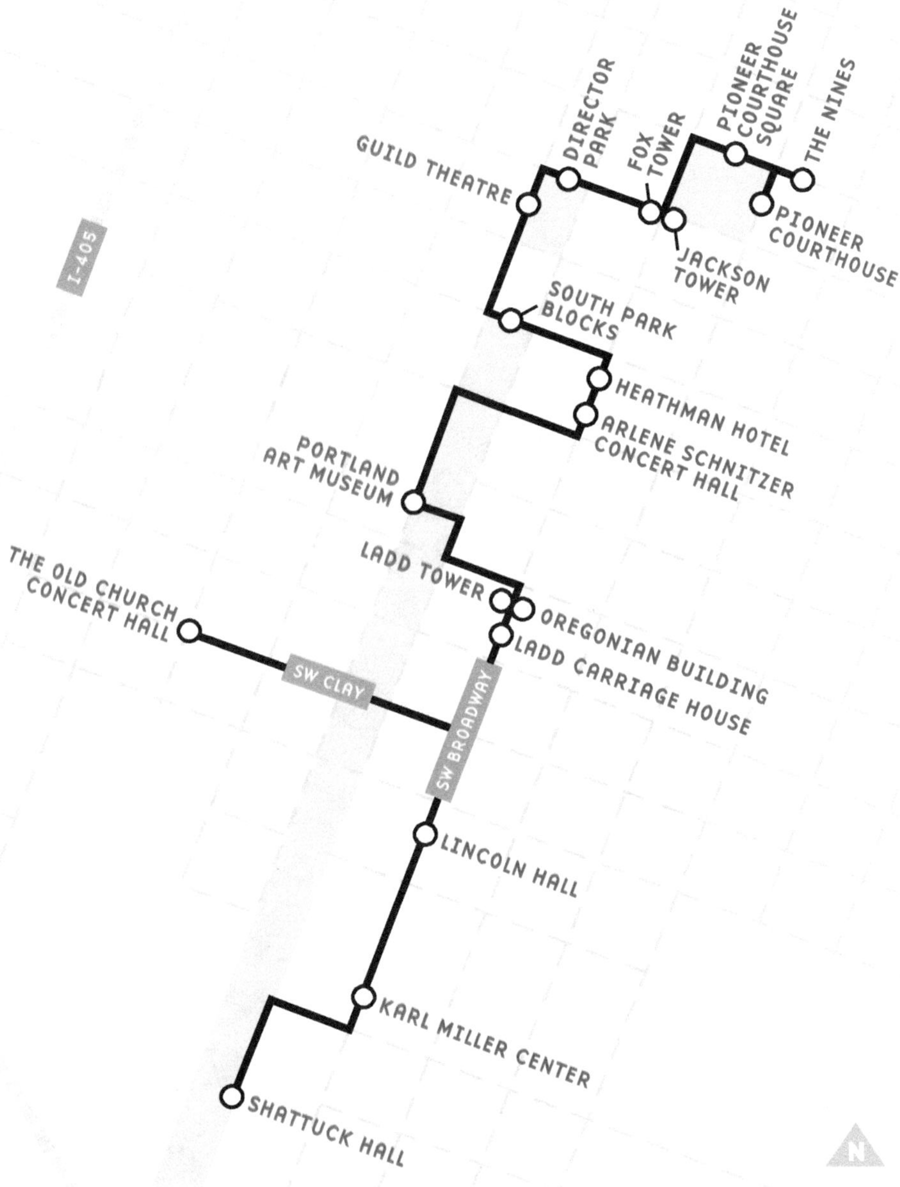

## *Circling the Square*

My journey has reached its center: **Pioneer Courthouse Square** (701 SW Sixth Avenue). While not officially or geographically the absolute center of the city, it's certainly the beating heart of downtown Portland. Completed in 1984 and designed by local architect Will Martin, it is a place for flower festivals and ice-cream socials, mass sing-alongs and celebrations of sporting

*Pioneer Courthouse Square*

glories. It is a ballot-drop site on election day and hosts the city's Christmas tree each December. It's where promotional booths tell us about Scientology or Poo-Pouri disinfectant spray, and where a stream of small festivals have occurred: the Portland Seafood and Wine Festival, the Pan African Festival, the Festival of Flowers, the Portland Winter Light Festival, the American Indian Day Celebration, and even a retirement party for a popular therapy llama, Rojo. By design, the center of Pioneer Courthouse Square was left open: no fountain, no statue. That's because it's complete when the square's center is full of people. In a certain sense, we are the fountain.

While Pioneer Courthouse Square is often referred to as the city's living room, it is many rooms and places at once: an outdoor community center, a spot for office workers to eat lunch, a place to rendezvous with friends, and, thanks to the MAX trains coming and going on three sides, a transit center. It also acts as a kind of foreground for the historic Pioneer Courthouse for which it's named. Pioneer Courthouse Square is both deeply idiosyncratic and universal, which enables its popularity. There are many parks and squares in Portland, but nothing else has so much human energy.

Three other structures preceded Pioneer Courthouse Square on this site. First was Central School, the first purpose-built structure for the Portland Public Schools system. Completed in 1858, it accommodated 280 pupils and three teachers. Though just three stories, it featured an Italianate-style observation tower.

Central School was demolished to make way for the Portland Hotel, opened in 1890: a gleaming symbol of Portland's rise during the late nineteenth century from muddy frontier town to ambitious city. Yet the hotel had a stilted birth. In 1882, owner Henry Villard hired New York City architects McKim, Mead and White to produce a design, but after the hotel's foundation was laid, construction halted as Villard lost his fortune. The building sat uncompleted for five years, until new owners recommissioned the hotel's former lead architect, William Whidden (having left McKim to co-found his own firm in Portland, Whidden & Lewis), to complete the project.

Once it opened, the Portland Hotel became the region's grandest, a preferred base for visiting dignitaries and celebrities.

In 1895, writer Mark Twain stayed here after regaling a packed audience at the nearby Marquam Grand Opera House. *Oregonian* reporter Lute Pease found Twain in the hotel's lobby the following morning, as the city was shrouded with forest-fire smoke, the author "surrounded by a medley of handbags, waiting for a carriage to the train. A blue nautical cap confined a part of his big mane of hair, but it bulged out at the sides and behind, a grizzly wilderness." As Twain left, he said, "Well, I haven't had an opportunity to see much of Portland. . . . I am compelled to leave it after but a glimpse. I may never see Portland again, but I liked the glimpse."

In 1903, President Teddy Roosevelt spoke from the balcony of his Portland Hotel room after laying the cornerstone for the Lewis and Clark Memorial Column at Washington Park. "All I shall say to you," Roosevelt told the crowd, "is . . . how I have enjoyed seeing this wonderfully fertile western Oregon. I have admired your farms, your manufactures; I have seen your great forests. . . . While I think I was a pretty good American when I came to Oregon, I shall leave the state an even better one."

Department store Meier & Frank purchased this block in 1951, demolished the hotel, and built a two-level parking structure that remained for over three decades. In the late 1960s, the store sought to expand the garage but was halted after public opposition. The City of Portland's 1972 Downtown Plan proposed a park or other public gathering space here, an idea that planning bureau members such as Richard Lakeman and Gordon Clark, as well as public activists, continued to keep alive over the ensuing years. "They were saying, 'Downtown is already dying. Creating more opportunities for cars may seem appealing, but what we really need is a reason for people to come downtown,'" explains Portland architect Mark Lakeman, Richard Lakeman's son. "There were wonderful park settings, but no distinct central heart of the city, which is a public square. It's the greatest of all the community-space archetypes. And they were absolutely right. It has profoundly helped reinvigorate the city and the region."

In 1979, Richard Lakeman hired architect Will Martin's firm, Martin, Soderstrom and Matteson, to create conceptual drawings of a potential square. That helped prompt a design competition the following year, which Martin's firm won against better-known competitors. Boston's Machado Silvetti, like Martin, proposed an amphitheater, but Modernist in style. New York's Peter Eisenmann, a rising star of the Postmodern architectural movement, proposed a pair of glass atriums. San Francisco's Lawrence Halprin and Charles Moore, who had collaborated on Lovejoy Fountain Park at the southern edge of downtown, proposed extending the American Bank Building across Morrison Street to front the square with retail. But Martin won with his version of a classical Greek agora, or gathering place: a versatile terraced curving amphitheater.

Martin knew the city better than his more famous competitors, which he believed was "a tremendous advantage. I was able to come up here at 2 o'clock in the morning and see what it was like, what the lighting qualities [are throughout the day]—I was here one night in the cold freezing rain—and the sense of Portland, the sense of what the people are all about," he told KOIN interviewer Mike Donahue on the eve of the square's opening.

Martin's team kept refining their design, right to the end. A week before the competition entry was due, the architect realized their proposal was crammed with too many functions. So Martin turned to an unofficial advisory group of artists and other creative minds, including sculptor Lee Kelly, landscape architect Doug Macy, and graphic designer Robert Reynolds. Reynolds in particular offered what became a key critique. "He said, 'Will, would you do me a favor? I want you to redesign it in thirty minutes: to cleanse your mind, simplify it, and see what you come up with.' So I did just that," Martin recalled. "I eliminated the elevator tower, the aviary, the café, and what was left of the conservatory, and wound up essentially with the scheme that we submitted. Bob came in and looked at it and said, 'That's it.'" By drawing the square from memory, Martin was able to find the essence of his design.

Before construction commenced, Pioneer Courthouse Square was nearly cancelled. Mayor Frank Ivancie and downtown business owners feared a public open space would attract crime; they preferred a private atrium with paid admission. "Will said, 'No, it needs to be open to everybody,'" remembers architect Cameron Hyde, who worked with Martin at Martin Soderstrom Matteson (now Soderstrom Architects) on the design. "He kept holding up examples of European plazas, and as we were working on the design, he even sent me to Tuscany, to see the public square in Sienna. Will was really taken with having different events in the square as the seasons change. In Sienna, on weekends they have farmer's markets, but it's famous for the horse race they have there once a year. Will knew Pioneer Courthouse Square had to be open enough so the activities could be very flexible."

As the square came under threat, popular former Oregon governor Tom McCall, then a commentator for local TV news station KATU, spoke up for the design. And an ingenious fundraising effort—inscribing people's names on individual bricks for $15 each—helped not only close the funding gap but demonstrate that Pioneer Courthouse Square was already too popular to cancel. Today the names on those bricks remain and are still being inscribed as an ongoing fundraiser; I bought one for Valarie's fiftieth birthday in 2021.

Martin was a colorful character. Though at the time professional men almost exclusively wore suits, "I never once in my entire life saw Will Martin even wear a tie," Hyde recalls. "He had a black turtleneck and a black velvet sport coat that he wore, always with a fedora, and had a big cigar in his mouth." In Martin's sketchbook, the architect drew himself in the fedora and wrote cheekily, "Would you buy a brick from this man?" Even in official architectural drawings, Hyde recalls, Martin "couldn't help but screw around. If you look closely in the Pioneer Courthouse Square drawing, he's got a bank being robbed on the corner. A couple was making love in another corner. Life is going on around the square. And he always had himself in these renderings, with his hat."

Martin's design reserved space in Pioneer Courthouse Square for several public art works and curiosities. There is the Weather Machine, which the architect conceived: a 33-foot metal column topped with a large silver-colored orb that at noon each day opens to provide the weather forecast using one of three symbols: a gold-leafed sun for blue skies, a silver heron for clouds, or a copper dragon for coming storms. There is also artist Seward Johnson's *Allow Me* statue, commonly referred to as Umbrella Man, featuring a suit-clad office worker with an umbrella. For about a year, the umbrella was removed for repairs, and I actually liked it better that way, because Oregonians almost never use umbrellas.

Pioneer Courthouse Square has undergone numerous renovations, mostly faithful to Martin's original design, but with one exception. The originally purple tile behind the fountain on the west side of the square was changed to a gray granite veneer in 2017. "It wasn't in the design competition entry," Hyde said of the purple tile. "Will got the idea in the shower. He said, 'We're going to change this travertine to purple tile.' I said, 'That's just fucking ridiculous. It's going to be hideous!' You couldn't talk him out of it." "It looks so much better now," Hyde says. But I disagree. The purple tile was part of the irreverence of the original Postmodern design. More importantly, it was Martin's clear preference.

Martin also helped create the annual Christmas tree display at the square, which had been proposed by developer and civic activist Bill Naito. "The engineers said, 'There's no way you can do a freestanding Christmas tree. You'd need cables to tie it to surrounding buildings,'" Hyde recalls. "Will stood his ground and said, 'No, we've got to have it.' And we figured it out. I had worked in the shipping industry, where we used oak wedges and sledges to raise and lower a double-hulled oil tanker up and down. I knew you could do quite a bit with an oak wedge. We designed a socket where you'd stick this tree in there and drove wedges around this metal collar. We avoided the guide wires. They still use the same thing today."

Thomas Lauderdale, bandleader of Pink Martini, has performed at Pioneer Courthouse Square more than anyone, including leading the house band for the annual Christmas tree lighting ceremony, "which is really great fun," he says. "We had the freedom to bring in this whole program of local musicians to join us, like the [Oregon National Guard] 234th Army Band, the Pacific Youth Choir, and choirs from Franklin High School, to curate an inclusive Christmas tree lighting, which had Jewish moments and maybe a couple of verses of 'Auld Lang Syne' in Arabic." Pink Martini has also hosted a series of sing-alongs at the square, inviting the public to join in. "Those have always been a little hectic, but kind of folksy: good clean American fun, singing songs," Lauderdale adds. "I think that singing together, dancing together, these are the important things to inspire people to be better, to be more open-hearted. And who cares if nobody can really sing? It's just a colorful kaleidoscope of characters. Not everything has to be perfect, and it's the vibe that is most important."

Lauderdale believes Pioneer Courthouse Square brings out a certain innocent spirit in the city. "Portland is a pretty podunk town. I mean, that's what I loved about it from the very beginning. Los Angeles is great as long as you don't want anything. San Francisco is almost too beautiful and therefore sketchy. Seattle has cosmopolitan aspirations and is trying really, really hard to meet them. Portland is great because it's podunk and it doesn't care. And that's what I've loved about Portland. It's possible to pull off really crazy things here because it is podunk."

Pioneer Courthouse Square turned out to be not only Will Martin's breakthrough project but also his last. Less than a year after the square's opening, the architect and his son were killed when the small airplane Martin was piloting crashed into a wall of the Grand Canyon. That tragedy makes the end of his 1984 interview with Donahue all the more compelling. "They say that politicians like to be in office when a major edifice is constructed so that their names can appear on the cornerstone," Donahue began. "Is there a certain amount of ego satisfaction in your work as well?" Martin replied, "I used to be young and arrogant, or more arrogant: very much caught up in what I was doing and believing that it was probably the best thing that was being done. I'm not so sure of that anymore, and I believe now that if we are not people-oriented, if we don't design for people, then we're missing the whole bit."

If Pioneer Courthouse Square is a place where Portlanders from all walks of life come together, the building it's named for, the **Pioneer Courthouse** (700 SW Sixth Avenue) across the street, is strangely quiet. Though it still serves as a seat of the United States Court of Appeals for the Ninth Circuit, its presence seems antiquarian; its halls are often empty. Today the Pioneer Courthouse is dwarfed by the taller buildings around it, but I remember seeing a photo of the building taken in 1875, the year of its completion, and noting how it was standing much

*Pioneer Courthouse*

taller than any of the modest mercantile buildings nearby. This courthouse is a beautiful talisman of Portland's past.

Daniel Lownsdale purchased the site in 1848 for $5,000 from founding fathers Francis Pettygrove and Asa Lovejoy, in hopes of building a public market. But Lownsdale's ownership was challenged by the City of Portland, which initially sought the land for its own and prevailed in court, but then sold the block to the United States government for $15,000. President Ulysses S. Grant then authorized funds for a combination post office, courthouse, and custom house to be built here.

The oldest federal building in the Pacific Northwest and the second-oldest federal courthouse west of the Mississippi River, the Pioneer Courthouse was designed by Alfred Mullett, supervising architect of the US Treasury Department. A combination of Greek Revival and Palladian revival styles, the courthouse's most notable feature is its wooden cupola, from which customs inspectors monitored ships coming in and out of port. Although initially criticized for being too far from the existing townsite, three years after its completion the courthouse survived an 1878 fire that destroyed twenty other downtown blocks. Eventually the city grew up around the courthouse, and a 1905 expansion added two new wings, creating the building's U shape. The courthouse was nearly demolished in the 1970s to make way for a parking garage, just as the Portland Hotel across the street had been torn down for one in 1951. In both cases, department store Meier & Frank was responsible, trying to compete with a new generation of shopping malls offering seas of free parking.

Inside the Pioneer Courthouse is a delightfully warm glow, perhaps thanks to extensive woodwork made from Oregon ash, as well as the gold chandeliers and Doric pilasters. As I walk the halls of this building, there must not be any court in session, for the place is almost completely empty. It's as if I'm wandering through the set of a movie about a court trial, but the cast and crew have completed filming for the day. Yet the cupola upstairs, accessible to the public, is a small delight. Octagonal in shape, it has an operable arched wood window on each side. With historic photos interspersed on the walls between the windows, it's possible to compare the view from the late nineteenth century and the early twenty-first while looking out. I especially love that the windows still have their original glass, in all its imperfections, slightly distorting the view. Fabricated in the manufacturing process of the time, the panes are wavy in places, thicker at the bottom than the top, and dimpled in spots.

As I exit the Pioneer Courthouse, its silence gives way to urban energy again as a MAX train passes on Sixth Avenue, headed north, and I can hear a guitarist playing across the street

The Nines

on the edge of the square. I take just a few steps to cross Morrison Street, toward **The Nines** (525 SW Morrison Street), which has been a hotel since 2008, although I still think of this as the Meier & Frank department store building. I should know better, having reported on the store's demise.

This handsome early twentieth-century building was completed in stages beginning in 1909 and represented the first major commission for architect A. E. Doyle. Meier & Frank was the first of many downtown buildings in this era clad in white-glazed terra cotta, its bright tone a suitable match for Portland's often overcast skies. As I approach, a homeless man with a cardboard sign is sitting on the ground with his dog, in contrast to the pricy cars pulling up to the hotel.

Aaron Meier opened the company's first store on nearby Front Street in 1857. It became Meier & Frank sixteen years later, when Meier went into partnership with one of his employees, fellow German immigrant Emil Frank. In 1898, under the leadership of Frank's brother Sigmund, Meier & Frank moved to a five-story building on the current site. The business was successful enough that a decade later, an expansion was planned. Before construction commenced, Sigmund Frank and A. E.

Doyle visited Chicago, where some of world's first skyscrapers were being built, inspiring Frank to commission an entirely new, full-block department store. Financial constraints necessitated construction in segments over a decade and a half, with today's fifteen-story building completed in 1915. Its Commercial style features residual Beaux Art façade detailing, including sunbursts and even tiny carved swastikas (before the 1930s regarded as a religious icon seen in cultures across Europe and Asia). The department store's offerings in the years after expansion ranged from apparel and consumer goods to a pet store, as well as the swanky Georgian Room restaurant on the top floor, and even an in-house radio station on the fifth floor. Pneumatic tubes were used to send messages and money between floors.

In 1922, future Academy Award–winning actor Clark Gable worked at Meier & Frank for a few months. The twenty-one-year-old Ohio native had hitchhiked to Portland from Montana after the traveling theater company he belonged to disbanded; fellow-actors told him Oregon had an up-and-coming theater scene. While working at Meier & Frank, Gable met the woman who would change his life: Josephine Dillon. She managed an acting school in Portland called The Little Theater, and trained Gable to better use his deep voice and paid for orthodontic and cosmetic surgeries to improve his looks. Dillon also suggested Gable (whose actual first name was William) go by his middle name, Clark. Despite their seventeen-year age difference, the couple married in 1924, the same year that painter Mark Rothko began taking acting lessons from Dillon, during a short-lived return to Portland from New York. Soon after, Mr. and Mrs. Gable moved to Hollywood so he could pursue a movie career. The couple divorced in 1930, four years before Gable's Oscar-winning role in *It Happened One Night* and nine years before starring in *Gone with the Wind*. Dillon continued to teach acting, including to future Hollywood stars Gary Cooper, Donna Reed, and Rita Hayworth.

The store continued to evolve. In 1950, when Meier & Frank installed what was then the largest escalator in the United States, curious shoppers formed a queue that filled up the entire ground floor. But soon this Meier & Frank flagship was, like other downtown department stores, competing unsuccessfully with suburban shopping malls. The store continued for several more decades, but with dwindling returns. In 2005, Meier & Frank was sold to the Macy's chain, which reduced the store to its first six floors, creating room upstairs for a new luxury hotel, The Nines. A new contemporary-style penthouse by Skylab Architecture was added, home to the Asian-fusion restaurant Departure, where acclaimed chef Gregory Gourdet would make his name before gaining notoriety on TV's *Top Chef*. Before Meier & Frank closed for good in 2016, I reported for *The New York Times* from the last iteration of its popular Santaland installation on the Tenth floor, where each December kids would sit on Santa Claus's lap.

Crossing diagonally back across the square, at its southwest corner I come to **Jackson Tower** (806 SW Broadway), one of downtown Portland's most handsome buildings. Completed in 1912 from a design by San Francisco firm Reid and Reid, the twelve-story office building's white-glazed terra cotta façade gives way to a distinctive clock tower.

Jackson Tower was originally known as the Oregon Journal Building, housing the newspaper of the same name, but in 1951 was renamed after the paper's publisher Charles Samuel Jackson. A Virginia native, he came to Portland in July 1902 as the hired publisher of the *Evening Journal*, which had been founded in March of that year and was already failing. He purchased the publication with a group of investors, changed its name to the *Oregon Journal*, and made it a success. Jackson's editorials were influential, building public support for Oregon's use of ballot measures, referendums, and recalls in the early 1900s, and then for Portland's unusual weak-mayoral system in 1912 (with four commissioners having nearly identical powers to the mayor, continuing until 2025). That same year, Jackson moved the paper to this building. With the paper's success and Jackson's ensuing wealth, he became a philanthropist, in 1917 donating 88 acres on Marquam Hill to what became part of the University of Oregon Medical School campus (now Oregon Health & Science University). Jackson remained the *Oregon Journal*'s publisher until his 1924 death.

Jackson's son Philip enjoyed an even longer tenure as *Journal* publisher, from 1924 until his passing in 1953. He was

*Jackson Tower*

succeeded by William Knight, father of future Nike co-founder Phil Knight. In 1961 he approved the *Journal*'s sale to S. I. Newhouse's Advance Publications chain, after the death of the paper's owner, Maria Clopton Jackson (Philip's widow). Her will had specified that the company be bequeathed to its employees, but in court was found to be written in non-legally-binding language. In 1982, Advance, which already owned *The Oregonian*, ceased publication of the *Oregon Journal*.

I now cross Broadway at Yamhill Street, briefly noting the Nordstrom store where I often shopped as a teen, before heading to the **Fox Tower** (805 SW Broadway), a twenty-seven-story glass office building completed in 2000. It's an early example of an architectural type that became commonplace in the early twenty-first century: a relatively slender tower rising from a multistory podium extending to the sidewalk.

*Fox Tower*

The Fox Tower was named for and replaced the Fox Theatre, one of the last in what had been a collection of theaters lining Broadway for most of the twentieth century (and one of two theaters on this block, along with the Music Box). The Fox, originally known as the Heilig Theatre and completed in 1910 for theater mogul Calvin Heilig, featured a Romanesque-style design by English-born architect E. W. Houghton and one of the largest performance spaces in the US west, with 1,500 seats. Its most unique feature was hidden behind the lower balcony: a private viewing box connected to Calvin Heilig's apartment, allowing him to watch performances from his living room. In 1917 the theater hosted the world's most famous dancer, Vaslav Nijinsky, who had recently been released from two years under house arrest in Budapest. Shortly after performing in Portland, Nijinsky's mental condition deteriorated, and by 1919 he was committed to a mental asylum, never to perform in public again.

From the beginning, the Heilig Theatre had been equipped to show movies. A 1913 advertisement pictured in Gary Lacher and Steve Stone's book *Theatres of Portland* mentions "Edison's Talking Pictures" prominently (fourteen years before the first Hollywood "talkie," *The Jazz Singer*). The formal switch came in 1919, when the Heilig changed its name to the Hippodrome. In 1929, it was leased by the Paramount-Publix chain and changed its name again, to the Rialto, with a new eye-catching marquee installed with a waterfall of neon lights. Yet the timing couldn't have been worse, for the Great Depression sank the new owners, who sold to the J. J. Parker chain. After just a year as the Rialto, in 1930 the venue became known as the Mayfair Theatre, which hosted both double-feature movies as well as stage shows.

In 1944, the great jazz saxophonist Coleman Hawkins headlined at the Mayfair, accompanied by a then-unknown future legend: pianist Thelonious Monk. After arriving by train, the all-Black group was refused service at every local hotel. A local minister helped find them local families to stay with instead. Ads for the Mayfair Theater show boasted an "All Colored All Star Jazz Symphony that could play everything from Brahms to Boogie!" After matinee and evening performances here, the group moved across the river for a weeklong gig at the Dude Ranch jazz club on Northeast Broadway.

The Mayfair became the Fox Theatre after a 1954 renovation made this the second-largest movie screen in the United States, boasting a new Art Deco interior, overseen by architect Carl G. Moeller. The new owner, Twentieth Century Fox studio, brought several famous actors to attend the August 12 premiere including Van Heflin, Mamie Van Doren, and Rita Moreno, as two thousand spectators filled bleachers outside on Broadway. The Fox continued as a popular Portland movie house and performance space for another thirty-five years. In 1990, after an initial plan to demolish the theater for an office building was abandoned, it continued to host live music, most notably an October 29, 1991, performance by Nirvana, just a month after releasing their classic album *Nevermind*.

The Fox Theatre's 1997 demolition came just a few months after I moved to Portland. I remember the giant pit there (to make room for an underground parking garage) before the tower was erected, which *Willamette Week* featured on its cover, sarcastically posing people in the pit sunbathing in swimsuits on lawn chairs. Many Portlanders also lamented the loss of a popular mural on the back wall of the Fox Theatre by artist Robert Wyland dedicated just four years earlier, called *Orcas of the Oregon Coast* (part of his Whaling Walls series).

Replacing the theater with an office building came at the instigation of owner Tom Moyer, who had grown up working in his family's movie theater in Southeast Portland's Sellwood district and went on to build one of the nation's largest movie-theater chains. As a young man, Moyer had been a successful boxer, in 1940 narrowly losing the US amateur-boxing title to the great Sugar Ray Robinson. After turning pro, Moyer won his first twenty-two bouts, then after the Pearl Harbor attack retired from boxing to join the army, serving in the 41st Infantry Division during World War II and receiving a Bronze Star. Over the ensuing decades, his Moyer Theaters grew to include more than 350 screens. After the company's 1989 sale, he retained the Fox Theater and nearby Broadway Theater because of their prominent downtown locations, redeveloping them into the 1000 Broadway office tower in 1991, then the Fox Tower in 2000.

The Fox Tower was designed by TVA Architects, founded in 1984 by Robert Thompson and Ned Vaivoda, best known for designing Nike's corporate campus in suburban Beaverton. Today Thompson sees similarities in his two career-making clients, Tom Moyer and Nike co-founder Phil Knight. "Both men were very soft-spoken gentlemen, surprisingly quiet yet clear and decisive in articulating their goals and vision," he recalls. "When they spoke, you listened."

Moyer had little interest in architectural beauty, which is why the Fox Tower's most distinct visual attribute, a curving northeast façade that visually enlivens the otherwise boxy form, was actually a response to regulatory constraint. "The zoning code did not allow any shadow from the tower to be cast directly onto Pioneer Square on March 21 [the spring equinox] at noon," Thompson recalls. But the restraint "quickly became a positive," necessitating the curve when Moyer would have preferred a rectangular form that utilized every inch of rentable space. For both the tower and the public space it overlooks, Pioneer Courthouse Square, a greater civic good prevailed.

### *Plaza to Park*

Behind the Fox Tower on the adjacent block is another outdoor public space: **Director Park** (815 SW Park Avenue), opened in 2009. Because Tom Moyer owned both properties, and no building existed here (just a surface parking lot), the tower's underground parking garage could be extended beneath this site. Since the late nineties, Moyer, along with former Portland mayor and Oregon governor Neil Goldschmidt, had also supported extending the South Park Blocks north, ideally to connect with the North Park Blocks, as had been proposed in the nineteenth century, or at least to recover the six blocks here initially conceived as part of owner Daniel Lownsdale's plan. Director Park represents the only block turned over to public space. Philanthropist Jordan Schnitzer donated nearly $2 million for the project, after which Director Park was named for his grandparents, Simon and Helen Director.

Director Park's design, by acclaimed Philadelphia landscape architect Laurie Olin in collaboration with ZGF Architects (led by partner Greg Baldwin), is complementary to Pioneer Courthouse Square. Despite its being called a park, this is a paved plaza or Italian-style piazza, packing a variety of functions into its

Director Park

confined 100-by-200-foot size. An interactive fountain anchors the southwest corner, with shallow waters attracting children and families in summertime. A 25-foot-high glass canopy shelters a terrace with café tables along the west side. Adjacent is a small pavilion offering food and drink. Curving wood benches add still more seating. And on the south side is a people-sized chess game.

I wish the canopy, Director Park's signature design feature, was twice its size, and I remember once being told off-record that a larger canopy was originally planned. Even so, maybe then the park's balance of uses might be lost. I think in its relatively short life Director has become a distinct place of its own, and is popular with the public. It indeed feels like an inviting European piazza, and its combination of modest square footage and myriad functions creates a pleasingly intimate setting. It's flexible, able to incorporate food trucks or host movie screenings and sports-watching watch parties on a big screen. Director Park is a quintessentially urban place, accommodating many uses together.

Facing the park is the marquee of the **Guild Theatre** (829 SW Ninth Avenue), a beloved former movie house now occupied by Japanese bookstore chain Kinokuniya. It was completed in 1927 as part of the Studio Building, which for decades housed more than a hundred music-rehearsal studios. Admittedly, the Guild was actually not a great theater-going experience. Its ceiling was low, and the ancient heating-cooling system roared. The theater's seating layout was reversed, with the front screen at the entrance, meaning anyone who came in during a screening became a visual distraction. Yet in an age of soulless multiplexes, the Guild, even with its sticky floors and dingy bathrooms, had personality. And during my years as a young *Willamette Week* movie critic at the turn of the twenty-first century, the Guild was the movie theater I visited most often in Portland.

Operated at the time by the Portland Art Museum's Northwest Film Center, the theater hosted the Portland International Film Festival, giving me early peeks at movies I went on to review like Christopher Nolan's *Memento* and Wong Kar-Wai's *In the Mood for Love*. I also covered the Guild retrospectives of classic directors like Andrei Tarkovsky, Michelangelo Antonioni, and Eric Rohmer. And there were wonderful programs devoted to Portland's burgeoning local-film scene, led by filmmakers who went on to national notoriety, like Matt McCormick and Miranda July, and who inspired me to become a filmmaker. Though I've been an architecture journalist for decades, those Guild screenings are a reminder that film was my first love.

Moving south past Taylor Street and Salmon Street, I'm stepping into the **South Park Blocks** (between SW Park and Ninth Avenues, Salmon and Jackson Streets), part of a network of linear parks across the central city, also including the North Park Blocks, the Plaza Blocks, the Open Space Sequence, and Tom McCall Waterfront Park, which collectively act as the city's lungs. It's no coincidence that I can suddenly hear birds chirping. A few years ago, when I flew in a small chartered Cessna plane flying over downtown Portland, the South Park Blocks caught my eye the most, rather than the skyline or individual buildings.

Dedicated in 1852, just one year after the city was officially incorporated, the South Park Blocks were the brainchild of developer Daniel Lownsdale, one of the city's earliest landowners. Lownsdale had come to Portland in 1845 and established the Pacific Northwest's first tannery, along what became known as Tanner Creek. He was a member of Oregon's first territorial legislature and the city's first surveyor, instrumental in establishing Portland's famously small blocks, as well as the Great Plank Road, the city's first major infrastructure project. Moving into real estate development, Lownsdale, influenced by cities in Europe as well as the row of park-lined city blocks in his native Louisville, Kentucky, envisioned an elegant mix of buildings and greenspace. He conceived the Park Blocks as an attractor for what was initially an affluent residential area, near homes owned by some of the city's most powerful civic and business leaders, including William S. Ladd and Simon Benson.

The land that became the South Park Blocks was just west of where the modest city grid ended, giving Lownsdale the freedom to build these blocks at just 100 by 200 feet, half the size of other downtown blocks. As mentioned in the context of Director Park, Lownsdale envisioned the South Park Blocks as six blocks longer than what remains today. After his 1862 death, Lownsdale's will, bequeathing the blocks to the city, was successfully contested in court by his heirs. The city purchased the southernmost twelve blocks, but six additional blocks were lost to development.

Because of their narrowness, the South Park Blocks feel less like a park than a kind of shared yard for the buildings between them. That intimacy also makes the Park Blocks a particularly shady respite from summertime heat, the tree canopy covering the entire greenspace. It's also a stage for interaction. Oregon Ballet Theater rehearsals used to take place here in the summertime, and the Portland Farmers Market is here weekly. At the southern edge of the South Blocks, on the Portland State University campus, is where you'll find a particularly youthful and culturally diverse presence.

In 1970, a half century before downtown Portland's 2020 racial justice protests, a similar incident occurred here, also violently curtailed by police, called the Battle of the Park Blocks. Earlier that month, National Guard troops at Kent State University in Ohio had opened fire on unarmed students protesting expansion of the Vietnam War; four were killed and nine wounded. Students nationwide began picketing, including at Portland State. After a student protester was hit by a car in a deliberate act of right-wing vigilante violence, demonstrators began erecting barricades of upturned tables and park benches to protect themselves. By the following Monday morning, as the protests were beginning to wind down, Mayor Terry Schrunk and parks commissioner Frank Ivancie (the future mayor) sent police officers in riot gear to break up the encampment. "It looked like an army coming down the Park Blocks," Kent Weiskopf, one of the student protesters, told *The Oregonian*'s Douglas Perry in 2022. More than two dozen students were hospitalized with injuries suffered at the hands of police. The next day, more than 3,000 citizens—this time not just students but people of all ages—marched on City Hall. "I hoped it would never come to this," a remorseful Mayor Schrunk, a Portland State alumnus, told reporters. Indeed, the Battle of the South Park Blocks may have marked a sea change, inspiring the election of a new generation of progressive leaders in the early 1970s.

Though the 2020 protests occurred west of here, the South Park Blocks were also affected. Protesters toppled two statues, of President Abraham Lincoln and President Teddy Roosevelt. After five years and counting, those statues have not been restored, but the City of Portland has announced its intention to bring them back. And the South Park Blocks remain a stage for student demonstrations, most recently in 2024, following Israel's invasion of Gaza. Even so, the everyday reality is so much more tranquil. More than any other place in the central city, the South Park Blocks are the place to become immersed in nature, evoking the Frederick Law Olmsted tradition of trees and greenery as sanctuary in the heart of the metropolis.

## *Parkside Culture*

Along the South Park Blocks and Broadway are numerous architectural landmarks, so my next few stops oscillate between the two places, starting with **Heathman Hotel** (1001 SW Broadway). Completed in 1927 for developer George Heathman and designed by DeYoung and Roald, the ten-story building blends Jacobethan and Italian Renaissance styles. I like how the upper portion of its brick façade is clad in a diamond pattern. The Heathman's interior showpiece is a eucalyptus-wood-paneled tea room near the lobby.

For its first six decades, this was known as the New Heathman Hotel, a sister property to the original Heathman Hotel at Park Avenue and Salmon Street; this one was more upscale, attracting lumber barons and railroad magnates. The New Heathman's opening included speeches from Governor I. L. Patterson and Mayor George Luis Baker, and an orchestra performance simulcast on KOIN radio from its new studios in the hotel's mezzanine. The *Oregon Journal* called the New Heathman Hotel's style "modern as human ingenuity and talent could possibly make it." Its namesake, George Heathman, died of a stroke only three years later.

By the time of the hotel's 1984 renovation, when the "New" prefix was retired, the Heathman had arguably supplanted the Benson Hotel as the most prestigious local accommodation, a place where touring authors, musicians, and artists frequently stayed. Lining the hotel's mezzanine, where the radio station used to be, is a library of first-edition books signed by its writer-guests. Endearingly yet somewhat absurdly, the Heathman was long known for the Beefeater costumes worn by its doormen, as if they'd come to the hotel directly from the Tower of London to hail taxis for guests (the costumes were replaced in 2019).

As a film critic, I would often visit the Heathman each winter to interview directors and actors promoting their work during the Portland International Film Festival. Many times I'd be talking to a director who seemed to be on the cusp of stardom, although that rarely came to fruition. One exception was in 2002, when I interviewed director Todd Haynes about *Far From Heaven*, which went on to receive several Academy Award nominations that year, including a Best Actress nomination for its star, Julianne Moore, and Best Original Screenplay for Haynes. What I remember most from the interview was not the movie itself, but Haynes's relocation to Portland. He had first come here to stay with his sister while writing the *Far From Heaven* script, and wound up moving. "This place engendered a real change in me," Haynes told me for a *Christian Science Monitor* article. "I started to enjoy myself again." He has now lived here for more than twenty years.

The Heathman's eponymous in-house restaurant was for my first two decades in Portland among the city's most talked-about dining destinations, especially when headed by chef Philippe Boulot, part of a generation who made the city a culinary destination. A Normandy native and former disciple of legendary French chef Joël Robuchon, Boulot moved here in 1994 with his wife Suzanne, a pastry chef from Portland, after they had worked together at London's Four Seasons Hotel. During his eighteen-year tenure at the Heathman, Boulot's cooking attracted attention from food writers like Anthony Bourdain (whom he took fishing in an episode of TV's *No Reservations*). I remember Boulot's French accent and warm cordiality as he walked the dining room in his chef's whites, chatting with diners.

Boulot was succeeded at the Heathman by another local culinary pioneer, Vitaly Paley, whose Northwest Portland restaurant Paley's Place had attracted equal attention, and who oversaw the newly rebranded restaurant Headwaters until 2020. "It rains nine months out of the year here, but when it stops raining, what came out of the ground for me as a chef is what mattered the most," Paley told me that same year. "It's not just the quality and range of ingredients here, but the fact that Oregon isn't ruled by tradition. You go to New England and it's clam chowder. You go to Louisiana and it's jambalaya. There are so many places you can go to and rattle off what they're famous for. We don't have that in the Northwest. That's precisely why I'm here." In 2011, Paley emerged victorious on Food Network's TV competition show *Iron Chef America*. "The mayor's office gave me a fork to the city," Paley recalled with a laugh. "I still have it hanging on the wall. I think it meant something to Portland."

Unfortunately, the pandemic forced the closure of the Headwaters, and Paley has since relocated to Hawai'i. While he and Boulot are no longer running Portland restaurants, there are other great chefs from their generation, such as Greg Higgins and Cathy Whims, and what they collectively established—a sense for the first time of Portland as one of the nation's great food cities, drawing from a bounty of ingredients in every direction—endures.

Next door to the Heathman and actually wrapping around it in back is the last of what once were many theaters lining Broadway: the **Arlene Schnitzer Concert Hall** (1037 SW Broadway). Known before its 1984 renovation as the Paramount Theatre, the "Schnitz," as it's commonly referred to today, is hard to miss, with its iconic PORTLAND sign hanging off the front

Arlene Schnitzer Concert Hall

of the building, retooled from what had read PARAMOUNT for more than fifty years, but originally had been PORTLAND, since the building's opening in 1928 as the Portland Publix Theatre.

The Publix was designed by Chicago firm Rapp and Rapp in an Italian Rococo Revival style, with a multistory wall of glass above its marquee, topped with decorative cast stone and pediments. The Publix originally hosted live vaudeville performances, and a Wurlitzer organ mounted on an elevator could be raised to the level of the stage. Its ornate baroque interior made this the most opulent of Broadway's many theaters, brandishing marble walls, furnishings from a French museum, and huge crystal chandeliers in the lobby.

While known as the Paramount from 1930 to 1984, the theater hosted a succession of superstars: the Marx Brothers in the thirties, Frank Sinatra and Buddy Holly in the fifties, Bob Dylan in the sixties; then in the seventies, Stevie Wonder, Bob Marley, Fleetwood Mac, Bruce Springsteen, and Queen; and in the eighties Madonna, The Police, and U2. I've seen the Oregon Symphony perform there many times, as well as Ray Charles, Wynton Marsalis, Itzhak Perlman, Mikhail Baryshnikov, Savion Glover, Jerry Seinfeld, and John Cleese. I particularly remember at the Ray Charles concert, preceded by an hourlong performance by the Oregon Symphony, a frustrated fan a row ahead of my dad and me grumbling, "I didn't come to see no symphony. I came to see Ray!"

By the sixties the Paramount was in disrepair and could easily have been demolished. In 1965, its cast-iron balcony collapsed. In 1970, two huge blocks fell from the facade, one crashing into the marquee. Five years later, owner John Haviland auctioned most of the interior architectural details including statues, the organ, antique furniture, and a sixteenth-century suit of armor. Luckily when a statue of a nude woman with her hands covering her face called *Surprise* failed to reach its minimum selling price, members of the audience pooled their resources to buy it and donate the statue back to the venue. It remains on display today.

"It was an old theater, and a lot was not up to snuff," remembers David Leiken of Double Tee Promotions, who booked the Paramount from 1975 until its 1984 renovation. "But it was a great venue, and for some reason, the acoustics were way better than they are now." Leiken particularly remembers producing numerous Grateful Dead shows here. "They were different from just about everybody—how they operated and how they treated their people," he explains. "They even stayed at the same modest hotel the rest of the crew did." Leiken particularly remembers a night in 1978 with two long Dead shows, the second lasting well into the morning. Finally, driving down Twelfth Avenue just before dawn, Leiken encountered a lone bicyclist riding down the street, sustaining a wheelie for the entire block: Trail Blazers legend Bill Walton, who that year won the NBA's Most Valuable Player award.

In 1984, to save the Paramount from demolition, arts philanthropist Arlene Schnitzer pledged $1.7 million, after which the venue was renamed in her honor. While famous names have continued to grace the Schnitz's stage over the decades, it has become best known for its anchor tenant, the Oregon Symphony. Founded as the Portland Symphony Society in 1896, it is the sixth-oldest orchestra in the United States, and oldest in the western United States.

When Valarie and I moved to Portland in 1997, the Oregon Symphony was still being conducted by James DePreist, who had become one of America's first major Black conductors upon taking the job in 1980. The nephew of famed opera singer Marian Anderson, DePreist got his start by winning an international conducting competition, prompting Leonard Bernstein to offer him the New York Philharmonic's assistant conductor job for the 1965–1966 season. By that time, DePreist had contracted polio, which made him another kind of pioneer: one of the first to conduct from a seated position. The Oregon Symphony under DePreist became a nationally recognized ensemble for the first time, and he continued to work around the world as a guest-conductor. DePreist became even more well-known in 1987, when childhood friend Bill Cosby invited the Oregon Symphony Orchestra to record a new arrangement for *The Cosby Show*'s opening theme, "Kiss Me." Before the conductor's 2003 retirement, I got to see DePreist conduct a few times, and when he passed away in 2013, my mind went back to a moment after one performance, when I was surprised to be walking behind DePriest as he slowly ambled up a side-exit hallway, guided by arm braces. He had such presence to me, proud yet vulnerable.

Leaving the Schnitz behind, I cross the Park Blocks heading west, anticipating hearing the birds again but instead coming across a heated argument between what appear to be a down-on-their-luck man and woman. But I've got my eyes on the wonderful **Portland Art Museum** (1217 SW Park Avenue). A site that has almost continuously expanded and evolved, today this is a complex of three interconnected buildings. The original Main Building, completed in 1932, is an early-Modernist gem that helped launch architect Pietro Belluschi's career. To the north is a former Masonic Temple, completed in 1924 and designed by architect Frederick Fritsch, now known as the Mark Building. In between is the Rothko Pavilion, completed in 2025 by Chicago's Vinci Hamp Architects and Portland's Hennebery Eddy Architects.

The museum's roots date to the 1892 founding of the Portland Art Association by a small group of business and cultural leaders including Henry Corbett, William Ladd, Henry Failing, Reverend Thomas Lamb Eliot, and attorney-writer C. E. S. Wood, with the purpose of building an art collection that could be shared with the public. One of the PAA's first actions was to open a museum in 1895, in an upper hall of the Portland Library Association on Seventh Avenue and Stark Street (today Broadway and Harvey Milk Street). The association's first director was Henrietta Failing, Henry's sister, just twenty-four years old when she began. Inspired by attending the 1893 World's Columbian Exposition in Chicago, she successfully organized exhibits with artworks on loan from local collectors. In 1905, Failing oversaw

*Portland Art Museum*

the museum's move into its own building at SW Fifth and Taylor, the first exhibition featuring paintings from that year's Lewis and Clark Centennial Exposition. After stepping down in 1908 because of illness (though continuing as a lecturer in art history for thirty more years), Failing was succeeded as director by Anna Belle Crocker, who over her twenty-eight-year tenure created an ambitious exhibition schedule, grew the museum's permanent collections, oversaw the opening of the Art School (renamed the Museum Art School in 1933), and helped make possible the museum's wondrous Belluschi-designed building.

To win the Portland Art Museum commission, the young Italian architect faced an uphill battle convincing the trustees that he could be trusted as much as his former employer, architect A. E. Doyle, who had died in 1928. As the Great Depression set in, the firm under Belluschi's leadership had struggled, shrinking to five employees. But he had been a regular visitor to the museum since his arrival, taking classes at its Art School and bonding with Crocker and instructor Harry Wentz. They convinced the museum's trustees to give this young architect a chance designing the museum's new home.

To Belluschi, a Modern interpretation of historic influences was a way to remember the past while still embracing function. His generation was determined "to shake architecture out of its lethargy . . . and clear the ground for a new era," as Belluschi later reflected in a 1951 speech at Reed College. "Of the ideals on which contemporary architecture is based, first and foremost is the right to free our thinking from the dogmas of the past." Even so, while the design was without architectural ornament, it drew from the architect's Beaux Arts training and his Italian heritage. The museum was clad in traditional materials like brick and elegant travertine, and configured with a tripartite base, middle, and top, as well as an axial floor plan, common to classical architecture. Today the original Portland Art Museum building reads like a fusion of old and new.

Yet the design was opposed by the museum's trustees, who preferred a classical Georgian-style building like nearby Central Library, which Doyle's firm had designed a decade before Belluschi's arrival. The adjacent Masonic Temple next door to the museum site, completed in 1924 (and later incorporated into the

Portland Art Museum campus), was more to their liking with its historical pastiche. Belluschi, undeterred, turned to the world's most famous architect, Frank Lloyd Wright, sending a drawing of the proposed museum for critique and asking for help in convincing the trustees. "My dear Belluschi," Wright wrote back in an encouraging letter, "I think your plan simple and sensible and the exterior would mark an advance in culture for Portland." The trustees, with whom Belluschi shared the letter, agreed to move forward with the Modernist design.

"He had a tremendous amount of natural talent, but mostly he had vision," says architect Anthony Belluschi, Pietro's son. "As an immigrant he had a certain wisdom because of travel and his education, growing up in Europe. He was very conscientious of his work because he was in a new land with a new language. But he was able to persuade clients in a gentle but strong direction, never pushing too hard. He was very good at conceptualizing projects, more so than detailing them. I think he got involved in the architectural details much later in his career, when he became more knowledgeable about construction and how buildings are put together. He was only thirty years old when he designed the Portland Art Museum, so that in and of itself is amazing. He really understood the quality of light, and he kept the building very clean-lined, with a welcoming entry. He used brick and of course travertine, which drew from his experience in Italy. Yet what I really love is its lack of pretentiousness." In 1940, eight years after the Portland Art Museum was completed, the American Institute of Architects chose it as one of the hundred best buildings constructed in the United States over the previous twenty years.

The museum has expanded numerous times during my nearly three decades living in Portland, to say nothing of the sixty-six years prior. The first space I regularly visited, the Berg-Swann Auditorium for movie screenings, has long since been demolished. In the early 2000s, the campus was expanded to include the aforementioned former Masonic temple next door.

Only in the past few weeks was I able to tour the Rothko Pavilion for the first time. When this glass-ensconced connection between the Belluschi and Mark Buildings was being conceived in the 2010s, I worried it might overwhelm Belluschi's original structure. But that turned out to not be the case. While such landmarks should never be torn down, they have to continue to work for their occupants; an underutilized old building is a building soon to be demolished. "He would agree that we're on the right track," Anthony Belluschi says today. "He would be in favor of combining the buildings to work in unison with each other." Actually, Pietro Belluschi even said so specifically, in an early nineties interview shortly before his death: "I have a dream that they could enclose that part that is between the museum and the Masonic Temple and build wings."

I was surprised that the Rothko Pavilion commission didn't go to Portland architect Brad Cloepfil, who has designed striking art museums all over the country. Yet there's no denying that the Vinci Hamp / Hennebery Eddy design successfully transforms the Portland Art Museum experience. It takes advantage of the original building's clear axial connections, making a visit here no longer solely a matter of going to a series of different rooms to see art, but instead of moving through space. Walking the main arterial path from the Rothko into Belluschi's Main Building, it's possible to experience a variety of different genres and periods—Native American art and cultural artifacts, Northwest artists, nineteenth-century European paintings—without even entering these galleries.

"I was on the streetcar in '06. The museum had its back to the streetcar. I overheard some students say, 'What's that?'" recalls Brian Ferriso, the Portland Art Museum's former director, who led the Rothko Pavilion effort and, shortly after its completion, was named head of the Dallas Museum of Art. "They were looking at these big brick facades. They said, 'I think it's a museum, but I don't think anything happens there.' I felt, how do we become more inviting? How do we become more of an invitation and a center?" With the Rothko Pavilion's completion, I think Ferriso and his collaborators have done just that. The transparency of its glass-ensconced form and the way it makes the museum an indoor-outdoor experience, with its terraces and plaza, make this venerable arts institution so much more open to the city. The design even preserves right-of-way through this former outdoor plaza, with the pavilion cantilevering over a bike-and-pedestrian passageway.

My first apartment in Portland, a block away from here and where this book began, had a view of the back walls of the museum, and I was only a few years removed from being a student like those Ferriso overheard. Had there been the plaza, the café, and the glass that's there now, as of the Rothko's opening, I would have spent more time there from the start.

While the Portland Art Museum's permanent collection is not on par with the Louvre or the Metropolitan Museum of Art, it contains a scattering of works by the masters: an early painting by Vincent Van Gogh, for example, called *The Ox Cart*, as well as pieces by Anthony Van Dyck, Gustave Courbet, Robert Rauschenberg, Alexander Calder, and others. Yet an art museum is not a competition to collect famous names or valuable works. It's about finding works that move us, and placing them in a space that people will want to come and interact with.

My favorite artwork in the Portland Art Museum's permanent collection is from a lesser-known name: an 1864 painting called *The Forest at Fontainebleau* by Virgile Narcisse de la Peña, who was part of the Barbizon School of landscape painters immediately pre-dating Impressionism. When I look at that painting, I'm transported, figuratively and literally speaking. It depicts a tree-lined path, beneath an enormous cloudy sky, thereby celebrating a beautiful natural setting and suggesting a journey beyond it. There is a hint of Impressionistic fuzziness, yet a greater clarity than that conveyed by Monet and Cezanne. It looks lucidly yet romantically at the path ahead, which actually serves as a guide for me writing this book. Yet the Portland Art Museum renovation of the Rothko Pavilion also brought about a wondrous new attraction: eight Mark Rothko paintings on long-term loan to the museum by his family. As I'll explain later in this chapter, the artist emigrated here as a child and took his first art classes at the museum. On my first visit to the museum after its expansion, I enjoyed a moment of wonder and solitude sitting in a room full of Rothko paintings, all by myself.

## *Laddville*

Returning to Broadway but needing a pick-me-up, I stop at Caffe Umbria for a double espresso and a cookie before continuing to a trio of buildings located on the former grounds of the nineteenth-century mansion belonging to mayor and self-made tycoon William S. Ladd. The largest of the three and my first stop, on the east side of Broadway, is the **Oregonian Building** (1320 SW Broadway), completed in 1948 from another Pietro Belluschi design, sixteen years after his Portland Art Museum. It occupies the site of Ladd's home.

In 1851, the year Portland was officially incorporated, a then twenty-five-year-old Ladd left his native Vermont for San Francisco to join former classmate Charles Tilton in the mercantile business. When it became clear that gold-rush-era California was already saturated with merchants, Ladd headed north to Portland, bringing a small consignment of liquor to sell

*Downtown from the Oregonian Building*

*Oregonian Building*

and a character-reference letter from his hometown minister. (If that doesn't symbolize Portland's duality of indulgence and innocence, I don't know what does.) Just three years later, Ladd became the city's fifth mayor and is still the youngest to have held that office. In 1858, he and Tilton founded Oregon's first bank. Ladd hadn't set out to be a banker, but during the Panic of 1857, many of his liquor customers fell behind in their accounts, so he began to loan them money.

By 1860, with the Ladd & Tilton Bank having made him wealthy, thirty-four-year-old Ladd and his family moved into their Italianate-style mansion here, designed by E. M. Burton. The Ladd mansion was later enlarged to thirty rooms by architect William P. Lewis in a Second Empire style, with a dramatic mansard roof and interiors paneled in rosewood, maple, and mahogany. The back of the home faced Broadway, and at the northwest corner of the property was a two-story circular greenhouse.

Ladd's business empire expanded in parallel to his mansion. Over the course of the 1860s, he co-founded the Oregon Steam Navigation Company, the Oregon Telegraph Company, the Oregon Iron Company, and the Oregon Central Railroad

Company, while also investing in Portland's first flour mills, as well as the luxurious Portland Hotel. Ladd became celebrated for his philanthropy, underwriting the construction of several churches near the South Park Blocks, several of which remain standing today. The Ladd mansion, however, was torn down in 1925, just over two decades before the site eventually became home to the city's largest and most venerable newspaper.

The *Weekly Oregonian*, as it was first known, had begun production in 1850 and initially struggled to break even, so publisher Thomas J. Dryer sold the paper in 1860 to the affluent Henry Pittock (the son-in-law of Ladd mansion architect E. M. Burton), who purchased a new steam-powered printing press and began daily publication of the *Morning Oregonian* in 1861, enabling its rapid growth. For a half century beginning in 1866, *The Oregonian* was dominated by editor Harvey Scott, the brother and political adversary of Abigail Scott Duniway, Oregon's celebrated women's suffrage leader. During the Civil War, his editorials were staunchly pro-Union and supported the nascent Republican party of President Abraham Lincoln. Yet Scott opposed many progressive causes such as state-supported free education, organized labor, and Oregon's system of direct-voting primaries and referendums, as well as the very issue for which his sister would become famous: women's rights. Yet under his leadership, *The Oregonian* also prospered as a business, continually growing its circulation and influence.

For sixty years before moving to this location in 1948, *The Oregonian* had been headquartered in a magnificent Romanesque-style downtown building at Sixth Avenue and Alder Street with a clock tower, the city's tallest structure for more than a decade. But after the building was damaged by fire in 1943, the paper's leaders began planning to build a new home.

The Belluschi-designed *Oregonian* headquarters, occupying a full-block site, took advantage of a 24-foot slope from west to east by burying two of its six stories underground on the Broadway side. In back, Belluschi added large expanses of glass so pedestrians could watch the paper's gigantic printing presses in action. News and editorial offices were consolidated on the third floor. Printed papers were sent by conveyors to the second-floor mailing room, then to loading platforms and delivery trucks waiting in the center of the building. There were also recording studios on the fourth floor for the paper's radio station, KGW, and a television studio. Visiting the building just after its completion, *Time* and *Life* publisher Henry Luce said this was the finest newspaper plant in the country.

Yet this headquarters may have cost *The Oregonian* its independence. Within a year of completion, the building was sold to the Connecticut Mutual Life Insurance Company, in a leaseback arrangement. Two years later, in 1950, New York–based newspaper magnate Samuel Irving Newhouse purchased *The Oregonian* itself. The headquarters had seemingly been a financial overreach, sapping the paper's resources. But under Newhouse, the paper continued to gain prestige. In 1957, *The Oregonian* won its first Pulitzer Prize, for William Lambert and Wallace Turner's reports on local corruption.

Beginning in 1999, editor Sandra Rowe and publisher Fred Stickel led the paper to five Pulitzer Prizes in less than a decade. During these same years, the newsroom was beginning to lay off many of its staff writers and editors. By 2014, enough people had been let go that the headquarters was sold, too large for the paper's needs.

The Oregonian Building's 2016 redevelopment into offices for Seattle developer Urban Renaissance Group was overseen by Allied Works, which was tasked with uncovering the original structure, just as the firm had done successfully at the Wieden + Kennedy World Headquarters. "It was brutal," architect Kyle Lommen told me for a *Portland Architecture* blog post. "The workspaces seemed almost like punishment. They had laid acoustic tile ceiling everywhere and knocked out all the double-height spaces. What was going on in the world when they said, 'We don't want any daylight'? But the bones of the building offered so much." The new lobby represents a kind of metamorphosis, with rows of curvy oversized lamps hanging from the newly exposed ceiling. An equally dramatic space is on the Sixth Avenue side, where architecture firm CannonDesign occupies the former location of *The Oregonian*'s printing presses, a double-height office space with a two-story wall of glass that offers a postcard view of three upcoming locations: the Wells Fargo Center, the KOIN Tower, and the Edith Green Wendell Wyatt Federal Building.

Standing outside the building today, I laugh a little thinking that I chose the worst possible time to become a newspaper journalist: in the nineties, just as the industry began its decline, undermined by the Internet's rise. Yet I'm glad I got to spend time freelancing for *The Oregonian* while it was still located here. Even today, I like visiting that lobby, not out of nostalgia for my brief days at *The Oregonian* but because its restoration feels like a small act of magic.

Across Broadway is one of downtown's oldest remaining structures, the **Ladd Carriage House** (1331 SW Broadway), the sole survivor from William S. Ladd's extended mansion grounds, and an example of the lengths people will go to for historic preservation when a work of architecture is truly beloved. Yet whenever I walk by this block, I'm reminded that preservation is often one step forward and one step back.

By the time the Ladd Carriage House was completed in 1883, the former mayor who commissioned it was in declining health, and paralyzed from the waist down. "That's why having horses and carriages was so very important to him," explains architect and historian Paul Falsetto, who co-founded the Friends of the

*Ladd Carriage House*

Ladd Carriage House in 2005 to save the building from demolition. "They said after a day of work he would get in his carriage and ride around the city. People would see him as a fixture going through the town with his beautiful horses."

The Carriage House's fanciful design by English architect Joseph Sherwin is a mix of late Queen Anne Victorian, Eastlake Stick, and English Tudor styles, with seemingly every inch of its façade decorated. The building's hipped roof is punctuated by a series of window dormers and gables, the insides of which are decorated with tracery. The trim work extends out from the windows to form a lattice pattern shading the top half of the window behind it. The exterior includes both horizontal and vertical shiplap siding, fish-scale and diamond shakes, embossed panels, and ornate brackets over the windows.

"It's too big to be a stable and storage for carriages. It's too ornate for that practical purpose. But there it is," Falsetto adds. "William Ladd spent a lot of time and effort and energy on that building. Truth be told, it's really a fully original design that's hard to classify other than calling it eclectic or fantastical. We ran out of names for all the elements on this building. You get the sense that the architect must have loved carpenters, because he gave them a full chance to show their craft and skill. But I think he must have hated roofers, because this is the most complex roof I have seen. And then they added this cupola on top that looked like something on one of the most ornate churches in Portland. The cupola was basically there to help vent the hay loft. This thing was incredible to look at, and from any distance you never would have guessed this was a stable."

The three-level carriage building was renovated in 1926 by Portland architect Morris H. Whitehouse into specialty shops. Later, the former hayloft was used as a dance floor and apartment. In 1972, it was leased as an office by architect Van Evera Bailey and remodeled as a law firm. Later tenants included the Portland Civic Theatre, the Portland Society of Arts and Crafts, and Hoffman Construction.

In 2005, First Christian Church, which owned the entire block, announced plans (in partnership with a local developer) to demolish the Carriage House, as well as the historic Rosefriend Apartments building next door, in order to build underground parking topped by a new condo tower. For the church, the parking was the point: their congregation was tired of circling the block looking for curbside spots. But First Christian seemed blindsided when Falsetto and about thirty others formed the grassroots Friends of the Ladd Carriage House. Reverend Rex Loy said the church was in the business of saving souls, not buildings.

Sensing the church would not show mercy, the Friends instead began to explore budging the Carriage House off its foundation and moving it to a new site. "We were trying to figure this out for over a year," Falsetto recalls. "If you moved the building, it would have left a slug-trail of demolition through the city: cheek to cheek with every building on every street; sidewalk trees would have had to have been removed, every telephone pole taken out of its way. It just didn't seem tenable. So we were stuck." But then another developer, John Carroll, joined the project team and offered what became the solution: move the 300-ton Carriage House temporarily onto an empty adjacent block (an abandoned gas station), build the desired five stories of underground parking on the Carriage House site, and move the building back there.

The church agreed to Carroll's plan, which is what has allowed the Carriage House to remain standing today. But the twenty-three-story Ladd Tower, built next to the Carriage House, necessitated demolishing the Rosefriend Apartments, which had been one of my favorite Portland buildings. Built in 1907 and designed by local architect David L. Williams, the U-shaped structure wrapped a central courtyard, and its red brick façade was contrasted beautifully with terra-cotta-clad bay windows.

I wrote a succession of blog posts arguing for the Rosefriend's preservation, earnestly believing I could make First Christian see the light. They were replacing much-needed affordable housing with a luxury condo, which seemed greedy and socially irresponsible. But all I really succeeded in doing was alienating myself from Falsetto and those who were saving the Ladd Carriage House, by accusing them of turning a blind eye to the Rosefriend.

The day of the Rosefriend Apartments demolition, I stood across Broadway recording with my video camera as a large construction crane tore away at the brick façade. I remember

*Rosefriend Apartments*

how easily the walls came down, and how a large crowd was assembled, somewhat gleefully, as if watching Godzilla ravage Tokyo. It was admittedly a dramatic sight, though. For many years, *Demolition of the Rosefriend Apartments* has been the most-watched of my approximately fifty short films. And the building's demise became a galvanizing moment for me: I determined to take a more active role, beyond simply writing, when architecture I loved became threatened. Two years later, when

Memorial Coliseum was slated for demolition, I co-founded a grassroots organization modeled after Falsetto's Friends of the Ladd Carriage House, called the Friends of Memorial Coliseum, which was eventually successful in saving the arena.

### *Stages and Classrooms*

I mentioned earlier that William S. Ladd had funded numerous churches in this neighborhood around the South Park Blocks. Two blocks west of the park is my favorite such work of ecclesiastical architecture in Portland and the city's oldest house of worship still standing on its original site: today known as the **Old Church Concert Hall** (1422 SW Eleventh Avenue). Designed by Warren Williams, it was completed in 1882, one year before the Ladd Carriage House, as the Calvary Presbyterian Church. This is Portland's best remaining example of the Carpenter Gothic architectural style: an application of Gothic Revival detailing applied to wooden structures, often built by house carpenters, possessing a natural dichotomy of decorative and rustic. The budget for Calvary Presbyterian was modest, and an initial design was rejected for being too elaborate. So Williams, who was also responsible for several Old Town buildings

*Old Church Concert Hall*

with gorgeous cast-iron ornamental façades, offered to design this church for free.

Seen from the street, the Old Church includes dramatic buttresses and pointed arch openings, but its signature feature is the belfry tower and spire on the site's southwest corner, marking the entry. Inside, the sanctuary's vaulted plaster ceiling is decorated with gilded wooden ribs and is supported by a pair of cast-iron columns spaced between the center pews. Forming a screen at the back of the east wall of the sanctuary are pipes and fittings of the original Hook and Hastings organ, which is still operable. The original hand-carved pews of fir and oak remain too, as do the jewel-like stained-glass windows.

The fact that the Old Church is still standing today is largely thanks to Lannie Hurst, who led an effort to save the building in 1967 when it was threatened with demolition. "I believe a city should be a delight," she told the *Oregon Journal*. "Portland can be this way and should be." A children's librarian, Hurst had no experience in historic preservation. But when the boarded-up church was offered for sale and attracted suitors planning teardown, she spearheaded an effort to purchase the building and turn it into a nonprofit performance space. Hurst also inspired others to help: one day, nearly fifty volunteers showed up to paint the church, including two future mayors, Connie McCready and Neil Goldschmidt.

The Old Church Concert Hall now hosts hundreds of performances each year, but it was threatened with closure during the COVID-19 pandemic. Yet executive director Constance Bracewell remained steadfast. "This building has stood through more pandemics than this one: through wars, through times of social upheaval," she says. "Buildings like this one, their context has changed so many times because the environment around it changes."

Bracewell's first day as executive director, in 2023, was same day that an arson attack destroyed the circa-1905 Portland Korean Church (originally the First German Evangelical Church), located just two blocks away. She'd previously spent a decade working in Hollywood as a visual-effects artist, for hit movies like *X-Men* and *The Fast and the Furious*. But this time

Lincoln Hall

the flames were real. "We had recently upgraded our sprinkler system," she says. "And it certainly felt good that night."

Though the Old Church Concert Hall is no longer a house of worship, its past seems to imbue the performances with a quietly spiritual ambiance. Bracewell says a colleague recently described this as "collective effervescence," a feeling of oneness and positive energy as people come together. Indeed, long after the Presbyterians have left, this building still has a congregation.

Back on the South Park Blocks, I arrive at another performance space: **Lincoln Hall** (1620 SW Park Avenue). Completed in 1911 as Lincoln High School, it was designed by Whitehouse & Fouilhoux in a Classical Revival style with high Corinthian columns marking its entry. Today it's home to Portland State University's film, theater, and music departments, with a 465-seat auditorium welcoming a variety of performing arts organizations, including White Bird dance company and Chamber Music Northwest. I particularly remember being riveted here at a touring dance performance by Australian choreographer Lucy Guerin in 2002 called *Melt*. It was so refreshingly simple: no narrative, no real set, even—just pairs and trios of dancers moving in rhythm with great energy and fluidity, to a theme of reacting to extreme temperatures.

No matter what performance I attend here, it is the building's past as Lincoln High School that always still first comes to mind as I enter. That's not only because vestiges of the original interior remain, such as a glass display case that seems meant for basketball trophies or honor roll lists. Lincoln Hall is also special to me because of three exceptional and iconic alumni: painter Mark Rothko, cartoon voice artist Mel Blanc, and poet Gary Snyder.

Rothko, born Markus Rothkowitz in Dvinsk, Russia (now Daugavpils, in Latvia), immigrated to the United States at the age of ten in 1913 with his mother, to rejoin his father, who had settled in Portland the year before. Yet the reunion was tragically short. Six months after young Markus arrived, his father died of cancer. "His time in Portland was at a very tender age," says local art critic and historian Jeff Jahn. "When you combine the culture shock of emigration with his father's death, it's literally *the* biographically most important moment in his life, and it shaped everything that came afterwards."

At Lincoln High School, Rothko was active in drama and the debating team, but he also struggled with classmates' antisemitism. In the school's 1921 yearbook, they named him most likely to become a pawn broker. That fall, Rothko left for Yale University but soon dropped out and moved to New York, spending more than twenty years as a largely unknown artist. But by the late 1940s he had developed a signature style: abstract color fields, deceptively simple yet powerfully engrossing. As part of the Abstract Expressionist movement (also known as the New York School), Rothko became one of the most famous US artists of the twentieth century, whose paintings today auction for tens of millions of dollars and are held in permanent collections of the world's leading art museums.

Rothko returned here often, including in 1933 for his first-ever museum solo show, at the Portland Art Museum. "[I spent my] youth in front of the endless space of the landscape of Oregon," he later remarked, "in front of the monumental emptiness that is nothingness and at the same time part of it all." One of Rothko's early watercolor paintings from the 1920s seems to prefigure his later abstract color fields: a landscape view looking from the West Hills toward East Portland, with Mount Hood in the distance. "Here he begins to find his language even though he won't fully realize it for nearly twenty more years," Jahn explains. "He wasn't painting the Oregon skies in those later works, but certainly there's something about how the clouds in Portland filter the light. They make you conscious of the depth of light and color and form, which you do see in his later works."

Lincoln High School alumnus Mel Blanc became perhaps equally well-known, or at least his voice did, bringing alive Bugs Bunny and Daffy Duck, Wile E. Coyote and Porky Pig, Sylvester and Foghorn Leghorn, among many other cartoon characters. When I was a child, Blanc's voice was my companion each morning as I watched scores of midcentury Warner Brothers cartoons on TV, in the afternoons as the voice of Barney Rubble on reruns of *The Flintstones*, and on Thursday evenings the voice of Twiki the robot on *Buck Rogers in the 25th Century* ("Beedee beedee beedee"). "Even as a child, I heard voices," Blanc wrote in his 1989 autobiography, *That's Not All Folks*. His South Portland neighborhood was "an ethnic mosaic," with not only a large Jewish population but also pockets of German, Mexican, and Japanese families, each with an accent that young Mel could mimic. At Lincoln, he was often disciplined for clownish behavior, which was really about finding his voice, both figuratively and literally. "Lincoln High had a cavernous hallway that produced a resounding echo," he recalled. "It was acoustically optimal, I determined, for trying out this new voice I'd been practicing: a shrill, cackling laugh." The school principal once caught Blanc in the hallway doing the laugh and yelled, "I should kick you out of school!" About fifteen years later, that particular cackle became the laugh of Woody Woodpecker.

Gary Snyder came from a family of writers. His mother, Lois Snyder Hennessy, was an *Oregonian* reporter, and young Gary worked for the paper as a copy boy. After graduating from Lincoln in 1947, Snyder went on to win a Pulitzer Prize for his 1975 poetry collection *Turtle Island*. Yet he is best known as a member of the Beat movement of the fifties, which included writers Jack Kerouac, Allen Ginsberg, and William S. Burroughs. A thinly fictionalized version of Snyder called Japhy Ryder is a character in one my favorite novels, Kerouac's autobiographical

*The Dharma Bums* from 1958. It is Ryder who introduces the author's fictional alter ego, Ray Smith, to Zen Buddhism and mountain-climbing. The book is a continuing series of dualities—city life and wild nature, hedonism and spirituality, kinetic jazz and transcendent silence—which spoke to my young-adult soul and helped set me on course as a writer.

Lincoln Hall was nearly torn down in the 2000s because of defects including water intrusion, asbestos exposure, and structural deficiencies. A basement extending underneath the sidewalk on Broadway was held up with two-by-fours and plywood. "Lincoln Hall was considered kind of the poster child for deferred maintenance in the state university system," recalls Michael Tingley, a principal with Bora Architects, which designed the 2010 renovation. "A group of state legislators toured it, and there was a big debate about whether the building was even worth saving, despite it being the very first building on the Portland State campus. I really think it was that legacy, combined with the fact that it's a beautiful building, that convinced them to save it, even though it would have been less expensive to take it down and replace it."

Now we're getting into the heart of the Portland State University campus, to which I always enjoy returning because of the diversity and energy brought by its students. In 2012 I taught a class here called Urban Discourses, a bittersweet memory. I was unprepared for the challenge, with overly long PowerPoint presentations full of too much text. During my last class of the term, while screening a film (appropriately titled *A Day Called X*), I stepped into the hallway to listen to a voicemail from Valarie telling me she had cancer. Yet the interaction with students was enlivening and humbling: I regret not ever having pursued additional teaching opportunities.

On Broadway two blocks south of Lincoln Hall, walking under the continuing sunny skies, I arrive at PSU's **Karl Miller Center** (615 SW Harrison Street), a hybrid of new and renovated buildings. Completed in 2018 from a design by Stuttgart, Germany, firm Behnisch Architekten in collaboration with Portland's SRG Partnership (now Cannon Design), the building was part of Portland State University's larger effort to create a true campus within its urban setting.

Since moving to the South Park Blocks in 1946, the former Vanport College has grown from a small commuter school to a university of more than 20,000 students. And while the South Park Blocks are an undeniable asset, giving this urban institution something like a leafy traditional campus, particularly in Oregon's rainy climate students need communal indoor gathering spaces, which the university had lacked. Perhaps that's why the Karl Miller Center, with its luminescent multistory atrium traversing two buildings, has quickly become a kind of living room for not just the School of Business but all of PSU. "We actually used to have MBA students practicing presentations in their cars," Cliff Allen, the business school's dean, told me for a 2018 *Metropolis* article. "Now that atrium is packed throughout the school year with students."

Karl Miller Center's multistory atrium, a sliver of which can be seen from the street as a glass pyramid (recalling architect I. M. Pei's Louvre entrance), fills the entire two-building complex with natural light, with walkways crisscrossing the top portion while, at the bottom, a terraced stairway doubles as a

*Karl Miller Center*

stadium-style seating. By arranging a variety of spaces around the atrium, the design maximizes connectivity while promoting an inclusive attitude toward learning. That the Karl Miller Center received a LEED Platinum rating from the US Green Building Council was particularly meaningful here. "Because this is Portland, sustainability is everywhere in our curriculum," said Allen. "Our mantra is 'business that matters.' The Karl Miller Center allows us to say we practice what we preach."

At the southern edge of campus and the end of the South Park Blocks, visiting **Shattuck Hall** (1914 SW Park Avenue) always gives me reasons for optimism. As home to the Portland State University School of Architecture, its studios and classrooms are filled with students' conceptual drawings and models—a hive of creative energy and a vibe of optimism—and its impact extends beyond the classroom to impact communities both locally and globally.

Completed in 1915 as the Shattuck Elementary School and designed by Portland Public Schools staff architect F. A. Naramore, the building was named for Erasmus D. Shattuck, a former chief justice of the Oregon Supreme Court, who also took part in the Oregon Constitutional Convention of 1857 and co-founded the Portland Library Association. This was the third elementary school to go by the name Shattuck, the first two having been destroyed by fire. Intended to be fireproof, the building was clad in brick and glazed terra cotta. Shattuck Hall's entrance features a small open courtyard facing the Park Blocks, with stairs on each side leading to twin entrances marked with curving Venetian windows. This remained a functioning elementary school until being closed in 1964, due to declining enrollment, after much of the neighborhood was razed for the South Auditorium urban renewal project and construction of Interstate 405.

Though only accredited since 2007 (thanks to the efforts of department chair Rudolph Barton), PSU's School of Architecture has already established its own culture, where faculty and students are encouraged to think independently yet with community always in mind. Its first director, Clive Knights, encouraged professors to shape curriculums to correspond with their own interests and investigations. Before coming to PSU, he'd taught at a university in his native United Kingdom where

*Shattuck Hall*

professors would "literally white out the dates of the syllabi and recopy them," Knights recalls. In Portland, "We wanted to stimulate the pleasures of teaching. The faculty needs to be inspired. That can't happen when something is handed to them."

PSU School of Architecture professors have done much to make an impact, not just on students but beyond the classroom, whether it's longtime Jeff Schnabel, who founded the popular Portland Winter Light Festival, or a group of professors participating in its Center for Public Interest Design. Assistant director Todd Ferry has overseen numerous local community-oriented projects including creating an alternative women's shelter from a cluster of tiny houses and a mobile performance space for Portland Opera from a delivery truck. Director Sergio Palleroni's efforts, meanwhile, have focused on housing and development for disadvantaged communities around the world, working with organizations such as the United Nations and the World Bank.

"I grew up in Latin America. When I came to the US, I thought, 'Here's a country with extraordinary resources.' I'd seen the other side of poverty, and when I went into practice I was driven by those people in need," Palleroni told me in a 2013 *Portland Architecture* interview. "It was my journey to take students to the other side of the railroad tracks, serving people we didn't see in architecture magazines. I could have spent the rest of my life designing one school or clinic after the other, but there was something missing. If we were going to make change it needed to be more systemic. What we teach and research in schools needs to lead to greater opportunities to address growing public need." Over a dozen years later, Palleroni is still leading the CPID.

I asked why he settled in Portland, when so much of Palleroni's work is a long plane ride away. "You have to go to places where people are trying to connect the dots," he said. "Some of the best conversations are happening here in Portland about re-imagining what a city might be like, ideas of social equity and how we can feed ourselves from within a city. In every era of history there are places like this, which are trying to advance human thinking. People are really actually questioning some of the fundamental things we do. Some things Portland doesn't do well. But enough people come here and bring ideas that I always find myself learning from the things that I'm seeing. Then the other thing is, you've got to find a place to live that is safe and where you can recharge your batteries and have a civil discussion about what you've experienced and get feedback from people who understand. Portland is magic in that way and I'm thankful."

Completing this walk, I've once again reached a kind of asphalt moat: Interstate 405, built as an open trench and curving around the south and western edges of downtown to connect with the Fremont Bridge. The trench is a less-intrusive solution than the tall overpass carrying vehicles from the Marquam Bridge along the east bank of the Willamette (as part of the same central-city loop). And both freeways are busy enough to seem essential arteries. Yet we now know that traffic rises to fill the roads and highways we build for it, and that in retrospect, cities all over the country were carved up by interstate projects, most often displacing neighborhoods home to persons of color. The din of the freeway in my ears provides all the more reason to do an about-face and begin walking north again.

# Interlude

## *Towering Presence*

*Downtown from the KOIN Tower*

As we look out at the view of downtown Portland from the top of the **KOIN Tower** (222 SW Columbia Street), I notice that Jeff Gianola still has his makeup on. A longtime news anchor for the TV station that gives this building its name, Gianola has just finished a late-afternoon KOIN news broadcast. As soon as the end credits rolled, he nonchalantly got up from the anchor desk and unplugged his lapel microphone, walked past the robotic cameras and teleprompters, waved goodbye to co-anchor Jenny Hansson and meteorologist Josh Cozart, and gestured for me to follow along. We were eager to get up here while there was still a little sunshine, between periods of light rain. During a commercial break a few minutes earlier, Cozart had assured us the next precipitation wasn't due for at least an hour.

This thirty-fifth floor view is panoramic yet its access hidden. We'd reached the little corner viewing platform by snaking with flashlights through an unlit room full of mechanical equipment, with the help of a building engineer, Duke. But we weren't exactly alone. Just after arriving, we caught sight of a hawk dive-bombing a smaller bird.

Traveling on foot from the South Waterfront district to the West End, from the Pearl District and Old Town to Pioneer Courthouse Square and the South Park Blocks, I've once again briefly left the street to seek a higher, broader vantage point, this time from the city's third-tallest building. Looking northwest, I can see several buildings I'm about to visit or have been to already: the Wells Fargo Center, which is the city's tallest structure, as well as the Portland Building, a global icon of Postmodern architecture, and the Standard Plaza, a sleek talisman of midcentury minimalism. Beyond them are Block 216, with its cleaved corners causing unusual sunlight reflections, as well as the arched form of the Fremont Bridge, and, in the far distance, a succession of industrial container-ship cranes along the river.

Arguably even more picturesque than any building or bridge are simply the clouds. Though I'd hoped for sunny blue skies, weather like this is often more dramatic, when a parade of clouds continuously floats by, with the sun repeatedly peeking through amid periods of intermittent rain—a Portland specialty. These are the cloudy skies that drew me back from New York, and that seem to have inspired the great Mark Rothko.

*Willamette River from KOIN Tower*

The KOIN Tower itself is perhaps downtown's most handsome and immediately recognizable tall building, with its red brick cladding and tapered top. Completed in 1984 and originally known as the KOIN Center, this was one of numerous downtown landmarks built during that decade, along with the Portland Building, Pioneer Courthouse Square, Tom McCall Waterfront Park, and the US Bancorp Tower. KOIN's design, by ZGF Architects, was led by partner Robert Frasca, who over his long career became one of the city's most accomplished architects. Frasca came to Portland in 1959 after graduating from MIT's School of Architecture and Planning, at the suggestion of his mentor, architect Pietro Belluschi, then the school's dean. He led ZGF's designs for the Oregon Convention Center, the MAX light-rail system, and Doernbecher Children's Hospital at OHSU, among many others.

Frasca and ZGF's KOIN design borrowed from the past, with references to Gothic, Spanish, and Art Deco architectural styles, but in a more timeless, restrained way than Postmodernist architects of the time like Michael Graves (who designed the nearby Portland Building). "He didn't want to do fads," recalls

ZGF managing partner Jan Willemse. "He wanted to do stuff that lasted. Bob was always very direct in saying that the work had bigger responsibilities than to itself or even to the client. He wasn't talking about making an object or a monument, but the responsibility of design to the city. He saw it in a bigger context, almost a physiological contact—a physical object with a psychological impact."

The building is called KOIN because the original TV studio was demolished to make way for the tower. In return, the developers gave the station a ninety-nine-year lease in the new tower's basement for $1 per year, renewable for another ninety-nine years. Subsequent building owners have tried to break the agreement, to no avail.

The KOIN Tower includes two floors of retail giving way to fifteen floors of office space and eleven floors of high-end condos at the top. In a time when major-city US downtowns were facing middle-class flight and an uptick in crime, the building was a kind of urban island, where one could live, work, park, and play without ever having to leave the property. Today, amid declining office presence, it's an example of the type of housing downtown needs. The project added energy to this heretofore quiet stretch of blocks, partly because of the KOIN Center Cinemas movie theater on the second floor, downtown Portland's first multiplex. In the late 1980s as a high school student going to these theaters I fell in love with a new generation of independent films, and a decade later it's where I got started as a *Willamette Week* movie critic, attending private matinee screenings. Today the closed multiplex has been converted to studios and a small performance space for classical radio station KQAC.

KOIN, Portland's CBS affiliate, still broadcasts from a basement studio. Its newscasts have seen a stream of anchors and reporters come and go, but one face has remained the same for nearly forty years: Gianola, who as of this writing is in his final year as a news broadcaster before retirement.

As a child in San Diego, Gianola worked two paper routes to earn extra money, one of which included a stop at television station KGTV. "I would go in there and drop the paper off at the front desk, and they had a little commissary area where I figured out how to steal ice cream sandwiches from the vending machine," he recalls. "They had a little viewing area there, and I'd watch them do the news. And I thought, 'This is what I want to do.' I was so mesmerized." Later, Gianola became an intern at the station and was mentored by Harold Green, a dynamic if unpredictable newscaster who became one of the inspirations for Will Ferrell's character in the 2004 comedy *Anchorman: The Legend of Ron Burgundy*.

In 1983, Gianola was hired by Portland's ABC affiliate, KATU, as a reporter and weekend weather forecaster. He remembers the biggest local TV personality of the day, meteorologist and talk-show host Jim Bosley, taking Gianola under his wing. "I was kind of shy meeting him," Gianola recalls. "I said, 'I want you to know I'm a team player,' and Boz said, 'Oh God, I hate that!' But ultimately Bosley was the one who said to me, 'You've got to just be yourself.'" Two years later, Gianola was promoted to main anchor for KATU, part of a venerable duo with co-anchor Julie Emery for a dozen years. In 1998, Gianola moved to KOIN, where he's been ever since.

In recent years, Meniere's disease has made his life and job difficult, causing recurrent dizziness as well as hearing loss. In past conversations, I've talked with Jeff about the vertigo symptoms he shares with my wife, who has long struggled with a similar condition. It occurs to me standing here at the top of the KOIN Tower that I've asked a man battling recurrent dizziness to show me a high-elevation view that even makes me woozy. Yet Jeff couldn't be a better sport, as he continually points out to me the history of different nearby buildings.

Several decades before the KOIN Tower was built, on this site was a house occupied by Oregon's greatest women's suffrage leader, Abigail Scott Duniway, and the headquarters for her Equal Suffrage Association. Duniway had traveled to Oregon with her family in a covered wagon in the 1850s, losing her mother and younger brother to cholera along the way (her other brother, future *Oregonian* editor Harvey Scott, survived). She married a Willamette Valley farmer, Benjamin Charles Duniway, who was later permanently disabled in a farming accident, prompting Abigail to open a millinery shop in the town of Albany. That's where the seeds of her activism were sewn. "She had women who came into the store to buy hats who would talk about how their husbands controlled everything," Jennifer Chambers, author of *Abigail Scott Duniway and Susan B. Anthony in Oregon: Hesitate No Longer*, explained to me in a 2019 podcast interview. "They didn't even get to control the money they made themselves selling eggs or making clothes. It motivated Abigail, and she started to read about the work of other women leading the suffrage movement."

The Duniways moved to Portland in 1871 to found the *New Northwest*, a weekly newspaper devoted to women's rights. From their house on Clay Street, Benjamin ran the basement printing press while Abigail did the writing, becoming an eloquent and passionate advocate for women's rights. It was a long struggle, but in 1912, more than forty years after founding the *New Northwest* and three years before her death, Oregon became just the seventh US state to pass an amendment giving women the right to vote.

It's time to reluctantly depart this top-of-the-KOIN-Tower perch with Jeff and continue the journey. I've still got many more stops to make. But while I may snicker at local TV news, with its blend of sensationalized crime reporting, soft-focus human-interest stories, and weather, there is something noble about my anchorman companion: how he has endured here over the decades to become beloved to generations of Oregonians. I'm going to miss Jeff Gianola when he's retired, just like I'm going to miss this tour of central-city Portland when it's complete.

# *Walk 5*

## Density, Open Space, and Power

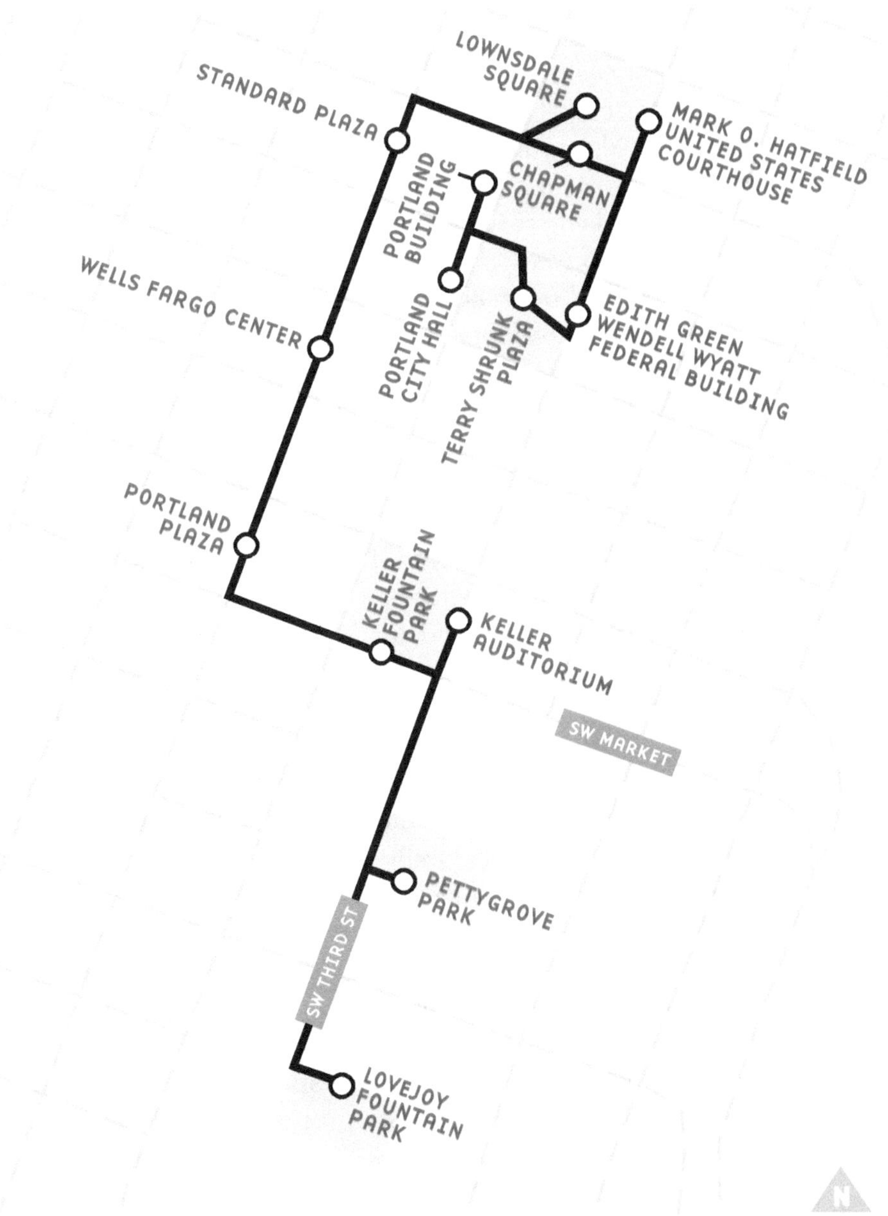

### *Urban Renewal*

In the mid-twentieth century, wide swaths of Portland on both sides of the Willamette River were demolished and rebuilt, as part of the nationwide phenomenon known as urban renewal. Federal legislation had given local governments power to clear away and replace "blighted" areas, which was disproportionately applied to neighborhoods populated by immigrants and people of color. Locally, city leaders began eyeing districts near the city center even before World War II ended; in 1943, shipping magnate Edgar Kaiser hired New York urban planner Robert Moses to create a postwar plan for Portland's growth. A team of two dozen planners worked from a ballroom at the Multnomah Hotel for two weeks, after which Moses unveiled a document called *Portland Improvement*, calling for a network of new freeways and new developments.

Over the ensuing two decades, on the east side came construction of Interstate 5, Memorial Coliseum and Emmanuel Hospital, replacing a large swath of Albina, Portland's principal Black neighborhood, as well as the industrial Central Eastside waterfront. On the west side, the old South Portland neighborhood, home to a diverse array of immigrant cultures, particularly Italians and Jews, saw fifty-four blocks condemned and more than 1,500 people displaced, for the I-405 freeway and the South Auditorium District: a cluster of office buildings, apartments, a renovated auditorium, and parking garages. It was characterized as a success story because the South Auditorium District brought a twenty-five-fold increase in assessed real estate value and brought 15,000 jobs to the city center. Yet not many of the buildings were architecturally distinctive, and even today the South Auditorium district feels sterile, lacks vibrancy, and is maybe even cursed, as if you can feel the presence of ghosts.

And yet there is something wonderful here, between the buildings: a sequence of small parks connected by pedestrian pathways that helped redefine urban landscape design in the United States. Known as the **Open Space Sequence**, the parks were designed by perhaps the most acclaimed US landscape architecture firm of the mid-twentieth century, San Francisco's Lawrence Halprin and Associates. The design symbolizes the journey of water through the Cascade watershed, from its

*Lovejoy Fountain Park*

mountainous source to the Columbia River, through a sequence of plazas and fountains.

As I enter from Lincoln Street at the south end of the development, I first come to the tiny Source Fountain, not much bigger than a bedroom nightstand. Completed in 1968 and co-designed by Angela Danadjieva, a member of Halprin's team, it's sometimes referred to as the Chimney and represents an artesian spring, with water bubbling up and over its square, waist-high, tiered brick top. It leads directly to Lovejoy Fountain Park (one block south of SW Harrison Street and Third Avenue), completed in 1966. Its design, led by staff landscape architect

Satoru Nishita, features water cascading down stepped terraces of board-formed concrete planes to mimic the rushing streams and cascades of the Cascade Range. Beside Lovejoy Fountain is a copper and wood canopy designed by Halprin's collaborator, architect Charles Moore.

Upon Lovejoy Fountain's opening, *Life* magazine published a photo spread titled "Mid-City Mountain Stream," describing "a piece of wilderness transplanted—wet and dry, glittering and static—which effectively invites wading and clambering and contemplation." Portland architect Mark Lakeman grew up visiting the Lovejoy Fountain regularly as a child, and actually prefers it to the more famous Keller Fountain. "To me the great experience was making your way into and through this cleavage up to the source of the water," he says, "like you were walking in a stream bed." Only the fountain's fairly secluded location, away from street traffic, makes it less popular, Lakeman argues. "There are people who have lived in Portland their whole live who don't realize Lovejoy is there. It's almost like a private space reserved for tower residents."

Pettygrove Park (one block north of SW Harrison Street and Third Avenue) is a more verdant companion to Lovejoy's hard geometry, with tall trees overlooking a series of earthen grass mounds encircled by winding pathways. It's a place of respite and shade, perhaps my favorite space in the Sequence to linger. Architect Will Bruder, who moved to Portland in the 2010s from Phoenix, lives in the Harrison Condominiums just off Pettygrove Park, where we've occasionally met to chat and sip drinks. Bruder, known for designing acclaimed art museums and libraries, and who early in his career worked under Italian architect Paolo Soleri on the experimental, quasi-Utopian settlement in Arizona called Arcosanti, was a friend of Halprin's and appreciates the Open Space Sequence. "Housing projects like this in St. Louis and Chicago left out the whole concept of working with the landscape," he says. But the Open Space Sequence "becomes the glue between these prosaic, rather simple inexpensive buildings. Halprin realized the importance of the spaces in between. That was the genius of this: the way each of the parks are these separate places, yet they connect to a larger idea about nature. It's just delightful."

For such an acclaimed work of landscape design, I admittedly rarely pass through the Open Space Sequence, which my friend Nolan Lienhart, the planning and urban design director at ZGF Architects, says is "an important part of this story—*why* you don't go in. There's a blessing-and-curse aspect to the way this was implemented. One thing we run into as urban designers all the time is people saying, 'Let's make car-free streets.' They're pretty hard to make work in North America, and they're really hard to make on the West Coast, where our regions tend to be car-dependent." Halprin's designs invite people to come together, but the development seems wary of urban life. "There was a sense that you needed to create a little difference between yourself and the city," Lienhart explains. "We laugh about it now, but that was a very serious consideration: 'We need to make people who don't want to be in the city feel comfortable.'" As a result, architecture and urban planning of the sixties seems to represent a low point for street-level vitality.

Before I leave them, it's worth noting that Lovejoy Fountain Park and Pettygrove Park were named for Portland founding fathers Asa Lovejoy and Francis Pettygrove, who famously flipped a coin to determine which of their home cities to name Portland after (Lovejoy's Boston lost out). Lovejoy came west in 1842 across the Oregon Trail and first opened a law practice in Oregon City, the new territory's seat. While at Fort Vancouver in 1843, he met William Overton, with whom Lovejoy agreed to travel by canoe back to Oregon City. Paddling south on the Willamette, they stopped to rest at a spot that local tribes had cleared of brush, possibly as a stopping point along the river between settlements. By this time, the Indigenous Multnomah people (a band of the larger Chinookan people), which numbered more than 3,000 at the tribe's height, had been decimated by malaria and smallpox, as had members of the nearby Kathlamet, Clackamas, Chinook, Tualatin Kalapuya, and Molalla tribes. Overton and Lovejoy decided this would be a good location for a town. Lovejoy filed a claim of 640 acres with the Oregon provisional government and the two became partners. But the more itinerant Overton sold his share of the land claim to Francis Pettygrove, who had come from his native Maine that same year to establish a store in Oregon City. Lovejoy and Pettygrove worked throughout

1844 to enlarge the clearing, and within twelve months they hired a surveyor to plat the Portland townsite: sixteen blocks, each 200 by 200 feet, the same proportions as downtown blocks today.

There is an odd, disquieting symmetry to Portland's founding fathers unhesitatingly claiming Indigenous land as their own in the 1840s, followed a century later by the destruction and displacement orchestrated by Moses's team and local city leaders in the 1940s. Yet my nearly thirty years in Portland has taught me that the city is being continuously remade, which means there is still opportunity to build not just a more vibrant but a more equitable twenty-first-century neighborhood here, among these otherwise great Halprin-designed parks.

The final piece of the Open Space Sequence, Keller Fountain Park (between SW Third and Fourth Avenues, Market and Clay Streets), is a masterpiece that arguably transcends its urban-renewal context. My earliest memory in Portland is coming to the fountain on a summer afternoon in 1979, at seven years old, accompanied by my mom. We'd driven from our home in McMinnville to see a musical at Civic Auditorium across the street (*The Wiz*, a reinterpretation of *The Wizard of Oz* with soul music). Yet the stagecraft inside couldn't compete with the urban spectacle I saw outside: the 13,000 gallons of water falling each minute over the fountain's 18-foot-high concrete cliffs, and lots of my fellow children frolicking in the pools below. I would have preferred to forget the musical and stay here.

When the Forecourt Fountain (as it was originally known) opened in 1970, *The New York Times* architecture critic Ada Louise Huxtable wrote that it "may be one of the most important urban spaces since the Renaissance," drawing comparison to Rome's Trevi Fountain. "The water starts as rivulets in a maze of concrete slabs at the top, at street level. As it increases in volume, it splashes and sprays with the sound of a dozen mountain streams to a sunken pool 10 feet below street level. It is possible to climb, crawl, walk or sit anywhere in this manmade landscape, including behind the falls," Huxtable wrote. "This remarkable exercise in art and environment happens in one Portland city block, 200 by 200 feet."

There had long been a three-story building here at Third and Market called the Auditorium Apartments, its ground floor occupied by first the Drop Inn and later the Spatenhaus Tavern (owned by future mayor Bud Clark). In 1967, the Portland Development Commission acquired this block and initially commissioned Skidmore, Owings and Merrill (the development's master planner) to design a conventional traffic circle and central fountain atop an underground parking garage. But the commission's architectural adviser, local architect Walter Gordon, protested the design. PDC then decided in 1968 to scrap the underground garage and invite back Lawrence Halprin to create what became a continuation and culmination of the Open Space Sequence.

*Keller Fountain Park*

The Forecourt Fountain design fit perfectly into Halprin's existing concept of a metaphorical watershed. In his 1964 notebook sketches are the initial idea: a fountain design that looked like the future Forecourt Fountain, arranged as a kind of proscenium stage giving way to chiseled walls over which the water cascaded. However, Angela Danadjieva, who became the fountain's lead designer, never saw Halprin's sketches. "At that time, Larry was very busy with other projects, so he was mostly out of town," she recalls. When shown SOM's traffic circle, she was not impressed. "I said, 'Holy moly! A plaza with a fountain?' That's how you've designed them throughout history."

The mountainous forms of the waterfalling fountain Halprin had imagined were communicated to Danadjieva by PDC chairman Ira Keller, who gave her a photography book of the Columbia Gorge and its waterfalls. Danadjieva knew she had to see the Gorge for herself. "At that time I didn't have money. I was sending half of my salary to my mom in Bulgaria. But I took the bus from San Francisco to Portland," she recalls, adding with a laugh, "and then I took a taxi from Portland to the Gorge. I didn't know what I was doing. But God, I loved the waterfalls so much." Her Forecourt Fountain design looked slightly different from Halprin's 1964 sketches: less rounded and more cubical, showing the influence of Russian Constructivist paintings. And her design burrowed farther into the ground, below street level. Danadjieva wanted to utilize the waterfall's sound and mist, to envelop visitors' senses. Before embarking on a landscape architecture career in the United States, in her native Bulgaria Danadjieva had designed theatrical stage sets; accordingly, here she wanted to take visitors on a journey, and create a respite from city life.

At the Forecourt Fountain's 1970 dedication ceremony, city leaders gathered for speeches at the foot of the fountain on the east side of the block, while several young Portland State University students—many of whom had clashed with police during recent Vietnam War protests—assembled uphill at the west end of the block. The mood seemed tense until the fountain's spigots turned on. While dignitaries politely applauded, the students began jumping into the fountain's pools. Halprin immediately grasped that the design was being validated. "As you play in this garden," he said at the podium, "please try to remember that we are all in this together."

Danadjieva, who was not present for the Forecourt Fountain dedication ceremony, saw Halprin receive full credit for the design. But in 2016, at a re-dedication ceremony following the fountain's restoration, she got her due. After being introduced as the project's lead designer and briefly addressing the crowd in her thick Bulgarian accent, the ninety-one-year-old designer received a standing ovation. Since then, I've had the good fortune to talk with her by phone many times, and I'd like to believe we formed a meaningful bond. But those calls also came with a purpose, for while Danadjieva is happy for the recognition she received that day, she still believes her story, and the proper design credit, remain unknown by many. I'm not sure how much I can help spread the word with this book, but Angela is one of my heroes.

Today as I visit, no children are frolicking in the water, just one couple who have stepped down to the edge base of the fountain, perhaps tourists (they eventually take a selfie together) and one man sitting to one side, reading his book. I think it's that kind of place, where you can be enlivened by the drama of the moving water and the striking beauty of its design, or simply calmed by its white noise, like traveling to a real Cascade fountain or to the beach.

Across Third Avenue is the aforementioned **Keller Auditorium** (222 SW Clay Street), which I first visited with my mom in 1979. More recently, on a 2022 tour, this became the only Portland performance venue I've extensively explored backstage: the stage manager's seat beside the curtains' edge, the dressing rooms, and the lighting booth behind the balcony. But the impetus for the tour was that the century-old Keller Auditorium has faced the possibility of closure.

The building opened July 4, 1917, as Public Auditorium, with an opening concert featuring the Portland Symphony (later renamed the Oregon Symphony) that took advantage of the venue's 5,000-pipe organ. Designed by Morris Whitehouse of Whitehouse & Fouilhoux, the auditorium featured a Classical Revival façade with brick pilasters. Less than a year after opening, the auditorium served as a temporary hospital during the

*Keller Auditorium*

Spanish flu epidemic of 1918. About eight hundred cots held patients on the stage and auditorium floor (where the seats had been removed); the basement became a makeshift morgue, as 169 patients died there.

Over the ensuing decades, the Public Auditorium welcomed a succession of illustrious names. Jazz saxophonist Charlie Parker and trumpeter Dizzy Gillespie played in 1954. President Dwight Eisenhower gave a speech during his 1956 reelection campaign; film footage of that event is the only known documentation of the venue's pre-renovation interior. John F. Kennedy spoke here during his successful 1960 presidential campaign. Martin Luther King Jr. told the audience during his 1961 appearance, "We must learn to live together as brothers, or perish as fools. . . . Americans must rise above the narrow confines of their individualistic concerns to the broader concerns of all humanity. They must rid themselves of the notion that there are superior and inferior races."

In 1967, the venue was almost entirely rebuilt (only 17 percent of the original structure was retained) and given a new name: Civic Auditorium. Its formerly brick exterior was now clad in glass and beveled quartz in a Modernist style, from a design by Skidmore, Owings and Merrill. Though most of the firm's work was well-received, *The New York Times* architecture critic Ada Louise Huxtable called Civic Auditorium "a building of unrelieved blandness." But that didn't stop a succession of memorable performers from appearing there. Shortly after the reopening, Led Zeppelin performed at Civic, followed over the ensuing decades by James Brown, Johnny Cash, Bob Dylan, New Order, and Public Enemy, among many others. In 2000, the venue was again renamed, this time as Keller Auditorium, after former Portland Development Commission director Ira Keller, not as a city-initiated honor, however, but as part of a $1.5 million naming-rights sponsorship underwritten by his son, Richard B. Keller.

In 2022, the City of Portland began exploring whether to renovate and seismically upgrade Keller Auditorium or build a replacement on another site at nearby Portland State University. "Don't pick at it too hard," operations director Ed Williams said jokingly as I ran my finger along one of the building's sidewalk-level quartz façade panels. "That started to deteriorate practically while they were installing it." Over the next hour, city administrators pointed out the building's many flaws, yet its history was just as resonant, perhaps most notably a wall of signatures in the control booth, signed by cast members from countless touring shows: *A Chorus Line* in 1981, *Evita* in 1983, *Cats* in 1987, the Joffrey Ballet in 1989, *West Side Story* in 1995, *Phantom of the Opera* in 2008, and *Anything Goes* in 2013. Portland's city council voted to fund both venue projects, seemingly assuring Keller's renovation and continuation; yet there is no budget for these efforts, and as of now, the auditorium's future is still uncertain.

## *Going Vertical*

Although Keller Auditorium and the Keller Fountain are, as their names suggest, of a pair, an unofficial third element is arguably the striking **Portland Plaza** (1500 SW Fifth Avenue) condominium building, looming over the fountain with its curving, cloverleaf form and sleek glass façade. Designed by Los Angeles firm DMJM and completed in 1973, this was the first residential building downtown to occupy a full city block, which despite the relatively high-density central location provides room for outdoor grounds including a swimming pool. Sometimes nicknamed the Norelco Building for how its shape resembles the electric shaver with three pivoting heads, the Portland Plaza offers 230-degree views of the downtown skyline. It was extensively remodeled in 2017 by local firm Opsis Architecture. "This building has such a strong voice," Opsis's Jim Kalvelage told me in a *Portland Architecture* interview. "You just want to listen to it."

The Portland Plaza was constructed with a pioneering glass cladding system conceived by DMJM principals Anthony Lumsden and Cesar Pelli (the latter of whom became one of the world's preeminent skyscraper designers). By reversing the mullions between glass panes so they faced inward rather than outward, the architects could wrap curving shapes in glass for the first time. Even today, over a half century after its completion, this tower seems futuristic, which was all the more true in its initial years. Early in the 1980 movie adaptation of author Ursula K. Le Guin's classic 1971 science-fiction novel, *The Lathe of Heaven* (aired on PBS television), a shot of the Portland Plaza fills the screen just before text fades in to set the scene:

PORTLAND, OREGON
the near future

Le Guin, one of the twentieth century's most acclaimed science fiction authors, moved to Portland in 1959, when her husband, Charles, began teaching history at Portland State University. Le Guin's first novel, *Rocannon's World,* was published in 1966, and her first consensus classic, *A Wizard of Earthsea* (part of a six-volume series), in 1968. She lived in Portland until her death in 2018, and remained an active citizen all the while, writing letters to *The Oregonian* while looking lucidly at the city's duality of small-town welcoming spirit and entrenched social problems like homelessness. In 2024, Le Guin's former home on Northwest Thurman Street was donated to the local nonprofit Literary Arts as the future site of an artists' residency. And I think *The Lathe of Heaven* is a particularly delightful tribute to

Portland: not simply because it's set here, but because it's about a dreamer who finds a way to change the future.

The Portland Plaza was the first contemporary downtown condo building, and with generously sized units offering panoramic views, it attracted affluent customers, including members of the Portland Trail Blazers. One resident was Lionel Hollins, starting point guard for the 1977 NBA championship–winning team. In fact, it was from his Portland Plaza home that Hollins, along with the team's two biggest stars, took in the ensuing melee.

Earlier that day, after a narrow series-clinching 109–107 victory in Game 6 over the heavily favored Philadelphia 76ers and their superstar guard Julius "Dr. J" Irving, "12,951 fans stomped, cheered, cried and stampeded," Robert Olmos and Steve Erickson wrote in *The Oregonian*. "A stranger in town would have thought Portland had gone mad. He would have been right. Blazermania had become a reality." That night, center Bill Walton and forward Maurice Lucas joined Hollins at his seventh-floor apartment in the Portland Plaza, looking down from its floor-to-ceiling glass walls.

"I don't remember if we had beer or what, but we sat there looking out the window, reflecting on what we had just accomplished," Hollins remembers. "We'd felt like we could win, but we were just like, 'Wow, we just beat one of the greatest teams in the NBA. We beat Dr. J.' And we were the youngest team in NBA history to win the championship, so it felt like the sky was the limit. We reflected on that, me and Luke and Bill, and we were just looking out the window at the crazy people, because they were crazy. There was no cops to be seen, but people jumping up and down on the top of their cars and honking and screaming. That went on 'till late night."

The Blazers' championship and the Mount St. Helens eruption were the two biggest local events of my childhood, each in its way changing the landscape and bringing worldwide attention. I was five years old when Portland won the 1977 title, slightly too young to truly grasp what was going on, but old enough to witness the community-wide euphoria. I wish I could somehow tell my childhood self that I would one day get to interview both Hollins and Walton.

Hollins, the sixth overall pick in the 1975 NBA draft, had been introduced to Portland earlier that year while playing for Arizona State University in two NCAA tournament games at Memorial Coliseum. "It was a nice downtown and you could walk," he remembers. After joining the Blazers, Hollins spent his first year living in the Hillsdale neighborhood southwest of downtown, near where the team practiced at the Mittleman Jewish Community Center. But then, "I made a decision," he remembers. "I wanted to live downtown." He chose the Portland Plaza most of all for its views, adding, "I loved the building—the cloverleaf design and the ability to see out to the mountains, even when it was raining. And I used to watch all the cars come up over the Marquam Bridge." Hollins's girlfriend at the time, Angela (now his wife of more than forty years), was working in the First National Bank Tower (now Wells Fargo Center) a block away; Hollins would take his dog and meet her in the nearby Plaza Blocks for lunch.

Hollins remained a Blazer through 1980, able to see the St. Helens eruption from here before leaving town; he only reluctantly gave up his Portland Plaza unit. "I would have continued to stay there but, as we got successful, people started to find out where I lived and coming to the building," he explains. "You couldn't get in, but you could ring the buzzer, and then in my apartment, a TV screen would light up and you could see who was there at the door wanting in. I got tired of answering the buzzer all the time." Three decades after the championship season, in 2007, the Trail Blazers retired his #14 jersey. Hollins went on to spend nearly four decades as an NBA assistant and head coach.

Two blocks north is the tallest building in Oregon: the forty-story **Wells Fargo Center** (1300 SW Fifth Avenue). Outside of Portland, this would not be considered a super-tall skyscraper, for at 546 feet it's less than half the height of New York's One World Trade Center and the Empire State Building. Even in Seattle, the Wells Fargo would not even crack the top ten tallest buildings. But that's not to say the Wells Fargo Center hasn't captured my imagination. Originally known as the First National Bank tower, it was completed the same year I was born, 1972. As a child, when my family would drive to into Portland on Interstate 5, I would wait for the top of this building to come

*Wells Fargo Center*

into view, like a first glimpse of the ocean when we'd drive to the Oregon coast. The First National was the only building tall enough to appear from this distance.

Designed by Los Angeles firm Charles Luckman and Associates for First National Bank (which vacated its historic headquarters on Fifth Avenue to move here), the tower expressed US economic might in the decades after World War II. At street level, however, it is arguably unwelcoming. Because of the building's sloping site from west to east, its entrance on Fifth comes via a bridge over the sunken base of the building, in what resembles a castle moat. Built during an era of suburban flight, its underground parking garage made the First National among the first buildings whose workers could come and go without ever entering downtown's streets on foot. Then there's the tower's full-block annex across Fourth Avenue, what's known as the Data Processing Building, historically an almost entirely people-free structure that was built to house backup generators and computer infrastructure.

Luckman's Los Angeles architecture firm, co-founded in 1950 with William Pereira, designed numerous landmarks, including the flying-saucer-like Theme Building at Los Angeles International Airport, the Disneyland Hotel in Anaheim, and New York's Madison Square Garden. And this was actually Luckman's second career, for he first became famous as a CEO. In 1937, while leading the Pepsodent company, Luckman was pictured on the cover of *Time* magazine and dubbed "the boy wonder of American business."

The First National Bank's façade, with dark anodized aluminum contrasting with white Italian marble fins, gives the building a distinctive look, compared to all-glass towers, and emphasizes its verticality. But it didn't impress *The New York Times* architecture critic Ada Louise Huxtable, who called the design feature "jazzy and schlocky enough to batter all sensibilities." And Huxtable wasn't alone. In a 2006 *Portland Tribune* survey of local architects, this was voted the city's most despised structure.

The Wells Fargo Center was renovated in 2019 by Portland firm West of West, which successfully made the building more inviting at ground level, with more transparent glass and a more spacious lobby, encouraging interaction among tenants. "Our interventions were surgical: to fit in and make it work," West of West co-founder Clayton Taylor says. "You're inserting something that goes against the original premise, but it needs to happen to keep these buildings alive."

Just over one hundred years before the Wells Fargo Center was constructed, located on this site was the Portland Colored

School, the city's first and only official segregated public school. Opened in 1867 with twenty-six Black students (twenty-one boys and five girls), it remained in operation for just five years. Portland had opened its Central School on the present-day Pioneer Courthouse Square site in 1858, but admission was denied to children of the city's approximately 130 Black residents. One parent, William Brown, appealed to the school board, made up of former mayors Josiah Failing and William S. Ladd, as well as Oregon Supreme Court Chief Justice Erasmus D. Shattuck. Brown's children were again denied access, citing a lack of funds. What they really feared, as Helen Marie Casey recounts in *Portland's Compromise: The Colored School, 1867–1872*, was that Portland taxpayers would revolt at the idea of their money helping to educate Black children. After all, just eight years earlier, Oregon had become the only state to be admitted to the union with a clause in its constitution prohibiting settlement by Blacks, which remained on the books until 1926. But when Brown threatened legal action, the board allocated $800 for the construction of a school for Black students.

That the city's tallest building and its greatest symbol of wealth and power (with a façade alternating white marble and black metal) would sit on the site of a school reluctantly built for Black students is, of course, ironic. Portland has long been the whitest US big city, and Oregon arguably has never fully reckoned with its history of excluding Black citizens and the struggle for Blacks to overcome prejudice and find prosperity in an overwhelmingly white area of the country has remained a constant struggle.

Walking on Fifth Avenue among some of the city's taller commercial buildings, I'm again struck by how relatively few people are on the street. This neighborhood has always lacked many residential buildings, over-relying on offices. And, granted, by this time it's fairly late, the afternoon sun no longer directly overhead. In fact, it has started to lightly rain again, the blue sky of an hour ago having temporarily disappeared. Certainly there is plenty of automobile traffic on some of the nearby arterial streets. But there just aren't many people walking these sidewalks. I suppose the transformation downtown ultimately needs will take years to accomplish, creating a better balance of places to live and work.

I'm headed now to my favorite downtown office building: the seventeen-story **Standard Plaza** (1100 SW Sixth Avenue) by Skidmore, Owings and Merrill. After it opened in 1963, this was the city's tallest building for nine years, until the Wells Fargo/First National's completion. The Standard Plaza was also the first office building in the city to occupy a full city block. Yet it's not the building's size that impresses, but rather its clean lines and distinctive golden-tinted glass.

The Standard Plaza, as its name indicates, was constructed for the Standard Insurance company. Originally known as the Oregon Life Insurance Company, it was founded in 1906 by German immigrant Leo Samuel to cater to workers in the burgeoning timber industry. On-the-job injuries were common, and most other life insurance companies were located on the East Coast, which meant claims were slow to be paid and customer service minimal. As the company grew, so did Samuel's community service. Portland's nickname, the City of Roses, has been attributed to him because Samuel grew roses outside his downtown Portland home and tied scissors to his fence so those passing by could be encouraged to clip and take a rose.

This building features a large public plaza on its eastern Fifth Avenue side, hence its name. Taking advantage of the sloping site, there is a sunken garden on the upper Sixth Avenue side, over which an entry bridge passes, similar to the Wells Fargo Center, yet more successful here. Instead of placing the building at the edge of the property, or doing so with a podium, like SOM did for its nearby Hilton Hotel on Broadway completed the same year, the Standard Plaza provides a generously sized public plaza on the Fifth Avenue side. Located here is also a unique entry sequence: up a central escalator and into a hybrid indoor-outdoor space on the second floor, walled in glass. Reaching the top of the escalator, there is an ideal view across Fifth to the Portland Building and its *Portlandia* statue.

The Standard Plaza possesses an exceptionally elegant simplicity and subtle details, which speaks to SOM's mastery of the form, having designed famous skyscrapers worldwide. Though this building's façade is a Mies van der Rohe–like rectilinear grid of glass and aluminum, its lateral floor beams are slightly tapered, with a gentle sense of curve, while the gold glass resembles a pair of sunglasses.

The Standard Plaza's best-known feature may be its illuminated rooftop weather beacon, which glows red if that day's high temperature is forecast to increase by five degrees or more, glows green if the temperature forecast is to remain the same, or white if the temperature is forecast to decrease. Flashing lights

*Standard Plaza*

mean rain is forecasted. (A wall panel in the lobby conveying this same information means you don't have to check the roof beacon.) Because of Oregon's temperate climate, the beacon remains green 90 percent of the time. In the future, however, we can expect far more red lights.

### *For the People*

I've now arrived at another of the central city's treasured stretches of greenspace: a multi-block foreground to several government buildings. They appear as one place but in reality are, depending on how you define it, two to three separate entities. The northern two blocks, known together as the **Plaza Blocks** (between SW Third and Fourth Avenues, Salmon and Jefferson Streets), are owned by the City of Portland and opened in 1869. The third and southernmost block is owned by the federal government.

The northern Plaza Block, called Lownsdale Square, was named for the aforementioned Daniel Lownsdale, whose land claim of 640 acres comprised much of present-day downtown Portland; he bequeathed to the city the South Park Blocks as well as the land here. The southern Plaza Block, called Chapman Square, was named for William Chapman, a Virginia native and attorney who came to the Oregon Country in 1847 from Iowa, where he had been the state's first elected member of the US Congress. Chapman remained politically active in Oregon and was elected to the Territorial Legislature in 1849. In 1850 he co-founded *The Oregonian* newspaper with publisher Thomas J. Dryer.

Though the Plaza Blocks are places of quiet respite, the proximity to City Hall and other government buildings has prompted many political protests here. In 1934, for example, pro-labor activists and members of the Portland Communist Party, sparked by the Great Depression's devastating hardships, put on a May Day march in what was then known as Plaza Park, as part of a national surge of radicalism to fight for economic relief. They even flew a large red flag over City Hall, which remained for most of the day thanks to a malfunction in the flagpole mechanism, much to Mayor Joe Carson's dismay. More recently, there were protests in 2000 against the Supreme Court's awarding of the presidency to George W. Bush, in 2003 opposing the Iraq War, in 2011 for the Occupy protests, and, in 2020, the demonstrations following George Floyd's murder.

The 2020 protests still loom especially large in my mind and Portland's collective memory. Months of continuous nightly Black Lives Matter demonstrations turned Portland into a national media stage, even as the COVID-19 pandemic made large gatherings a health risk. While thousands of citizens protested police brutality, including a popular "Wall of Moms," police in riot gear and eventually federal Department of Homeland Security troops sent by President Donald Trump responded with tear gas, and in many cases seemed to initiate violence, as if looking for a fight. Even Portland's mayor, Ted Wheeler, was tear-gassed by federal troops while standing in solidarity with protesters.

During these protests, award-winning *Oregonian* news photographer Beth Nakamura was hit by a police baton while following a police order for protesters to retreat north; she had merely kept taking pictures as she walked. "I was holding up my press pass and saying, 'Press, press!'" she remembers. "It's very violating, and it's gratuitous. I was just trying to do my job." Eventually, Nakamura and others started donning armor. "I got a stab vest. Later we all got Kevlar bullet-proof vests. Eventually I got a gas mask. We all had helmets. A lot of that stuff we had at *The Oregonian* from past protest coverage, but we had to update our gas masks," she says. "It didn't all happen right away. But protesters, you could see them change. They went from T-shirts to looking like warriors."

In 2022, a US Department of Homeland Security investigation found that, in 2020, under then-Acting Secretary Chad Wolf and Acting Deputy Secretary Ken Cuccinelli, intelligence operations in Portland had become improperly politicized and biased. The investigation also found that Acting Under Secretary for Intelligence and Analysis Brian Murphy had improperly characterized the protests as "violent Antifa anarchist-inspired," even though this was not grounded in any of the department's intelligence collection. It was a foreshadowing of the tactics that would become even more widespread in the second Trump administration.

The Plaza Blocks have long contained numerous works of public art. A bronze tablet in Chapman Square commemorates the first electric power transmission line in North America, on June 3, 1889, which terminated at Chapman Square after originating from a generating station 13 miles away at Willamette Falls in Oregon City. At Lownsdale Square's center is the Spanish-American War Soldier's Monument, erected in 1906, honoring the Second Oregon Volunteer Infantry. During the 1898 conflict, they were the first US troops to enter Guam and the first to land in the Philippines. The monument was created by California sculptor Douglas Tilden, several of whose statues remain on public display in San Francisco and Berkeley.

A statue erected in 1993 and known as *The Promised Land*, designed by David Manuel to commemorate the 150th anniversary of the Oregon Trail, is no longer here. It depicted a pioneer family (a mother, father and son) with a wagon wheel and leaning rifle behind the father, who is holding a Bible. The statue was controversial from the start, and opposed by many in Portland's arts community. In a *Los Angeles Times* article, Art Alexander, a member of Commissioner Mike Lindberg's staff, called *The Promised Land* "a whitewashing of the truth." After being vandalized during the 2020 protests, *The Promised Land* was removed and stored out of public view. Four years later, the City of Portland announced the statue would be deaccessioned from its collection.

The other statue that disappeared from view after the protests (but thankfully has since returned), known as the *Thompson Elk* (or simply *Elk*) and located between Chapman and Lownsdale Square on Main Street, is my favorite work of public art in Portland. Erected in 1900, it is the city's second-oldest work of public art, pre-dated only by the circa-1888 Skidmore Fountain. The statue, created by sculptor Roland Hinton Perry and sitting atop a fountain by E. G. Wright, was commissioned and donated to the city by former Portland mayor David P. Thompson, and cast at the Henry-Bonnard Bronze Company foundry in New York City. Thompson, an Ohio native who came to Oregon in 1853, was a successful businessman and civic leader, establishing the state's first railroad (around Willamette Falls in Oregon City) and also serving as Portland's mayor from 1879 to 1882. Additionally, he had served as the first president of the Oregon Humane Society, perhaps explaining why he commissioned a

*The Elk statue*

relatively uncommon statue honoring not some political or military leader but wildlife.

Before creating the *Elk* statue, Perry had been best known for the Neptune Fountain at the Library of Congress in Washington, DC. Even so, his statue had early critics. The local Exalted Order of Elks refused an invitation to participate in the dedication ceremony, calling Perry's work "a monstrosity of art" because it was not anatomically accurate, adding that the elk's neck would be "the envy of a giraffe." There have also been repeated attempts to move it as a traffic hazard. Though fountains are traditionally located at the centers of greenspaces, and this one is too, it's also in the middle of Main Street, bisecting the Plaza Blocks. Photographs from the 1930s show a traffic sign tacked on its flank.

The *Elk* is perhaps best known for appearing in Gus Van Sant's 1991 film *My Own Private Idaho*. The first Portland-set scene begins at the base of the fountain, with Keanu Reeves's character, Scott, cradling River Phoenix's character, Mike, the latter having succumbed to a narcoleptic seizure. But in the movie, the statue an altered version of Perry's artwork, topped with a human rider; its base is inscribed with the name of another statue Thompson had donated to the city, *The Coming of the White Man*. That's an inside joke, because the latter statue's location near a public restroom in Washington Park made it for many years a well-known gay cruising spot, which in turn made that statue's title a double-entendre.

Van Sant chose the *Elk* for a *My Own Private Idaho* scene in part because near the Plaza Blocks was another popular cruising site too. "They called it 'Camp,' and we didn't know why. Nobody seemed to know why," the director recalled in a 2024 interview. "Eventually an older member of that scene explained it to me. Just a few blocks away, between Fourth and Fifth, there was this big bus station; we actually shot a scene from *Drugstore Cowboy* there, with Matt Dillon walking through the bus station, before it got torn down. Next to that was an empty block. He said in the Depression there was an encampment there—tents and vehicles where people lived. It was also where prostitution would happen between different characters: the rich guys that would come down from the hills and pick people up at Camp. And so, the modern hustlers, they all referred to it as Camp. And so the *Elk* statue is just within a block or two of Camp, and was part of the environment."

During the 2020 protests, protesters deliberately toppled numerous statues in downtown and beyond, and some mistakenly think the *Elk* was among them. It was a gathering place for protesters, some of whom ill-advisedly lit bonfires in the then-waterless fountain, causing burns and cracking. This prompted city inspectors to preemptively remove the artwork and place it in storage. When I visited the *Elk* at an undisclosed storage facility later that summer, it turned out to be in perfect shape, except for a few specs of paint. But it was only the statue I saw, not the fountain. In the meantime, the *Elk* site on Main Street was turned into a kind of shrine, with different variations of elk toys and homemade elk statues placed on the empty base of the statue, and even performance artists taking turns standing there frozen in place. Yet its full return was initially threatened by the City of Portland, which planned to bring back only the statue itself without the large water fountain serving at its base, in order to make room for a bike lane. After citizen opposition, the city reversed course, pledging to restore the fountain and rerouting the bike and automobile lanes here. But municipal workers had actually destroyed the fountain as they removed it in 2020, necessitating a complete rebuild. Now that it has returned, perhaps the *Thompson Elk* can become a symbol of downtown Portland's rebirth.

Facing Chapman Square is the **Mark O. Hatfield United States Courthouse** (1000 SW Third Avenue), which opened in 1997 just after Valarie and I moved to the city. During a public open house we attended, I remember looking out at downtown from the sixteenth floor, through a wall of glass. The city had no tall buildings with observation decks, so this became our way to get a sense of downtown Portland as a whole, just as I'd done in 1990 from the top of the World Trade Center after arriving for college in New York.

Mark Hatfield, for whom this courthouse was named, served for more than thirty years in the United States Senate and, before that, was a two-term Oregon governor. A World War II veteran, he had fought in the pivotal battles of Iwo Jima and Okinawa, victories that had cost some 75,000 combined US lives. In 1968, he was on a shortlist of candidates for Richard Nixon's vice-presidential running mate, but Hatfield's opposition to the Vietnam War, unique among Republicans, meant the party's more conservative southern members would not support him.

The Hatfield Courthouse, designed by New York City firm Kohn Pedersen Fox in collaboration with Portland's Bora, is clad primarily with limestone, meant to recall traditional civic architecture. Yet on its upper floors such as the one I had looked out from, the west-facing courtroom lobbies were intentionally given floor-to-ceiling views. "The judicial process is so stressful for people, so the intention when you come out of the courtroom

*Mark O. Hatfield US Courthouse*

was to give you as much of a relief as possible," explains Kohn Pedersen Fox co-founder William Pedersen. "The design of the building was specifically developed to reveal the components of the judicial process, as opposed to the classical period when you'd hide it behind some classical façade. One of the fundamental assignments is for the building to be able to express the dignity and solidity of the government. That was quite easy in the classical era. But in our era, the issue of transparency is extremely important as well."

Pederson also laments the violence emanating outside the Hatfield US Courthouse in 2020, and the role federal troops had played. "It's painful to know that a building that was designed to be a symbol of justice has become somewhat a symbol of injustice," he says.

I twice reported on courtroom proceedings here in 2002. First as a stringer for *The New York Times* I observed (for a story written by Timothy Egan) a federal grand jury indictment of the "Portland Seven," a group of US Muslims attempting to join Al Qaeda terrorist forces and Afghanistan's Taliban government in fighting the United States military following its attack on Afghanistan a year earlier. I sat with a pool of other reporters in the gallery as the indictment was being issued, and particularly I remember a nearby courtroom sketch-artist near me depicting the stoic faces of the accused. Two months later I was back at the Hatfield to report for *Bloomberg* on a class-action suit against Wal-Mart, the world's largest retailer. More than 400 employees from twenty-four of the chain's twenty-seven Oregon stores collectively accused Wal-Mart of violating federal and state wage laws between 1994 and 1999. I watched scores of plaintiffs testify under oath that Wal-Mart pressured them to work off the clock. The jury sided with the plaintiffs.

Making a clockwise loop around the Plaza Blocks, which are relatively quiet this late afternoon, I'm next headed two blocks south to the **Edith Green Wendell Wyatt Federal Building** (1220 SW Third Avenue). It was named for former US House of Representatives members Edith Green, a Democrat representing east Portland, and Wendell Wyatt, a Republican representing the west side. Originally a drab 1974 office building by Skidmore, Owings and Merrill, it was transformed in a 2013 renovation from a design by Cutler Anderson Architects and SERA Architects.

Shortly after the building's reopening, I remember standing on the roof, enjoying views of Mount Hood and the West Hills beneath a huge, slanted roof shade, covered in solar panels and lifted off the roof itself to prevent thermal heat transfer; from afar it looks like a graduation cap worn at a jaunty angle. Even

Edith Green Wendell Wyatt Federal Building

more eye-catching are the exterior sun shades affixed to the west façade, further blocking the glass from afternoon sunlight. These aren't aesthetic moves, at least not primarily; the renovations have helped reduce the building's energy use by 45 percent. But they also communicate the federal government's symbolic intent to be sustainable, which in a certain respect now makes it dated, for today's national leadership openly disdains such strategies.

A decade ago, however, during the Obama administration, it was different, and so was the city, which was a leader in sustainable design and construction. "I felt Portland is maybe the greenest city in North America. If there was any place I could convince people to do a building that was both technically and emotionally green, it would be there," architect James Cutler told me for a 2013 *Architect* article. Known for several award-winning house designs, including the estate of Microsoft founder Bill Gates in Seattle, Cutler began his career under legendary architect Louis Kahn. "The very first project that I did with Lou, I discovered that we don't do buildings. We do clothing that houses institutions," Cutler recalled. "And we have to tailor the garment to each particular institution's anatomy." The Edith Green Wendell Wyatt renovation is just that: a retailoring of an old suit to better fit its occupants, and its owner's utility bill.

Cutler collaborated with Portland's SERA Architects to fine-tune the exterior shades and the position of their vertical metal reeds to craft the right balance of aesthetics and interior-daylight levels. "We didn't want to have an evenly spaced series of reeds," recalled former SERA associate principal Lisa Petterson (now a principal at CannonDesign). "We needed something more biophilic and rhythmic."

My favorite view at the Edith Green Wendell Wyatt is not on the rooftop, picturesque as the vantage point may be; it is standing outside the ground floor, just beneath those exterior screens. The lush array of native plants there today, created by PLACE Studio, makes it not easy to see, but looking straight up at the screens is like viewing an abstract sculpture.

One block west is a block-sized park that's both a companion to the Plaza Blocks and legally separate from them: **Terry Schrunk Plaza** (between SW Third and Fourth Avenues, Jefferson and Madison Streets). It's owned by the federal government and sits atop an underground parking garage for the Edith Green Wendell Wyatt Federal Building. Schrunk Plaza is by far the least frequented of the three park blocks, lacking a pathway through. Yet the park, named for former Portland mayor Terry Schrunk, also sits directly across Fourth Avenue from Portland City Hall, and its small amphitheater occasionally comes alive for civic celebrations.

One such moment at Terry Schrunk Plaza overshadows all others. On June 6, 1977, more than 150,000 people descended into downtown Portland to celebrate the Portland Trail Blazers' NBA championship with a parade, concluding at Schrunk Plaza with speeches by members of the team and by Mayor Neil Goldschmidt, on whose head star Blazers center Bill Walton poured a beer. "It was a thing to behold, and I will forever be able to say I was there," Walton told me in a 2021 podcast interview (he died in 2024). "It's what you live for; it's what you play for—that sense of community, the sense of collective effort and purpose, the sense of participation in something that is bigger than your own individual life and the way that our fans would be so ready."

The top pick in the 1974 NBA draft, Walton had won two national championships at UCLA as part of coach John Wooden's ten-championship dynasty. He turned down a lucrative offer from the American Basketball Association to come to Portland, which had received the first draft pick after a coin flip with Philadelphia (the same team the Blazers would face in the NBA Finals three years later). "I knew I wanted to come to Oregon," Walton recalled. "I was just blown away by how remarkably beautiful and gorgeous it was—the rivers and volcanoes and mountains and gorges and canyons, hot springs—and no people." When he wasn't playing basketball, he was often out hiking and camping.

If the 1977 championship turned out to be a fleeting moment for Walton and the Blazers, its star player may be all the more admirable for how he so often overcame injuries and adversity, with countless different surgeries. "My career was marked by meteoric climbs to the top, followed almost immediately by catastrophic health crises that have taken me right down to the bottom. And that happened a number of times in Oregon," he said. "Some of the things didn't turn out so well, but a lot of them did. And those are the memories that I focus on because it was a place where I played my best basketball, and I had the most remarkable teammates. Basketball was the easiest part of my life. It was a safe place, a place of joy, for me."

It's still hard to believe Bill Walton is gone, as is his co-star on the championship team, Maurice Lucas. "He was like the molten lava that's underneath the surface of the Earth, just looking for a big volcanic eruption to come right out," Walton said of Lucas. "His very first game at the Memorial Coliseum, he threw down a reverse slam dunk in Kareem's [Abdul-Jabbar] face at the buzzer to win an exhibition game. And the rest is history. We never lost another big game while we were both healthy. Maurice Lucas was the greatest Blazer of all, the greatest teammate that I ever had. He was such a towering pillar of strength. And whenever there was a crisis, whenever there was a catastrophe, whenever there was a decision that had to be made and responsibility that had to be assumed, Maurice Lucas would lean into the group, look around, and he would say, 'I'll take care of this.' And he did.

And when things still did not go his way, Maurice would ramp it up a little bit more. We won the championship because we had Maurice Lucas, we had [head coach] Jack Ramsay, we had the Blazer maniacs, and nobody else did."

Ramsay, Walton added, "was just the man. He was just brilliant at knowing the pulse of the team, to get you up into the focus and the enthusiasm and the energy, the concentration. Jack had a different understanding of the role of the coach than the other coaches I played for. He wasn't a past player of significant historical import. But he was a teacher. You should have seen his masterful use of the blackboard. That's really the ultimate challenge for a young dreamer is to search for or find and learn from the master teachers. Jack taught me things that I did not know existed."

Today the Trail Blazers face a much different situation. The 1977 championship gave way to over a quarter-century of playoff runs (including two NBA Finals appearances in 1990 and 1992), as well a succession of great players, from Hall of Fame members Clyde Drexler and Arvydas Sabonis to the buzzer-beating virtuosity of Damian Lillard. But the team's new ownership group appears to be distressingly penny-pinching and (unlike Lillard) possess little loyalty to Portland.

I remember once attending a small ceremony at Schrunk Plaza in 2007 to commemorate the thirtieth anniversary of the Blazers' championship. It was raining that early June afternoon, and there were just a few members of that 1977 team in attendance, along with local leaders and about fifty fans. But, like the public memorial service for Maurice Lucas in 2010, I rarely turned down an opportunity to pay homage to my heroes.

Now, as I cross busy Fourth Avenue, my attention turns to **Portland City Hall** (1221 SW Fourth Avenue). It's a relative anomaly in this neighborhood at just four stories, but the building has presence, not only for the power it represents but with its Italian Renaissance style, with a sandstone and granite exterior including Tuscan columns, dentil moldings, and keystones.

City Hall's 1895 completion came after four decades with no such building. After Portland's 1851 incorporation, each newly elected mayor was required to find a temporary headquarters for city business. Finally, in 1890, funds were raised to purchase this full block site between Fourth and Fifth Avenues. Located here previously had been St. Helen's Hall, an all-girls private school (which relocated to Raleigh Hills in Southwest Portland and eventually became the co-ed Oregon Episcopal School). Architect Henry Hefty won the City Hall design competition with an ambitious proposal for a bell tower rising several stories over its four-story base. But after the building's foundation was poured, builders determined it would require twice the estimated budget to complete, and construction was halted. Two years later, construction began on a more modestly scaled city hall designed by architecture firm Whidden & Lewis, on the previous building's foundations.

Architect William Whidden came to Portland in 1883 as an architect for famed New York firm McKim, Mead and White, commissioned to design the Portland Hotel. After Whidden's colleague at McKim, Ion Lewis, joined him here in 1889 to form this new firm, Whidden & Lewis designed a succession of major downtown architectural works, including the Imperial Hotel, the original Portland Library Association (demolished), and the Multnomah County Courthouse.

Inside, the main chamber, where city council members (known as commissioners) hear testimony and vote, is a two-story volume that feels like a small theater, with a rounded mezzanine balcony often filled with activists. When I testified before city council in 2009, to argue for Memorial Coliseum's preservation after Mayor Sam Adams announced its demolition, I remember struggling to keep calm as my heart raced. There had been scores of other citizens speaking that day; honestly I don't know how city council members have the patience to continually sit through hours of testimony. Speakers are seated before council two at a time, and it turned out I had a much better-known co-speaker also arguing for the Coliseum's preservation: former Oregon governor Victor Atiyeh. He addressed council not as a retired politician, Atiyeh said, but as a veteran, arguing that the entire Coliseum was a veterans memorial.

When I visit or pass by City Hall, I still think of Vera Katz, who, when I moved to Portland, was in the first of a three-term run as mayor (1993–2005). She is the most celebrated local leader of my time here, and the first Portland mayor I ever interviewed. Though downtown Portland's rise to a pedestrian-friendly urban planning success attracting creative workers from around the nation had already begun in the seventies and eighties, Katz oversaw a kind of renaissance, in which new neighborhoods like the Pearl District and the Central Eastside came alive.

As a child she had immigrated to the United States with her Jewish parents, as refugees fleeing Nazi Germany (who, before that, fled Russia after the revolution of 1917), and settled in New York City. As a young woman she aspired to be a professional dancer and studied under the legendary impresario Martha Graham. Katz came to Portland in 1962 with her husband, artist Mel Katz, from Brooklyn, New York. "There was some kind of almost square patriotic impulse she felt, which really flowed from a deep debt of gratitude to the US for rescuing her," explains her son, Los Angeles journalist Jesse Katz. "I think she had a real need and a calling to give back, and to work towards a more just society." Amid the cultural awakening of the 1960s, Katz took her

*Portland City Hall*

first steps into political activism by protesting local businesses and organizations that excluded women, including the Portland City Club and the Lipman-Wolfe department store's bar. "There was something about her that people responded to," he adds, "and was allowing her to help shape the future of what Portland was going to look like."

For most of the city's history, before a 2022 vote creating a twelve-member city council, Portland's government was based on a system that's uncommon for a large US city, in which the mayor is just one of five voting members. It was meant to emphasize consensus and prevent the mayor from becoming overly powerful, which was particularly important given how the Portland of past generations was gripped by corruption. Yet certain mayors still wound up leaving an outsized fingerprint on the city. Now, we've just begun a new era, but an encouraging one, I think, for the larger city council gives more representation and advocates for marginalized communities and those living far outside the central city.

Crossing Madison Street, it's time to unwrap a birthday present. At least that's the way the **Portland Building** (420 SW Main Street) looks from outside, because of its façade decorated with faux garlands and long colorful ribbons. Designed by Michael Graves and serving as an administrative headquarters for several local government bureaus, this is the city's most famous building, and not just because the country's second-largest statue, *Portlandia* by Raymond Kaskey, is perched above the entrance. The Portland Building was one the nation's first major works of Postmodernism, which briefly flourished in the seventies and eighties: a playful interpretation of classical, traditional architecture, but often crossing over into caricature.

Graves's design reflected an exuberant sense of showmanship: a desire to stand out from the crowd. And indeed, at the Portland Building's 1984 dedication, Mayor Frank Ivancie suggested this would become the city's equivalent of the Eiffel Tower. But the Portland Building wasn't built to last, largely because of budget austerity Ivancie had imposed: it was largely devoid of natural light and leaked profusely. Its style also makes the Portland Building an anachronism. Yet after an extensive

*Portland Building*

renovation completed in 2020, the building has not only endured but looks and functions better than ever.

Before I say more about the Portland Building, I want to mention the jazz club on this site from 1926 to 1959: McElroy's Spanish Ballroom. Several of the all-time jazz greats performed here, including Duke Ellington, John Coltrane, Dizzy Gillespie, Lionel Hampton, Ella Fitzgerald, Louis Armstrong, and Cab Calloway, which for me, as a longtime jazz lover, makes this sacred ground. Yet great music was only part of the inspiration. The club's founders—J. Cole "Pop" McElroy, a white musician and dance hall manager, and Stanton Duke, a Black business promoter—intentionally built one of the first integrated venues in Portland, where Black and white customers could dance together.

"They were humanists," Robert Dietsche, author of *Jumptown: Portland Jazz, 1942–1957*, told me for a 2001 *Willamette Week* story. "Pop McElroy was not as interested in making money as he was in integration. It was the main reason he did what he did with Stanton Duke. But Duke was an indefatigable promoter. They would poster whole streets promoting this, because the white media wasn't interested." Though the ballroom was elegant and large for a jazz club, with its crystal chandelier shimmering above a springy, ball-bearing-mounted floating wood dance floor, "it was thought by some to be the den of iniquity," Dietsche added. "White people were picking up these so-called primitive Black dances there. It was believed that mixed dancing would lead to mixed marriage, and this town was paranoid about that."

In December 1941, Duke Ellington's band played for a week at McElroy's, after the Pearl Harbor attack canceled a string of upcoming gigs. This particular ensemble was the most critically acclaimed of Ellington's long career, the Blanton-Webster Band. The bandleader enjoyed the extended gig enough to later celebrate two birthdays with concerts at McElroy's, which were recorded and later released as *The Birthday Sessions*, a five-album set from Laserlight Records. In 1954, John Coltrane played McElroy's with Johnny Hodges' band. "He was a backup guy then," said Dietsche. "Nobody knew he was going to be a revolutionary." Three months after playing in Portland, Coltrane got one of his biggest breaks, joining a new band led by Miles Davis.

A quarter century after McElroy's closed, the City of Portland commissioned a work of architecture that was, in its way, akin to jazz. Just as jazz musicians improvise new interpretations of pop songs, standards, and showtunes, so too did Postmodernism reimagine classical building styles. For much of the twentieth century, Modernism, with its emphasis on functionality and a dogmatic lack of ornamentation, had dominated the design of commercial and civic buildings alike. By the 1970s, a new generation of architects including Michael Graves, Robert Venturi, and Peter Eisenmann were ready to rebel. Graves's Portland

Building delights in the historical references that Modernism rejected.

An Indianapolis native who spent his career in New Jersey teaching architecture at Princeton University in parallel with designing buildings, Graves got his start working for celebrated industrial designer George Nelson (famous for his bubble lamps and ball clocks), learning the value of boldly playful, eye-catching design and prefiguring Graves's late-career success designing household products for Target. A two-year fellowship at the American Academy in Rome from 1960 to 1962 inspired in Graves a romantic affection for classical architecture, and a desire to channel its influence.

Graves spent the first two decades of his career mostly designing houses (and teaching), and the Portland Building was Graves's first major public commission. It came via an international design competition, held by the City of Portland in 1979. When architect Philip Johnson—a convert from Modernism to Postmodernism, and a fan of Graves's work—was hired as an adviser to the selection jury, "Michael knew he would have a chance," recalls architect Lisa Lee Morgan, who had been one of Graves's Princeton University students and joined his office that summer.

From the start, Graves's design had vocal critics. The city's most celebrated architect, Pietro Belluschi, called the Postmodern design an "oversized beribboned Christmas package" and warned that "today's shock value may well be tomorrow's drag." But it wasn't just bold style the City of Portland was looking for. Graves's was the only competition entry to meet the tight budget constraints and programmatic requirements. "He was absolutely convinced that if he offered one shred of practical reason why they might reject his submission, they would take it," Morgan says, "because awarding the contract to such an unusual design was a risk. And I think he was right. Michael said to me over and over, 'Lisa, you've got to make sure that every inch of square footage, every space that is needed by the program, every bit of the schedule, is all to their specifications.' So it became my job to say to the other architects and the contractors, 'No, we can't do this,' 'No, we can't do that.' Responsiveness became a very, very important part of the submission."

Once Graves won the competition, getting the Portland Building built so cheaply compromised the end result. Graves and his team had designed a terra cotta façade, for instance, but instead they had to settle for a polymer coating over bare concrete, which contributed to the building's years of water intrusion. The Portland Building's small windows—a response to newly stringent energy codes following the energy crisis of the 1970s—also made the building largely devoid of natural light. Administrative staff working here were later found to take sick leave more often than those working in other City of Portland facilities.

The *Portlandia* statue's arrival in 1985, via a Willamette River barge, was one of downtown's most memorable moments, attracting many to the riverside, including pioneering author and journalist Tom Wolfe. "I looked, I blinked, I looked again, I blinked some more, I rubbed my eyes... Great Godalmighty.... A gigantic woman, made of hammered copper, glorious, goddess-like, gleaming in the sun, her hair pulled back, a Greek toga draped from her shoulder, her immense right arm reaching down, down, down toward the multitudes," he wrote in *Newsweek*. Wolfe described hundreds taking to the river, to "meet her in tugboats, patrol boats, fire boats, yachts, sloops, schooners, skiffs, dinghies, ketches, yawls, dories, gigs, kayaks and canoes, horns and whistles blowing, flags waving and voices screaming every cry of homage known to man," including Mayor Bud Clark in a canoe, "his King of Diamonds beard unmistakable even from the shore, had taken to the river in a canoe. He was wearing lederhosen. As he closed in on the great copper goddess in midriver, he cried out, 'Whoop-whoop!' Then he cried again, for good measure, 'Whoop-whoop!'" Two days later, with *Portlandia* now in place atop the building's entrance, Raymond Kaskey, who had modeled the goddess after the lady of commerce on the city's seal, was hoisted in a cherry picker to the brow of the statue for the christening with champagne.

In 2014, city council contemplated demolishing the Portland Building, questioning the prudence of spending up to $200 million (including $100 million for a year's worth of employee relocation) to repair a "white elephant," as Commissioner Nick Fish called it. As if on cue, Graves returned to Portland that year for a speech, only the second time he'd been to town since the building was completed thirty years earlier. The eighty-year-old Graves, wheelchair-bound since becoming paralyzed from the waist down in 2003, joked to sold-out Portland Art Museum ballroom that audience members might have been tempted to buy tomatoes from the nearby farmers market to throw at him. "I've done 350 building designs," Graves said, "and I don't have this controversy anywhere else. I don't know where the hostility comes from. It hurt when people said, 'Tear down the building and keep the statue.' It's tear-making." Yet Graves also made clear his unapologetic affection for the Portland Building. Recalling a visit earlier that day, "It was shimmering. It was so uplifting," he said. "I had the biggest smile on my face. It was joy."

That same afternoon, when I interviewed Graves at his hotel, he made clear that the building's controversy did not impact how he saw the city. "It's surprising to me how green it is," he told me for an *Architect* magazine interview. "Portland is a gentle city. It's a city where you could imagine spending the rest of your days, because like Boston, like New Orleans, like San Francisco, there's a *there* there. And you can't say that about very many cities. You can't say that about Des Moines."

Graves fondly recalled winning the Portland Building design competition. "I came here with this idea that we could have a building with symbolism in it, that had color. And it wasn't a glass box. America had grown tired of that, and it was ripe for a change," he said. Still, Graves acknowledged the building's shortcomings. "We were in the midst of an energy crisis, and they wanted us to add tinted glass," he said. "People don't remember, but I got extra points for having windows that were smaller than usual."

Graves had never experienced one of his buildings being torn down (although one house was destroyed by fire), and he shuddered at the thought. "I would be devastated, I know, if any of my buildings came down. Not just in my lifetime, but I don't want them to come down ever," he says. "They are your children and you love them all." He also expressed his pragmatic willingness to make major changes to the design as part of a potential renovation, adding, "Buildings all need care, and so does the Portland Building."

Soon after that visit, Graves passed away, not knowing for sure whether the Portland Building would be restored. But at a dinner for Graves I attended, I saw him be unofficially promised that his building would survive. Indeed, the city decided against demolition, in part out of a belief that the building's problems—not only the leaks but the lack of light—could be rectified. The restoration, overseen by DLR Group in consultation with the late Graves's firm, made substantial changes to the building's design and appearance, including a new aluminum façade and switching out its shaded windows for clear glass. This rankled some historic preservationists. "Re-interpretations of history are always problematic," Theo Prudon, president of Modernist preservation organization Docomomo, told me for that same *Architect* article. "I think there is a concern that the new interpretation will be seen as the real thing. It's an age-old discussion in preservation. How far do you take it?"

When DLR Group interviewed for the Portland Building redesign commission, the firm encouraged the city to think beyond just fixing leaks and seismically stabilizing the building. "One of our key messages was how important it was to think about this project not just in terms of fixing a building and a project but telling new, positive stories," recalls former DLR Group principal Carla Weinheimer (now retired). "We said, 'No one's going to get just excited about fixing something. It needs to transform.' That's something we brought to the interview and something we kept in mind all the way through the project. This needed to become something bigger and better than a fix."

The restored Portland Building, reopened in 2021, was stunning to behold. Entering the lobby, which had been one of the building's spaces most devoid of natural light, it is now possible to see through the building in all four directions. Upstairs offices, where previously dark glass had been replaced with clear, were now full of light. Best of all, from certain conference rooms, it's now possible to look out at Fifth Avenue from behind the *Portlandia* statue. "I always felt like we were uncovering what was meant to be," Weinheimer adds. "You're listening to the building: the history of it, the scale, the materiality, and when the design is right, you feel it."

# *Walk 6*

# Take Me to the River

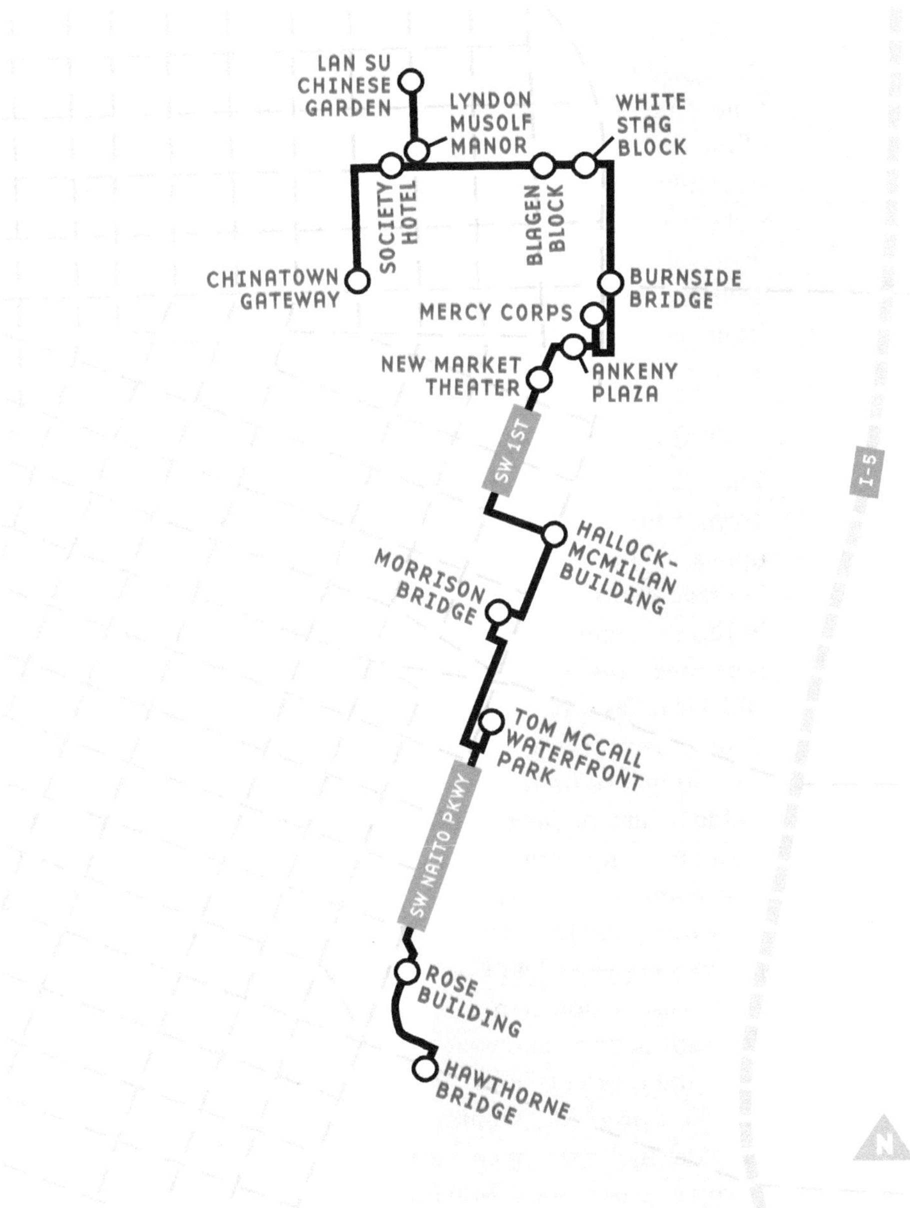

Several times in this book, I've reached the Willamette River only to move on. Aboard the Portland Aerial Tram, after enjoying a panoramic view of the waterway as it passed through the central city, I touched down at the terminal a few hundred feet from the river's edge. After walking through the Pearl District, I arrived at the base of the Fremont Bridge. Walking a half-mile down Naito Parkway, I took the stairway onto the Broadway Bridge and was able to stand directly over the river for the first time. But each of these visits was brief; there was still so much of the central city to see.

Only now, nearing the end of the journey, will I focus on the waterfront itself. As I move from Old Town into the Skidmore historic district, there is still some architecture to see. And there are three more bridges. But this walk's centerpiece is the waterfront itself, a beloved public amenity for recent generations, after more than a century as a commercial and industrial nexus.

## *Chinatown and Japantown*

The city's oldest neighborhood, today known officially as Old Town Chinatown, has always been a place of struggle and upheaval, but it possesses some of the city's greatest cultural heritage and architectural beauty. During Portland's early days in the mid-nineteenth century as a rough-and-tumble frontier port town, this is where seasonal workers from logging camps and farms as well as sailors between voyages would coalesce during the winter months in cheap lodging and brothels, patronizing some two hundred saloons. As the city grew, its upper-class residents moved farther away from the waterfront, and this area became an immigrant district, home to both Japanese and Chinese communities over time.

From 1860 to 1880, the city's Chinese population grew from just 22 people to 2,480, as immigrant workers filled jobs in railroad construction, agriculture, logging, and canneries, as well as domestic service, and were often persecuted for supposedly taking white residents' jobs. At first Chinese persons lived throughout the burgeoning central city, but as their population grew, pressure increased to corral the community into specific Chinatown neighborhoods. Initially Chinatown developed downtown between SW First and Second Avenues and SW Washington and

Alder Streets, but eventually stretched farther north and south. By the 1880s, Portland had a population of about 4,500 Chinese people, second only to San Francisco.

That growth halted after the federal government's passage of the first Chinese Exclusion Act of 1882, which banned Chinese laborers' entry into the United States after several incidents of anti-Chinese violence (not the first or last time the United States has rewarded its criminal vigilantes). A subsequent influx of Japanese immigrants provided similarly cheap labor and created a demand for hotels, laundries, and additional services. Eventually present-day Old Town between Broadway and the river became known as a Japanese enclave, Nihonmachi. These immigrants tended to be young bachelors who would eventually marry and start businesses here. Nihonmachi grew rapidly into the early 1920s, until federal immigration law was changed in 1924 to exclude Japanese immigration. By that time, many Japanese immigrants and their children had become naturalized citizens and were able to remain here. This changed dramatically, however, after the US entry into World War II. On February 19, 1942, President Franklin D. Roosevelt signed Executive Order 9066, authorizing the US government to issue exclusion orders in several West Coast states. Between May 1 and May 4, Nihonmachi emptied out, as citizens were forcibly removed to internment camps. In 1943, the Chinese Exclusion Act was finally repealed, and Old Town became a relocated Chinatown.

This neighborhood has also long been associated with homelessness and addiction. Passing at Burnside Street from downtown into Old Town, I can quickly see homeless people camped on the street and feel a familiar pressure on my chest: of empathy but also indecision, at whether I should try to help them with a few dollars or be on guard (the latter sensation I'm not proud of). Instead, I focus on the **Chinatown Gateway** (2 NW Fourth Avenue) I'm here to see.

I've always been drawn to historic city gates and arches, no doubt because of their historic, symbolic, and sometimes spiritual meanings, but also because a gateway is a kind of portal. Just as certain stairways feel powerfully experiential to me, so too does passing through the Chinatown Gateway. When it was erected in 1986 by the Chinese Consolidated Benevolent Association

*Chinatown Gateway*

(with financial support from Bill and Sam Naito's company, Norcrest), this was the largest such Chinese gate in the country, at 38 feet tall. In China such gates are known as *paifang*, referring to the ceremonial entries of ancient neighborhoods encircled by protective walls. Their architectural characteristics include multi-tiered roofs and upward-swinging eaves, which are part of Portland's version, along with a pair of bronze lions sitting at its base: a male and female representing yin and yang.

The Chinatown Gateway was designed and built in Taiwan in pieces by Ting Hwa Architects, then shipped to Oregon for assembly. The project was spearheaded by Liu Chi, a Taiwanese immigrant and Chinese Consolidated Benevolent Association member. Back home, he had been a basketball referee, and immigrated to San Francisco in the mid-seventies to earn a master's degree in physical education. To pay bills, he worked as a cook in Chinese restaurants, but this became his career. Liu bought a restaurant of his own in Berkeley, in part because owning a business helped expedite permanent US residency. "That was when my daughter was born, in 1978. I remember I had to make her a little cradle in the storage room on the shelf. I'd put her to sleep and help in the kitchen," recalls his wife, Rebecca

Liu. Eventually the couple were offered the chance to own a restaurant in Portland, Lung Fung, a better business opportunity because the Bay Area was saturated with Chinese restaurants. The family relocated to Oregon and eventually owned numerous restaurants here, including the eponymous Liu Chi in downtown's Jackson Tower.

In the eighties, the couple became active in the Chinese Consolidated Benevolent Association; Chi spoke both Cantonese and Mandarin, giving him a role as translator and connector. When discussing how to improve the neighborhood, "they talked about needing a gate, and my husband said that's a good idea because everybody would know it's Chinatown," Rebecca Liu remembers. "Taiwan has a lot of those gate designs, and my husband was able to use his connections to bring an architect who had designed a lot of Chinese-style gates."

To assemble Portland's Chinatown Gateway, a team of workers came from Taiwan, staying in the Liu family's home for the duration. Liu Chi convinced a local Chinatown accountant to give up his office next to the gate's construction site so the building materials could be stored there. For the gate's dedication, he borrowed the San Francisco Chinatown's 132-foot dragon costume as centerpiece of a parade, renting a container truck and driving it to Portland himself.

While today Old Town Chinatown has lost much of its Chinese population, with residents of Asian ancestry fanning out into the rest of the city (particularly near Southeast Eighty-Second Avenue), the Chinatown Gateway is not the last vestige of Chinese American culture in the neighborhood. "A lot of older Chinese people have stayed in the old Chinatown," Rebecca Liu says. "It used to be they weren't allowed to go to other places; property owners wouldn't sell to Chinese. This became home. And it's important to keep this Chinatown going."

Before moving on, I want to point out a sign for the Chinese restaurant Hung Far Low, one block north of the Chinatown Gate on a boarded-up building at Fourth Avenue and Couch Street. It's a fun piece of kitsch, with the restaurant's name written vertically between the words CHOP SUEY and COCKTAILS and a pagoda at the top. Hung Far Low (Cantonese for "Red Flower Restaurant") operated from this location from 1928 to

2005, a lengthy run for an industry in which 80 percent of businesses fail within five years of opening.

What makes me smile, though, is not necessarily the sign itself but knowing that, in 2010, the Hung Far Low sign was brought out of storage, restored, and rehung on the building's corner to mark the opening of *another* restaurant, Ping (located here until 2013). Ping's owners, John and Janet Jay, Kurt Huffman, and chef Andy Ricker, erected only a small sign for their own establishment. They knew the Hung Far Low sign was something more: a cultural artifact and a reminder of the neighborhood's vibrant past. Many Chinese restaurants were located in this neighborhood during the latter half of the twentieth century: Fong Chong, House of Louie, Rickshaw Charlie's, Great China, Tuck Lung. But how many business owners would be willing to erect a much bigger sign for the departed business than for their own?

John Jay, whose wonderful art-and-artifact-filled Studio J occupies the second floor of a nearby former warehouse at Fifth and Couch, is just that kind of person. Now an executive with the Japanese clothing brand Uniqlo, in the early 2000s when I got to know him, Jay was the executive creative director for advertising agency Wieden + Kennedy, but he always seemed more passionate about supporting arts and culture. "Everything we do has a cultural context," Jay told me for a 2005 *Oregon Business* profile. "We have to be connected to not just advertising and media and corporate people, but to the people making culture move. Far too often, advertisers are observers in the culture, not participants. You need to get your hands dirty and live it yourself."

My next stop, the **Society Hotel** (203 NW Third Avenue), is part of the city's greatest architectural heritage: the cast-iron era of the late nineteenth century. After the Industrial Revolution, iron became relatively inexpensive, both as a structural support and for exterior ornamentation: balconies, fences, and especially decorative façades. Because Portland became a prosperous economic port in these years, its ambitiously decorative cast-iron-fronted buildings were rivaled in number only by San Francisco and New York City's SoHo neighborhood. I love the cast-iron buildings of Old Town Chinatown, both the remaining ones and those I've only seen in photos. While the Society Hotel is far from the most ornate local cast-iron building, today it's looking better than ever thanks to a 2015 renovation, which also provided seismic stabilization.

Originally known as the Mariners Building, it was constructed in 1881 by the Seaman's Friends Society, as a safe haven for itinerant sailors. In those days, many ship captains colluded with hotels to lure sailors into debt, necessitating their continuing loyalty to the job. The Mariners Building became a trustworthy place for sailors to stay the night. It was successful enough that, ten years after completion, the building's first three floors were lifted up to create a new ground floor.

In the early twentieth century, the Mariners Building was bought by Japanese-immigrant owners and was rebranded as the California Hotel. Three decades later, with the internment of Japanese American citizens during World War II, the hotel changed hands again, becoming property of the Chinese American Citizens Alliance. For many years, it served as a Chinese community dance hall. Between 1975 and 2015, the building was mostly unoccupied, save for several weeks in 1990, while serving as a location for an Alan Parker–directed Hollywood romance called *Come See the Paradise*, starring Dennis Quaid and Tamlyn Tomita.

In 2015 the Mariners Building was renovated into the Society Hotel by Integrate Architecture for owners Jonathan Cohen, Jesse Burke, Matt Siegel, and Gabe Genauer. "I thought, 'Old Town Chinatown is the only part of town that makes sense to me,'" Siegel remembers. "This is the one spot in the city where the existing buildings actually have character and stories. That is really what I like to use as the basis for any project: What is the building's story, and how do we continue it on?" At least one local developer warned Siegel not to invest here. "He said, 'Do it somewhere else. It's a losing cause here in Old Town. It's not going to get better,'" Siegel recalls. "Like the young ignoramuses we were, we said, 'You're old school, we're new school. It's going to change.' I think we were both right, as it turns out. He certainly had a point. For some reason, Old Town seems to be the most difficult spot to keep a positive trend going. But I don't think that gritty is necessarily a bad thing. I think if everything was super-polished, then it wouldn't have the flavor that an authentic, 150-year-old part of town should have."

The Society Hotel was renovated on a tight budget, with Siegel acting as general contractor and all four owners contributing labor. Over 1 million pounds of new concrete foundations and walls were added to bolster the original brick structure. Today, the hotel features an inviting wide-open lobby with natural light pouring in from storefront windows. The building's original balustraded staircase remains, as do additional interior details like the rooms' transom windows. Original wood studs were used to fabricate benches, and original doors were transformed into wall panels at the reception desk. The classic cast-iron, brick, and stucco exterior was also fully preserved. Upper floors were left almost completely untouched, exposing not only the original brick walls but a host of artifacts they found, from old newspapers (some of which were framed and hung in the rooms) to roller skates and even a large jug of wine hidden in the floor during Prohibition. They also found a message scribbled on one upstairs wall from generations ago: "The Frisco Kid stopped here . . . headed south."

The Society Hotel was closed for nearly a year from 2020 to 2021 because of the COVID-19 pandemic. Though Old Town, like much of the central city, has struggled to rebound, the hotel's owners have persevered. "Old Town has always wrestled with what its identity is. It's a place of many different communities who have called home here, and it's been a very transitional place," says Jonathan Cohen, who today manages the Society Hotel with his wife, Jesse Burke. "Just everyone trying to lay claim to a little piece of the American dream. But if there's anything we've learned from the pandemic, I think it highlighted for people how much we need each other. We're social creatures, and even though sometimes it's easier to stare at a screen all day long, it's not the same as the conversation we're having in person right now."

Before crossing Third Avenue, I pause to let a bicyclist zoom past me in the bike lane by the curb. I notice myself gazing not at the spandex-clad cyclist but instead at his shadow cast by the late-afternoon sun, gliding down the block. It reminds me of a favorite description in Homer's *The Iliad*: of a flying spear's shadow moving across the ground. It's a small moment of beauty, yet the brick apartment building I'm headed to next, **Lyndon Musolf Manor** (216 NW Third Avenue), is actually drab and plain compared to Old Town's cast-iron architecture. However, it's worth stopping here to commemorate two very different heroic figures.

Completed in 1910 as the Foster Hotel, this was an affordable place to live for Japanese immigrants and first-generation Japanese Americans. In the 1940s, a young attorney named Minoru Yasui resided here and operated a small law practice. A native of Hood River, Oregon, he'd been the first person of Japanese American descent to graduate from the University of Oregon's law school in 1939. After the Pearl Harbor attack in December 1941, Yasui, who was also a second lieutenant in the US Army's Infantry Reserve, reported for duty but was not allowed to join. A few months later, General John L. DeWitt of the Western Defense Command issued a curfew ordering all persons of Japanese ancestry (as well as German and Italian nationals) in Pacific Coast states to remain in their homes between 8 p.m. and 6 a.m. Then in February 1942, President Franklin Roosevelt issued Executive Order 9066, authorizing these same citizens' evacuation and incarceration. "It had in my opinion no basis in law," Yasui explained in a 1983 interview. "This certainly strengthened my resolve. . . . I knew that we had to protest this. Because what is done to the least of us can be done to all of us."

*Lyndon Musolf Manor*

On the evening of March 28, 1942, Yasui waited at his Foster Hotel unit until the curfew, then began walking up and down Third Avenue, intentionally seeking to be arrested. Approaching a police officer, "I had my birth certificate with me that proved that I was a person of Japanese ancestry," he recalled. "I asked the officer to arrest me and the officer said, 'Look, you'll get in trouble. Go on, run along home.' That certainly didn't serve my purposes. So I went down to the Second Avenue police station. The sergeant obliged me, and he threw me into the drunk tank." An *Oregon Journal* headline two days later read, "Jap Leader Here Paid by Tokyo," with federal authorities erroneously suggesting that Yasui had acted in cahoots with the Japanese government, based on his having worked for the Japanese consulate in Chicago.

Sentenced to a year in jail, Yasui spent nine months in solitary confinement at the Multnomah County Courthouse, while his appeal made its way to the US Supreme Court. Meanwhile, his family in Hood River was sent to the Tule Lake internment camp in California, among the 120,000 US citizens of Japanese ancestry forcibly displaced. On June 21, 1943, the Supreme Court ruled that while Yasui should not lose his US citizenship, his rights could be overridden in time of war. After Yasui's initial sentence ended, he was transferred to the Minidoka War Relocation Center in Idaho and remained there until 1944; upon release he moved to Denver, establishing a long and decorated legal career, including as executive director of the city's Human Right's Commission.

In 1984, Yasui filed a motion in federal district court requesting his conviction be reversed and his indictment dismissed because of unconstitutional governmental misconduct. The court vacated his conviction but declined to address the unconstitutionality claims. Yasui's case was waiting to be heard in the Ninth Circuit Court of Appeals when he died in 1986. In 2015, President Barack Obama posthumously awarded Yasui the Presidential Medal of Freedom, the first ever given to an Oregonian. In 2021, Yasui's former jail cell was relocated from the Multnomah County Courthouse to the Japanese American Museum of Oregon on Second Avenue and restored over several months for display by artist Brian Borrello.

On Lyndon Musolf Manor's ground floor is the Darcelle XV Showplace nightclub and cabaret, its marquee reading FEMALE

IMPERSONATORS. The business was founded by Walter Cole, better known as Darcelle XV, who in 2016 was certified by the Guinness Book of World Records as the world's oldest drag queen. Darcelle's odyssey had begun nearly a half century earlier, after purchasing the Demas Tavern on this site in 1967. "I didn't have a two-day plan," Darcelle told *The Oregonian*'s Lee Williams in 2017. "I thought, 'What have I done?' But that didn't last long."

In 1969 Darcelle made a first foray into female impersonation, taking this stage name, which honored French singer and actress Denise Darcelle. The "XV" suffix came in 1972, when Darcelle was elected Rose Empress XV for 1973 by the International Imperial Court System (one of the oldest and largest LGBT nonprofit organizations), which historically held drag balls that, each year, crowned a queen. At the end of the yearlong reign, on New Year's Eve, Demas Tavern was renamed Darcelle XV Showplace, continuing as a Portland fixture for nearly a half century. In 2020, it became the first Oregon business designated a national historic site for its place in LGBTQ history. As its application explains, the cabaret "reflects the improvised, low-budget, and self-reliant illusion of glamour that resulted from its development during this era when drag was celebrated mostly behind closed doors due to gay discrimination and the threat of harassment." Darcelle XV passed away in 2023.

The building was renamed Lyndon Musolf Manor in 1998, to honor the founding board president of Innovative Housing, Inc., the nonprofit organization that has operated from here since 1991. It provides ninety-five studio apartments for elderly and disabled individuals with very low incomes. Not only do we need Lyndon Musolf Manor today, we need a hundred more.

The fulcrum of this walk, from where I turn toward the riverfront for good and head south, is the **Lan Su Chinese Garden** (239 NW Everett Street), which opened in 2000 as the Portland Classical Chinse Garden. Occupying a full city block between Second and Third Avenues, Flanders and Glisan Streets, Lan Su is said to be the most authentic Suzhou-style garden in North America, almost completely hand-built by a team of more than seventy artisans from Suzhou, China. Its 40,000 square feet include more than four hundred species of plants, from orchids and water plants to perennials and bamboo trees. The sound of its cascading water, like at the Keller Fountain, drowns the noise of the city. I always remember its cobblestone path, because once when I visited Lan Su with a friend, writer Brett Campbell, he took his shoes off in order to feel the stones with his bare feet.

Lan Su's opening culminated a decade-long effort led by city council member Mike Lindberg, developer Bill Naito, and Mayor Vera Katz. Lindberg first had the idea in 1986 while visiting

*Lan Su Chinese Garden*

Suzhou to finalize a new sister-city relationship with Portland. The delegation was taken to an event at Suzhou's Master of the Nets Garden, a UNESCO World Heritage Site dating to the year 1140. "It was an overwhelming emotional experience," Lindberg told *The Oregonian*'s Randy Gragg. "I thought to myself, 'We've got a great Japanese garden [the Portland Japanese Garden west of downtown]. Why not build a great Chinese garden?'"

A site in Old Town was preferred, given the neighborhood's association with the Chinese American community. The local gas company, Northwest Natural, ultimately agreed to give up the surface parking lot across from its headquarters. Bill Naito, whose family company owned several nearby buildings, agreed to throw his support behind the project. Naito and his brother Sam, who had led the revival of Old Town after the end of World War II by renovating several historic buildings in the neighborhood, were of Japanese ancestry, but that didn't stop Bill Naito in particular from getting behind the project.

"In his mind, it was a companion to Pioneer Courthouse Square," recalls Bill Naito's granddaughter and biographer, Erica Naito-Campbell. "It was a place where people in that part of the city could come together and share an experience. Once he heard about it, he said, 'Yeah, obviously, why wouldn't I want to support that?' The fact that it was Chinese, that didn't matter to him." And, Naito-Campbell adds with a laugh, in reference to the brothers' rivalry, "My grandfather and my great uncle never worked on the same project; that was how they kept sane. My great uncle Sam was heavily involved in the Portland Japanese Garden, so my grandfather wasn't ever going to touch that with a ten-foot pole. But he loved gardens. The idea of a Chinese garden was perfect to him." Bill Naito engaged in a kind of shuttle diplomacy between business and city leaders to elicit support and raise funds for the garden. Though he would not live to see its completion, before Naito died in 1996, Mayor Katz promised him that the garden would be completed.

Walking Lan Su's pathway today, I pass through a series of pavilions, each festooned with poetic carvings and, like the cyclist a few minutes ago, casting long shadows. One carving features a poem by sixteenth-century poet Wen Zhengming that speaks to Lan Su's role: "Most cherished in this mundane world is a place without traffic. Truly in the midst of the city there can be mountain and forest."

While hand craftmanship makes it special, the garden still had to meet local building codes, despite not having contemporary blueprints. But Robertson Merryman Barnes, the city's first major architecture firm with all-female ownership, had developed a reputation for being good listeners and collaborators. "We got the job because we told them we saw ourselves as the watchdogs of the Suzhou Institute's design," recalls co-founder Linda Barnes. A few days after her firm received the commission, "I was in a conference room with the structural engineer going, 'How is this wall connected? How do you support these big stones?' We wound up having so many calls to China in the middle of the night, trying to figure out the details."

Barnes and her business partner, architect Nancy Merryman, also acted as cultural translators. "The idea of taking extra steps to make the garden wheelchair accessible was something the Suzhou team did not understand at all," remembers Merryman. Other times, the Portland architects had to infer was what wasn't being said. "You'd have these meetings where you thought everyone was aligned and that they'd agreed to create a new set of drawings. But the new drawings would never come," Merryman explains. "They'd say 'yes' even if they meant 'no.' There wasn't an exact word in Mandarin for 'no,' and it would be rude for them to say, 'We can't meet that deadline.' The drawings just wouldn't show up, and you'd realize they'd never truly agreed." There was so much back and forth that when Merryman and Barnes calculated their hours worked compared to their fee, their firm's profit was only about one dollar.

Even so, the two teams came together cordially. "There were always these cultural exchanges," Merryman recalls. "The design team would come from Suzhou for a big dinner with all of us. They didn't like any of the Chinese food in town, so they brought their own chef, who cooked a huge, incredibly delicious meal. I remember at the end, there was all this food left on one platter: tripe that the Americans didn't want to eat. But it was worth something spending that time together and beginning to make friends."

In 2000, I got to meet Lan Su's lead designer, Kuang Zhen, as well as the institute's director, He Fenghung, when they spoke at a lecture I'd helped organize, while working at the local American Institute of Architects chapter. Afterward, they gave me a small book of Chinese ink wash paintings, a treasured keepsake that sits on my office bookshelf as I write this. And a quarter century after its opening, Lan Su remains a delight. More than any other central-city park, this is a true destination: not just a place you wander into impromptu on the way to someplace else, but where people meet with intent, to temporarily escape city life and regain a sense of wonder.

As I approach the home stretch, it's time to refuel once more, this time with a double espresso at Café United near First and Couch. The colorful interior is fun, as is the café's logo, a kind of disco ball made up of international flags. Besides—I want to be fully alert and caffeinated as I show you some truly gorgeous cast-iron waterfront buildings.

Just across the street, is the **Blagen Block** (30 NW First Avenue), a veritable wedding cake of ornamentation and color, designed in an Italianate style by Warren H. Williams. Completed in 1888 for the W. C. Noon company, makers of bags, tents, awnings, and sails, this might be the prettiest building in the city. The Blagen's ground floor is lined with a succession of T-shaped columns and beams shouldering three-foot arches, said

*Blagen Block*

to be a Victorian interpretation of late Baroque Corinthian order. Its pilasters are decorated with acanthus leaves, stars, stripes, arrows, and laurel leaves. Above the capitals are projecting lions' heads, the last of which can also be found at the fourth floor and in the pediments of the roof's cornice. Each floor has a different arch form at the windows and a different series of details.

The Blagen Block was named for its builder, Niels Jensen Blagen, who emigrated from Denmark to the United States in 1871 and arrived in Portland six years later by way of Astoria, where he had been a successful commercial fisherman. Turning to general contracting, his company first built the Portland Flouring Mills on the east side of the Willamette River in Albina for financier William S. Ladd, then a series of railroad lines between Puget Sound and the Midwest, including some treacherous crossings through the Cascade mountains. The Blagen Block, its intricate façade notwithstanding, was comparatively easy-peasy.

Warren Williams was one of this city's most accomplished nineteenth-century architects, although his time here was relatively short. After beginning his career in San Francisco, Williams came to Portland in 1873, perhaps sensing opportunity after a large fire that year had destroyed twenty-two blocks along the west side of the Willamette River. Initially with partner Elwood Burton and later on his own, Williams designed several exceptional cast-iron commercial buildings in the central city, such as 1879's Union Block and 1884's Cambridge Block, both demolished in the mid-twentieth century, as well as 1882's Morris Marks House, which still stands after being moved in 2017. Williams also designed 1874's Portland's Good Samaritan Hospital and 1885's Villard Hall at the University of Oregon in Eugene.

I used to regularly visit the Blagen Block in the early 2000s while it was occupied by an advertising-agency client I was freelancing for. The building's exposed brick and copious natural light made being there more pleasant than the typical sterile, corporate office building. In 2014 this building was leased by the vacation-rental company Airbnb, its open office configuration by Bora gaining national notoriety. But like so many commercial tenants, Airbnb left center-city Portland during the COVID-19 pandemic. Yet no matter the tenant or even a long vacancy, all it takes is a quick glance to see what an enduring treasure the Blagen Block is.

*White Stag Block*

Next door is another cast-iron gem, the **White Stag Block** (70 NW Couch Street), which is actually a trio of renovated, interconnected buildings—the Bickel Building, the Skidmore Block Building, and the White Stag Building—that from 2008 to 2024 were home to the University of Oregon's small Portland campus. (It has since relocated to Northeast Portland.) Bill and Sam Naito, through their Norcrest company, are credited with saving these buildings in the mid-twentieth century when so many other cast-iron beauties met the wrecking ball.

The Gothic-style Bickel Building, facing the river on Naito Parkway, was designed by Justus Krumbein and completed in 1883 for German candymaker Frederick Bickel, but for two years it also housed Portland City Council, while City Hall was being completed. To my eyes, the Bickel is the most beautiful of the three that make up the White Stag Block, with its geometry of exposed pilasters and of columns marking ten bays along its ground-floor Naito Parkway frontage, as well as engraved leaves on its pilasters. The circa-1889 Skidmore Block, at First Avenue and Burnside Street, was designed in an Italianate style by William McCaw as a warehouse for Charles Sitton and named for Sitton's late business partner and benefactor, Stephen Skidmore.

The White Stag Building at Northwest Naito Parkway and West Burnside Street, dating to 1907 and originally known as the Hirsch-Weiss Building, is this block's largest and the most industrial in character, with a brick and concrete façade. It originally housed Max and Leopold Hirsch's Willamette Tent and Awning Company, which in the 1930s changed its name to White Stag after Max's son Harold Hirsch, an avid skier, convinced them to begin making ski apparel. The new name was based on an English translation of the German names Weis and Hirsch.

The White Stag building is best known for the neon PORTLAND OREGON sign on its roof, an enduring civic icon that has had four different iterations. The sign was created in 1940 as an advertisement for White Satin Sugar, then occupying the building, its name comprising the sign's original script displayed within a neon outline of the state of Oregon. In 1950, animation was added to show the shape of the state filling with sugar. In 1957, after White Satin abandoned the sign, the script was changed to White Stag as that company moved in. The silhouette of a vaulting deer was added, and beginning in 1959, each Christmas season a glowing red nose was illuminated, evoking Rudolph the Red-Nosed Reindeer. The building was sold in 1973 to the Naito family, who for nearly a quarter century kept the sign going even though the White Stag company was long gone. But in 1997 the script was changed to MADE IN OREGON, after the Naitos' retail chain of the same name. The University of Oregon, after taking ownership in 2008, sought a text-change to its name, which was discouraged by local leaders (perhaps protective of nearby Portland State University). Thus the City of Portland instead purchased the sign outright in 2010, enacting the PORTLAND OREGON script.

Bill and Sam Naito, whose company owned these buildings for a half century, helped save and redevelop not just the White Stag Block but also about twenty buildings in Old Town and downtown. Bill Naito even coined the name Old Town, to replace Skid Row. The brothers were US-born children of Japanese immigrants, who grew up mostly in Southeast Portland. In 1942, when Bill was seventeen and Sam twenty-one, Executive Order 9066 was signed by President Roosevelt, changing their lives. The family was forced to either find residence outside this region or be placed in internment camps. The Naitos had relatives in Salt Lake City, so they avoided the latter fate. But their father's Japanese-import business was ruined. "You just feel really like you've been betrayed," Sam Naito recalled in a 2003 oral-history interview for the Oregon Nikkei Endowment. "You were told all along that you are an American citizen, you were born here, you're just as much an American citizen as a German second-generation born here or Italian born here. . . . And so it was very difficult. Many of us became very bitter."

After Sam and Bill's World War II service, they operated the Norcrest China Company, a successor to their father's business, importing dinnerware and souvenirs from Japan. By 1962 they bought their first Old Town buildings: the circa-1906 Fleischner-Mayer building, a handsome brick warehouse, and then the circa-1895 Globe Hotel across the street, anchored by their Import Plaza store. The brothers quickly saw potential in real estate redevelopment and went on to purchase and restore nineteenth-century cast-iron buildings like 1885's Merchants Hotel and the aforementioned Bickel Block. "Everybody told us, 'You are crazy, and it's never going to work,'" Sam Naito recalled to Jane Comerford in a 2003 Densho Digital Archives interview. "Even our real estate man who sold the property says, 'Those people are fools thinking they're going to open up a retail store down here in Skid Row and think that anybody would come in. We put out the newspaper ad . . . and we were just packed." Besides Import Plaza, which my mom took me to when I was a child, the Naitos also operated stores like How Sweet It Is, Old Town Emporium, and eventually the popular Made In Oregon chain.

The Naitos' office, on the second floor of the White Stag, was a cinematic scene. "There were no partitions: just three rows of desks that spanned the floor," recalls Erica Naito-Campbell, Bill Naito's granddaughter and author of his biography, *Portland's Audacious Champion*. "My grandpa's desk was in the middle. He put in these giant rearview mirrors to keep an eye on the employees without turning his head. My great-uncle Sam was at a desk up to the right. They could hear each other, and what was happening with meetings at each other's desks, but they were not next to each other, which was important."

Entering the space, there would be the constant sound of a money-counting machine for the Naitos' retail businesses. There were scores of desks but no receptionist. "You'd stand there and eventually somebody might see you, and just yell across the rows of desks, 'Bill, someone here to see you!'" says Naito-Campbell, who spent much of her childhood in this office, where employees routinely brought their kids. "Women had their babies, and in a couple weeks they'd be back at Norcrest with a bassinet at their desk. If you had a phone call, the woman at the next desk would take care of your baby."

All the while, some of the city's most powerful politicians and business leaders would be streaming through to see Bill and Sam Naito. Inevitably, they would see pinned to a column behind Bill's desk a poster of Executive Order 9066. "Every time you sat down for a meeting with Bill Naito, you saw it," Naito-Campbell says. "It was not subtle. But he would never point it out to you. I consider this part of the way Portland handles race. They don't like it if you aggressively talk about race. But if someone saw it and said, 'What's that poster?', he would tell you. He would talk about what it was like as a high schooler to experience that level of institutionalized degradation. That's how he kept it fresh in his mind, and that was what was driving him." Executive Order 9066 was for Bill Naito a kind of caustic Rosebud, the obsession and fuel for an ambitious man, almost like Charles Foster Kane's lost childhood sled in *Citizen Kane*. Yet Bill Naito didn't seem bitter. He was a civic booster who helped rally community support for restoring landmarks like Central Library and Union Station, and building beloved new public spaces like Pioneer Courthouse Square, Waterfront Park, and the Lan Su Chinese Garden.

When the Naitos began buying property in Old Town, homelessness was rampant, yet Bill Naito never judged. "I never heard him say one negative thing about homeless people, ever," his granddaughter adds. "He had been mentored by [Nobel Prize–winning economist] Milton Friedman at the University of Chicago, who had a very radical economic view of the world, in which the free market solves everything. One of the upsides was that there was never moral judgment. Everything had an economic reason, not a moral one."

As with Pietro Belluschi, who died a few years before I moved to Portland, I feel like I've spent my career chasing Bill Naito and his legacy. He passed away in 1996, just before my arrival. Yet I'd like to think our paths crossed or at least that we occupied the same building complex at the same time, back in the seventies, when my mom and I were at Import Plaza, perhaps while he was at his desk upstairs.

In 2007, developer Art DeMuro and his company, Venerable Group, bought and renovated the White Stag Block. As workers stripped away a faux brick over-cladding from the 1950s, they discovered remnants of iron detailing that once graced the façade and decided to restore its original style. They joined these adjacent buildings with a new atrium, where the patina of formerly exterior brick walls can be seen as part of interior space. It made a vibrantly urban yet historically rich campus for the University of Oregon, and I remember coming here numerous times to see the work of its architecture students or meet professors. Now that the UO has moved across town, I come here less often, and here today there are noticeably fewer people outside. But the beauty of these buildings transcends.

Before heading back into downtown, I want to briefly cross Naito Parkway into the northernmost portion of (and a later addition to) Tom McCall Waterfront Park. I'll talk about the park itself later in this chapter, but right now my focus is the **Japanese American Historical Plaza** (Waterfront Park at NW Couch Street), with its blend of public art, landscape, and storytelling amid a row of cherry trees. The park was dedicated in 1990, and its thirteen engraved stones of basalt and granite, designed by landscape architect Robert Murase, tell how persons of Japanese ancestry were incarcerated during World War II. The plaza's centermost stone lists the ten internment camps. The base of this stone is surrounded by flagstones with jagged sides laid out in irregular patterns reflecting the broken dreams of the internees. Other stones are inscribed with poems composed by Oregonians Lawson Inada, Shizue Iwatsuki, Masaki Kinoshita, and Hisako Saito. A bronze plaque on the last stone has excerpts from the Civil Liberties Act of 1988, which includes an apology for Japanese Americans' unlawful imprisonment.

Murase, a San Francisco native and third-generation Japanese American, had as a young child been interned with his family during World War II. Later, after a landscape-architecture career that began as an intern for the great Lawrence Halprin, then continued with a decade spent living and practicing in Japan, he moved to Oregon in 1977, first to teach at the University of Oregon in Eugene and later relocating to Portland, founding his own firm in 1982. He proposed and designed the plaza while attending a Day of Remembrance memorial, which Japanese American communities hold throughout the country to remember February 19, 1942, the day President Franklin D. Roosevelt signed Executive Order 9066. Encouraged by Bill Naito, and with funding from the Japanese American Citizens League (for which the Naito family are longtime benefactors), Murase had his design accepted as part of the Waterfront Park expansion in 1988.

The location of the Japanese American Historical Plaza is also the place where, a half century earlier, Portlanders once welcomed the Nazis. In 1936, at a dock here, a crowd gathered to greet the German naval cruiser *Emden*. It was three years after Adolph Hitler's National Socialist party had taken power in Germany. An *Oregonian* editorial described the occasion as a demonstration of "peace on earth, goodwill to men." When the local chapter of the American League Against War and Fascism's members planned to protest the Nazi ship's mooring, the Portland police arrested them preemptively for failing to obtain a license. The protesters remained jailed for the duration of the *Emden*'s weeklong stay, then were released without charge. Portland mayor Joseph K. Carson, a World War I veteran, visited with the *Emden*'s officers, the local Chamber of Commerce held a banquet in their honor, and the ship's chaplain officiated a local wedding and christened a local baby. Two days before the *Emden* departed, its crew marched through downtown Portland. Out of deference, the German soldiers refrained from goose-stepping.

That the Japanese incarceration is commemorated on the same site where members of Hitler's armed forces once set foot in Portland is, in my mind, not just a coincidence, but a reminder that while conflicts like World War II can be taken as a morality play pitting good and evil, in reality any democratic society can succumb to and be seduced by authoritarianism. Standing at this plaza as evening approaches, I think of my late grandfathers and what they fought for: Ted Lehman, who as a US Army quartermaster under General Patton was part of the D-Day invasion of 1944 as well as the Battle of the Bulge, and the aforementioned Donald Libby, who as a US Navy chief machinist's mate participated in 1942's Battle of the Coral Sea and, at war's end, passed through atomic-bomb-ravaged Nagasaki.

### *Bridge to Bridge*

I was inspired to write this book partly by the pace of buildings being demolished over my twenty-five-plus years here, but now something bigger is about to be torn down and, admittedly in this case, for good reason. My next destination, the **Burnside Bridge** (Naito Parkway at W Burnside Street), is within a few years scheduled to be replaced for the second time in Portland's history. The city needs a bridge that's able to withstand the large Cascadia Subduction Zone earthquake predicted for this region, and during such an event, it's anticipated that all the existing downtown bridges would collapse. Planning, engineering studies, and design for the new Burnside Bridge have been under way for several years, but as I write this, on what was supposed to be the eve of construction, the project has been delayed until at least 2028, with Multnomah County citing "significant uncertainty at the federal level."

The first Burnside Bridge was completed in 1894, three years after what had been known as B Street was renamed Burnside. The moniker was to honor not the Civil War general Ambrose Burnside, but local businessman Dan Wyman Burnside, who had campaigned for dredging the Willamette River in 1866 to make Portland a viable deepwater port, enabling the city's subsequent economic growth. That first Burnside Bridge was a swing-span, accommodating river traffic by twisting half of its center span 90 degrees to make way for passing ships. I remember seeing a 1920 photo looking across the swung-open span during a bridge opening, a line of early-era automobiles waiting to cross; the gap made it look like the bridge was only half-completed. After this bridge was decommissioned, two of its spans were reused, not for the next Burnside Bridge, however, but for the Bull Run River Bridge and the Sandy River Bridge in Clackamas County.

The second, and current, Burnside Bridge was completed in 1926, but in a slightly different location, after what was known as the "Rotten Bridge" scandal. Three county commissioners backed by the Ku Klux Klan had awarded the bridge contract at $500,000 more than the lowest bid (about $8.9 million in 2024) and moved the bridge location in order to sell the original bridge's land and make a profit. The commissioners were recalled, but the new bridge construction went ahead on the adjacent site. It was initially designed by Kansas City engineer Ira G. Hedrick in partnership with local engineer Robert E. Kremers, using a double-leaf bascule lift mechanism (two counterweighted spans that rotate upward to open) designed by Joseph Strauss, who later designed San Francisco's Golden Gate Bridge. However, Hedrick and Kremers were eventually replaced by New York City engineer Gustav Lindenthal, who also supervised the bridge's construction. Though largely flat, this new Burnside Bridge was distinctive, thanks largely to its pair of octagonal turreted towers serving as operator's houses for the bascule lift span. For this Burnside Bridge's first quarter century, streetcars passed over it every few minutes, until removal in 1950.

The Burnside is also noteworthy for the placemaking beneath its bridgeheads. On the east side is the Burnside Skate Park, an initially unauthorized concrete construction begun in 1990 that was eventually accepted by city leaders, as it became a landmark internationally renowned among skateboarders. Beneath the west bridgehead for thirty-four years was the location of Portland Saturday Market, founded in 1974 and credited with revitalizing Old Town. Public markets are so often the beating heart of cities, full of food and crafts for sale from scores of vendors. It was enough to attract my mom, who would drive us from McMinnville to Portland to visit Saturday Market in the late 1970s, providing, along with The Galleria and Civic Auditorium, my first memories in the city.

Saturday Market was founded by artists Sheri Teasdale and Andrea Scharf, who were inspired by a market in Eugene of the same name. While living in Portland, Teasdale and her husband had been driving the 110 miles south to Eugene on weekends to operate a small grilled-kabob stand. "But then they had a child and the whole idea of driving down there didn't work anymore," recalls Scharf. "We were sitting in her kitchen and I just said, 'Portland needs a market.' We just looked at each other and said, 'Let's do it.'"

Scharf and Teasdale began lobbying civic and business leaders to consider an open-air market featuring handmade food and crafts. Most at City Hall were uninterested, but Bill Naito listened. "He was chewing on his old cigar and he was just funky, wearing this loose old cardigan sweater. We were very nervous," Scharf remembers. "He tossed the proposal on the desk and said, 'I'll tell you what I'm going to do.' He was so smart. He knew that area needed something that would bring people down there, despite of all the bums." Naito let them use the parking lot of the family's Fleischner-Meyer Building, across from the Naitos' Import Plaza store, which would benefit from the market's foot traffic if it proved successful. That first year, however, the market was slow. "But eventually people started showing up and on it went," Scharf recalls. "It became its own thing." Saturday Market moved to a site under the Burnside Bridge in 1976, where it stayed until establishment of a new home in 2009, under a canopy at Waterfront Park and in Ankeny Plaza.

The new Burnside Bridge design, by British firm BEAM Architects and as yet unbuilt, is unlike any other bridge in Portland, not only for its unusual inverted-Y variant of the cable-stay bridge type, but also because of its asymmetry. Early in the bridge-replacement process overseen by Multnomah County, the National Park Service ruled that because of the bridge's proximity to the Skidmore-Old Town Historic District, no above-deck structure should be built on the west side of the bridge, because it would violate the district's height limits and block views of the historic buildings here. So an inverted-Y tower, once built, would be erected only on the east side of the bridge, and east of the Willamette River itself, because the bridge must also span Interstate 5 and an adjacent railroad on the east side. In effect, the Burnside may seem more like a bridge over the freeway than over the water. Yet the inverted-Y form would make the most of the bridge's asymmetry. Compared to a tied-arch bridge, the other type Multnomah County considered, the inverted-Y is not only a more uncommon bridge type but substantially taller, essentially celebrating the asymmetry rather than minimizing the effect.

Yet as BEAM Architects partner Keith Brownlie reminded me in a 2024 *Oregon ArtsWatch* interview, bridges aren't designed according to how they will look from afar. "We design journeys," he said. "It's all about putting yourself into the seats of those bridge users and saying, 'Where are the high points? What are the objectives? Where can we pause? What happens when you're stopped and this bridge opens? What's your experience like?' That builds up from something simple into quite a complex net of experiences." And this is not just any Portland span. "The Burnside Bridge is particularly significant," Brownlie added, "because it's the pivot of the city. It's the spine. It's what the whole city folds out from. So I couldn't think of a more important bridge location than that one."

On Naito Parkway beside the Burnside Bridge is the **Mercy Corps Building** (45 SW Ankeny Street), a hybrid of old and new architecture by Hacker Architects completed in 2009 for the worldwide humanitarian organization. Although from Naito Parkway this appears to be an entirely new metal and glass structure, it's an expansion of the adjacent circa-1892 Packer-Scott Building: not a fanciful cast-iron gem, but a former warehouse that had stood the test of time and, through its weathered brick, showed it. "The whole face of it was pitted and grooved, almost like a landform," explains Hacker Architects partner David Keltner. "So we did this extensive restoration process of carefully replacing certain bricks and not others." In 2010, Hacker's design was named one of the country's top ten green projects by the American Institute of Architects' Committee on the Environment. More than a third of the building's power comes from alternative energy, and the building uses 75 percent less water than an average office.

Hacker Architects has always been one of my favorite local firms, especially because of its late founder, Thomas Hacker, who possessed both wonderful personal charisma and, as an architect, a gifted touch. Before coming to Oregon from Philadelphia, Hacker had studied under and worked for the great architect Louis Kahn. "I have never lost the deep belief in the power of architecture that he instilled in me," Hacker recalled to me in a 2011 interview. A University of Oregon professor in the 1970s before founding his Portland firm, Hacker was also a mentor to

*Mercy Corps Building*

some of Portland's greatest architects of the succeeding generation, such as Brad Cloepfil, Rick Potestio, and Nancy Merryman, which means that he influenced the city's built environment even beyond his own firm's excellent buildings (including a succession of beautiful local libraries). "Portland has an amazing civic sensibility, and a sensibility about making places in a city that is alive and vibrant and public," he told me. "It's a big deal."

Mercy Corps began in 1979 in Seattle as Save the Refugees, which Dan O'Neil founded to help Cambodian and Vietnamese people fleeing the Vietnam War and its aftermath. A Seattle-area native, O'Neil had first volunteered as a young man in east Africa and the Middle East, including on an Israeli kibbutz during the 1973 Yom Kippur War. "I saw what war did to people and places. It was not a pretty sight," he told me in a 2019 podcast interview. "I wanted my life to be about something larger than me, something humanitarian."

The organization expanded internationally by 1982, and O'Neill was joined by Ellsworth Culver, who initiated a rebranding as Mercy Corps. Now with a greater reach, the organization began humanitarian work around the world. In the 1990s, Mercy Corps aided refugees of the Yugoslavian civil war and the Armenia-Azerbaijan war. At the turn of the twenty-first century it helped earthquake victims in India, refugees of the Iraq War, and victims of the Indian Ocean tsunami that devastated South Asia. Then came aid after Haitian earthquake of 2010, the Syrian civil war from 2012, and the Nepal quake of 2017. In recent years, Mercy Corps' work in Sudan helped feed and support more than 220,000 people.

However, the organization's reputation, reach, and presence have been decimated. Shortly after I interviewed O'Neill in 2019, Culver (who had died in 2005) was posthumously accused by his daughter, Tania Culver Humphrey, of sexual abuse during her childhood. O'Neill, who had known of the allegations since the nineties and demoted Culver but did not fire him, retired. Today a new era is under way, led by CEO Tjada D'Oyen McKenna, who has emphasized aiding victims of climate change as well as refugees of warfare. But in 2025, Mercy Corps was forced to cut more than forty of its sixty aid programs, due to lost federal funding. Even the Mercy Corps building itself has been put up for sale. However, I think a new owner will be attracted to Hacker's architectural binary of historic and contemporary, as well as to this site—a nexus where Old Town and downtown, city and river, bridge and park, all converge.

Beside the Mercy Corps headquarters is also one of the city's most historic public spaces and a marker of our architectural past: **Ankeny Plaza** (18 SW First Avenue). At its east entrance facing Naito Parkway is a row of arch-connected columns salvaged from the demolished Smith & Watson Building, which stood nearby. At the plaza's western edge is a colonnade consisting of cast-iron components salvaged from the demolished north wing of the adjacent New Market Theater building. I can almost imagine Giovanni Paolo Panini or Hubert Robert, the eighteenth- and nineteenth-century painters of decayed Roman ruins, finding inspiration here.

Opened in 1948, Ankeny Plaza was named for one of the city's founding fathers, entrepreneur Alexander P. Ankeny. He arrived in Portland in 1850 and built a house on Oak Street but left just over a year later for Yamhill County. After fighting for the first regiment of the Oregon Mounted Volunteers in the Yakima War (pitting the United States against the Yakama people), Ankeny remained active in Portland, operating a steamboat line taking passengers up and down the Columbia and Snake Rivers. This earned him the funds to build 1872's New Market Theater. Captain Ankeny, as he was commonly known, spent the final two years of his life, from 1989 to 1991, in the Hawthorne Asylum.

Ankeny Plaza's centerpiece is the Skidmore Fountain, dedicated in 1888 and named for local businessman Stephen G. Skidmore, who bequeathed $5,000 in his will for a fountain to provide clean drinking water. Designed by New York sculptor Olin Levi Warner, it was styled after fountains that Skidmore encountered at Versailles palace in France. The Skidmore Fountain's three upper tiers, meant to provide water separately for people, horses, and dogs, rest on a central granite shaft with bronze caryatid figurines holding above them the uppermost bowl, like the mythological figure Atlas bearing the weight of the world. Initially, metal drinking cups were attached by chains to the figurines' heads. For the Skidmore Fountain's opening-day dedication, brewer Henry Weinhard famously offered to run beer through it instead of water. Perhaps that's why the *New York Tribune* suggested the fountain was too fine a work "for a western city with its bewhiskered, bepistoled lot of frontiersmen."

The Skidmore Fountain is associated with author, attorney, and artist C. E. S. Wood, who secured the services of Warner, his friend, and who wrote the inscription at the base of the fountain: "Good citizens are the riches of a city." A true Renaissance man, Wood was described by writer Tim Barnes in *The Oregon Encyclopedia* as "the most influential cultural figure in Portland in the forty years surrounding the turn of the twentieth century." He co-founded the Portland Art Museum, where his paintings are part of the permanent collection, and played a key role in making the Multnomah County Library a free and public institution. Wood counted among his friends authors Mark Twain and John Steinbeck, activist John Reed, attorney Clarence Darrow, filmmaker Charlie Chaplin, and poet Langston Hughes. He was also a progressive activist; in 1908 Wood resigned from the Oregon Bar Association for its refusal to admit a Black attorney. He also spoke out in support of women's suffrage and vocally opposed the US entering World War I. A West Point graduate, Wood first came to Oregon while serving as an army lieutenant in various campaigns against Native American tribes, including the Nez Perce War of 1877, where he recorded and translated Chief Joseph's surrender speech ending with the now-famous words, "I will fight no more forever." It has even been suggested that Wood may have taken liberties with the transcription. In any case, Wood and Chief Joseph became friends.

Facing Ankeny Plaza from the west is one of Portland's finest remaining works of cast-iron architecture: the **New Market Theater** (50 SW Second Avenue), or at least most of it. Completed in 1872, this was once a three-wing complex, but its north wing was demolished in 1956. The theater's architects, Elwood Burton and William Piper, had designed the first Multnomah County Courthouse, an 1866 structure known for its lavish glass dome (it was demolished in 1910). The New Market Theater was modeled after Venice's fifteenth-century Ca' Loredan Vendramin Calergi palace, with Corinthian columns and archways at the entrance giving way to two tiers of arched windows separated by brick and iron pilasters. "We doubt if any city on the Pacific Coast can show anything like a parallel," gushed *The Oregonian* when the building was completed, adding that the New Market Theater "proves conclusively and in the most appreciable manner the rapid strides of our city toward wealth and greatness."

The building was originally known as Ankeny Hall, but became known as the New Market Theater because on its ground floor was the city's first public market, arranged along a 200-foot

*New Market Theater*

arcade lined with twenty-eight marble-clad vendor stalls, while upstairs was the city's first performance venue on the second floor, where a hundred gaslit crystal chandeliers illuminated a 35-foot-high space. Though the building was completed in 1872, the theater's operations were delayed after the Panic of 1873, for another two years. Perhaps appropriately, its first performance was a theatrical production of *Rip Van Winkle*. Among those who took the stage in its first decade were Helen Modjeska, considered US theater's leading female Shakespearean actress of the time, and boxer John L. Sullivan, the last bare-knuckle heavyweight champion. In 1882, the New Market Theater also hosted an inaugural performance by the Portland Orchestral Society, a forerunner of the Oregon Symphony.

The theater's best-known attendee was former president and Civil War general Ulysses S. Grant in 1879. Two years after leaving the White House, as part of a world tour, Grant was in town for a reception held in his honor. But he left the event early to see a play at the New Market Theater called *Ours*, the proceeds from which were being donated to the charitable Hood Orphan Fund, to care for the orphaned children of former Confederate general John Bell Hood. In today's divided times, I can't help but marvel at how the country's most decorated Union Army general came to Portland's New Market Theater to honor one of his old adversaries.

The New Market closed as a performance venue in 1887, just twelve years after its first show, relegated to serving first as a warehouse and later, in the twentieth century, as a parking garage. The building was restored in 1984 as a mixed-use office building under the supervision of architects George "Bing" Sheldon of SERA Architects and George McMath of Allen, McMath and Hawkins. Sheldon in the 1970s chaired the influential Portland Planning Commission and co-founded the housing nonprofit Central City Concern; his firm would go on to lead the restoration of Portland City Hall. McMath, grandson of the city's most acclaimed early twentieth-century architect, A. E. Doyle, was "really the father of preservation in Portland," says architect and author William J. Hawkins III, McMath's former partner. After witnessing the demolition of several historic Old Town buildings in the 1960s, McMath lobbied city council to pass Portland's first historic-landmark protections and establish the Historic Landmarks Commission. "He pushed and pushed for it," Hawkins says. "George was a force." Allen, McMath and Hawkins restored many of Portland's most important historic structures, including the Pioneer Courthouse, the Old Church, and Central Library.

When the two firms went to work restoring the New Market Theater, "It was kind of grim inside: stripped of everything," Hawkins remembers. "Now and then you'd see a fragment of something historic peeking out. But everyone was thinking this would be the anchor project to get the district going again." Cast-iron building materials were no longer being manufactured, so to replicate the façade details, replacements were made from fiberglass, which McMath had first attempted on a restoration of the nearby Powers Building. The New Market Theater's ground floor after restoration became a hub of shops and eateries that seemed to signal better days ahead for this long-downtrodden neighborhood. Today most of those businesses are gone, and a 2016 plan to rebuild this building's north wing was abandoned. Yet the New Market Theater was renovated again in 2019.

Now in the final stretch of this tour, I'm walking near the riverfront along Naito Parkway, renamed from Front Avenue in 1996 for Bill Naito. My mind is on Oregon's beginnings as I come to the city's oldest remaining commercial structure: the **Hallock-McMillan Building** (237 SW Naito Parkway), completed in 1857. The building is named for its architect and builder, respectively, Absalom Hallock and William McMillan, who formed a partnership in 1849. Hallock went on to design eighteen early Portland buildings, while also serving as both county sheriff and a member of Portland City Council.

The Hallock-McMillan Building is also associated with one of the country's most acclaimed twentieth-century photographers: Minor White. A Minnesota native, White settled in Portland after college to start a commercial photography business. In 1938, he began a two-year commission for the Oregon Arts Project (a division of the Works Progress Administration) to document historic downtown buildings near the riverfront, including the Hallock-McMillan. Most of the buildings were scheduled to be demolished for Harbor Drive, but thanks to its location on Front Avenue, slightly away from the path of the new riverfront highway, this one survived. Though this was documentary photography, White's artful eye was clear. In 1942 the Portland Art Museum gave the photographer his first museum exhibition.

*Hallock-McMillan Building*

Later that year, White was drafted into the US Army and World War II, leaving Portland; he later earned a Bronze Star for valor. Moving to New York after the war, White was tutored in photography by the great Alfred Stieglitz before settling in San Francisco, where he achieved stardom. Today his landscape and portrait photography is included in the permanent collections of the Museum of Modern Art in New York and the National Gallery in Washington, DC, among others.

Soon after White documented the Hallock-McMillan, an ill-advised 1940s renovation stripped away its cast-iron façade, making the building look like a small jail. But it remained continuously occupied. A 1953 photo by Marion Dean Ross shows the May Hardware Company located there; a shot from 1976's *The Grand Era of Cast-Iron Architecture* by William J. Hawkins III shows a sign for the International Organization of Masters, Mates & Pilots.

Developer John Russell, who purchased the Hallock-McMillan Building in the late 2000s, had been eyeing it since the mid-1980s, after acquiring the historic and arguably more beautiful cast-iron Feichheimer & White building next door, as well as Dielschneider Building around the corner on Oak Street. "Then the question became obvious," explains Russell, who also developed the PacWest Center near city hall, and had previously led both the Portland Planning Commission and the Portland Development Commission. "How do I get ahold of the building that connects them?"

Although in previous decades historic cast-iron architectural detailing had been replicated using fiberglass, as had been the case for the New Market Theater, the Hallock-McMillan restoration actually went back to actual cast-iron. "The problem with fiberglass is it can be damaged easily," Russell says. His second choice, cement, was more durable but even harder to repair. "At first I said, 'Cast-iron: this old, old, old, technology? You've got to be kidding me.' But it is the best material." Architect-historian William J. Hawkins III worked with Emerick Architects to create new architectural drawings based on historic photos, from which new moldings were created for the cast-iron façade.

Early-evening rush hour traffic is thick along Naito Parkway as I reach the **Morrison Bridge** (SW Naito Parkway at Morrison Street), where the sidewalk ends to make room for

Morrison Bridge

the bridgehead's curving entry and exit ramps. Completed in 1958, this is the third Morrison Bridge on the site, preceded by two wooden swing-style spans. The first, completed in 1887, was Portland's original Willamette River crossing and the longest bridge west of the Mississippi River. The second opened in 1905 and remained in operation until this replacement was completed, necessitating its doglegged alignment.

The current Morrison is, like the nearby Burnside, a bascule-style draw bridge, flat on top to allow the two halves of its centermost span to tilt upward as ships pass underneath. The draw bridge is powered by the largest mechanical device in Oregon, with two 950-ton counterweights hidden within the wooden supports bookending the Morrison's center arch. The bridge was designed by St. Louis engineering firm Sverdrup & Parcel, which was also responsible for the Superdome in New Orleans. Co-founder Leif Johan Sverdrup was the US Army's chief engineer in the Pacific during World War II.

The Morrison Bridge's west-side ramps occupy the sites of two historically significant nineteenth-century buildings. To the south, where cars begin exiting downtown, stood the Italianate-style Esmond Hotel, which within months of its 1880 completion hosted President Rutherford B. Hayes. This was the first time a sitting White House occupant had visited Portland, and came four years after Hayes had won the presidency in a disputed vote that involved one of Oregon's electors. In exchange for Democratic Party nominee Samuel J. Tilden accepting defeat, Hayes, the Republican, agreed to the Compromise of 1877, which led to the dismantling of numerous Reconstruction-era racial reforms.

Where I'm standing now, beside the Morrison Bridge's northwest off-ramp, was a modest two-story mercantile building where the first Black-owned business in Portland was located. Brothers Abner Hunt Francis and Isaac B. Francis had grown up as free men in New Jersey, then worked as clothiers in Buffalo, New York, while Abner found his voice as a writer and activist. He became a contributor to *The Liberator*, abolitionist William Lloyd Garrison's newspaper, and in 1848 addressed the national antislavery convention alongside Frederick Douglass.

In 1851, the Francis brothers and Abner's wife Sydna migrated west and opened a mercantile store here, to challenge laws passed in 1844 and 1849 by Oregon's territorial government forbidding settlement by Black citizens. Just a few weeks after the store's opening, Abner was arrested, and territorial associate justice Orville C. Pratt ordered the brothers to leave Oregon

*Francis brothers' store*

within four months. But the expulsion was not carried out because of a petition signed by more than two hundred white Portland residents, many of them appreciators of the brothers' place in the city as merchants and especially as tailors. An advertisement for their business in the *Oregon Weekly Times* describes "the best assortment of Dry Goods, Clothing, Fancy Articles, Perfumery, Toys, etc., ever offered in this city, and will sell at prices fully corresponding with the times." The ad goes on to list Hungarian cowhide boots, Colt revolvers, embroidered silks, and cashmere for sale.

Over the next few years, Isaac managed the store from day to day while Abner continued writing, including a series of letters published in Douglass's newspaper, the *North Star*. "Distance does not damp his zeal," Douglass wrote, "in the cause of his people's freedom and elevation." But then Isaac Francis died in 1856, and a year later, delegates to Oregon's constitutional convention submitted to voters a Black exclusion clause along with a proposed legalization of slavery. Voters disapproved of slavery by a wide margin but approved the clause. In 1861, Abner and Sydna relocated to Victoria, British Columbia, where the provincial government welcomed Black people as full citizens. Abner Francis died there in 1872, followed by Sydna in 1889. Meanwhile, Oregon's Black exclusion clause was never enforced, though there were several subsequent attempts to pass an accompanying enforcement law. The clause was rendered moot with the US Constitution's Fourteenth amendment, ratified in 1866, but was not officially repealed by the State of Oregon until 1926.

Today Portland is one of the country's least-racially-diverse large cities, with a Black population of just over 6 percent, suggesting that the state's nineteenth-century exclusion laws made a lasting impact. I feel a personal commitment to racial justice partly because one of my ancestors, Solomon Fitzhugh, was a delegate to Oregon's constitutional convention of 1857. Fitzhugh, though he built a respectable career as a judge, was privy to and probably a supporter of these reprehensible exclusion policies.

### *Down by the Water*

Now I've finally reached **Tom McCall Waterfront Park** (98 SW Naito Parkway), the front yard of downtown Portland. Its

*Tom McCall Waterfront Park*

30 acres stretches for a mile, from the RiverPlace marina to the Steel Bridge. Opened to the public in 1978, this was perhaps the ultimate symbol of downtown Portland's rebirth, even more than Pioneer Courthouse Square. I've long enjoyed riding my bicycle along its seawall sidewalk, or occasionally just standing here and meditatively gazing out at the Willamette flowing by.

Initially called simply Waterfront Park, it was renamed in 1984 for Tom McCall, Oregon's popular former governor from 1967 to 1975, who was among the first leaders of his generation to advocate that Portland's downtown riverfront be devoted to public space. A Massachusetts native and the grandson of former governor and US congressman Samuel Walker McCall, he began his career (following US Navy service during World War II) as an *Oregonian* reporter and KGW radio news announcer. After an unsuccessful run for Congress in 1954, McCall scored his first election victory ten years later, becoming Oregon's secretary of state. In 1966 he defeated Robert Straub in the gubernatorial race. A moderate Republican who would seemingly be out of step with his party today, Governor McCall signed into law popular initiatives like 1967's Beach Bill declaring Oregon's coastal shores public land, 1971's Bottle Bill establishing container deposit, and 1973's Senate Bill 100, which created statewide benchmarks for city planning and growth management and enabled Portland to limit extensive sprawl.

A park along the downtown side of the Willamette had been first suggested by the Olmsted brothers in 1904. Frederick Law Olmsted Jr. and his stepbrother, John Charles Olmsted, had taken over the New York City landscape architecture firm founded by their father, Central Park designer Frederick Law Olmsted Sr., and over two generations they created more than seven hundred park designs and plans for cities across the nation. With plans proceeding for 1905's Lewis and Clark Centennial Exposition, local leaders brought John Charles Olmsted here to not only design the fairgrounds but also create a comprehensive city park plan. It was the time of the City Beautiful movement, when US and European cities, increasingly overcrowded following the Industrial Revolution and entering the age of the automobile, embraced public parks and grand boulevards. However, the younger Olmsted was prescient when, following a Portland visit, he wrote to his wife, "I have enjoyed my park reconnaissance very much as the landscape is fine and the possibilities for parks, as far as land is concerned, are excellent. But I fear the money will be deficient."

In 1912, city planner Edward Bennett's Greater Portland Plan called for the riverfront park recommended by Olmsted, which voters approved later that year. Yet little action resulted. Instead, in 1923, the city widened Front Avenue, then built a new seawall and a public market between the Hawthorne and Morrison Bridges. The Public Market Building opened in 1933, with a hundred shops, three hundred produce stalls and two miles of counters. In 1940, voters approved a new six-lane riverfront expressway beside it, Harbor Drive, completed two years later and then widened in 1950.

During the late 1960s, activists began campaigning for the long-discussed waterfront greenway. In the summer of 1969, a group called Riverfront For People staged a series of so-called family picnics in the median strip between Harbor Drive's six lanes of traffic, with hundreds participating. The following year, the Public Market Building was demolished and city council resolved to phase out Harbor Drive, which had become expendable following construction of the nearby Stadium Freeway

(I-405). Harbor Drive finally closed for good in 1974 and planning began for the park.

ZGF Architects and San Francisco landscape architecture firm Royston, Hanamoto, Beck & Abey created three potential development schemes. The first, drawing from the Olmsted tradition, consisted primarily of trees, grass, and walkways. The second scheme featured a theater and exhibition hall in addition to open space. The third made the park more of a commercial center like Ghirardelli Square in San Francisco. Extensive public outreach showed most favored the first scheme, the simplest and most explicitly park-like.

After its 1978 dedication, Waterfront Park was expanded in both directions. South of the Hawthorne Bridge, a lawn-covered amphitheater was added, where popular events like the Waterfront Blues Festival now take place annually. In 1988, city council approved a northern extension of the park beyond the Burnside Bridge into Old Town (where the Japanese American Historical Plaza is now located). That same year, Salmon Street Springs was completed beside the Hawthorne Bridge, a popular attraction designed by Robert Perron Landscape Architects and Planners, able to send about 5,000 gallons of water per minute into the air from 137 ground-based jets.

Part of what makes Waterfront Park so successful is its flexibility and lack of clutter. "As soon as the park was built, the city was getting proposals from people who wanted to put in memorial trees and shrines and benches," recalls John Nelson, a retired land use planner and landscape architect whose firm, Mitchell Nelson Group, consulted on Waterfront Park's design. "How do you address that? People didn't want it to look like a grandmother's attic with stuff everywhere. The thought was, 'We have to leave it as a park for the people, and big enough to accommodate celebrations, and when it's not being used it's a green lawn rather than this collection of components that have no relation to each other."

This flexibility allows a succession of events to be held there each year and, at other times, fosters a surprising calm. During Cinco de Mayo in May, Rose Festival in June, and the Waterfront Blues Fest each July, Tom McCall Waterfront Park is teeming with people. There have been numerous political gatherings here too. Tens of thousands came to at a rally for then-presidential candidate Barack Obama on May 19, 2008. Valarie and I were part of an estimated 100,000 at the Women's March on January 21, 2017, one day after the first inauguration of President Donald Trump.

Waterfront Park can also feel relatively empty if not oddly isolated at times. The adjacent multilane Naito Parkway seems to discourage the restaurants, bars, and shops that would increase activity. In recent years there have been calls to redesign Tom McCall Waterfront Park to add myriad individual new spaces. A new outdoor spectator venue is being built into the natural bowl between the Hawthorne Bridge and RiverPlace, and a skate park planned for the north end. Besides proposed small interventions like playgrounds, pop-up markets and picnic areas, more ambitious ideas include pedestrian-only green streets or even a canal leading from the park into downtown, or removing a portion of the sea wall to enable kayaking, swimming, or even a water taxi that could carry passengers to Sellwood, Milwaukie, or St. Johns. "Incremental thinking is not gonna get us there," PSU architecture professor Jeff Schnabel told me for a recent *Portland Monthly* article about reinventing Waterfront Park. "The bigger ideas are the ones that capture people's imaginations." But funding is limited. And besides: I don't think Waterfront Park's success must be measured by its always being full. I like that it's possible to find solitude here along with boisterous crowds, just as Oregon Coast beaches may often be nearly empty compared to sunny Southern California oceanfront areas yet are no less beloved. Ultimately this wonderful waterside greenspace is a blank canvas onto which we project our desires, ambitions and moods.

The lone work of architecture within the park's confines is the **Rose Building** (1020 SW Naito Parkway). Designed by one of Portland's greatest Modernist architects, John Yeon, it has served many purposes over time. The building was completed as 1949 as the Portland Visitors Information Center for the local chamber of commerce, then converted to city offices in 1965. It operated as a restaurant called McCall's Waterfront Café from 1988 to 2005, spent five years empty, then in 2010 became the headquarters for the Rose Festival Foundation, as denoted by a neon rose on its roof. "We get people who think it's

*Rose Building*

still a restaurant," Marilyn Clint, the Rose Festival Foundation's recently retired CEO, told me in a 2021 interview. "They'll walk in and go, 'Can I get a table?'"

Yeon began his career working alongside his friend Pietro Belluschi in the office of architect A. E. Doyle. Together they fell under the influence of one of Doyle's former clients, Portland Art Museum educator Harry Wentz, whose cabin near Manzanita on the Oregon Coast provided Yeon and Belluschi the template for what became the Northwest Modern style of house design. Yeon went on to design 1937's masterful Aubrey Watzek House, which within a year of its completion was featured at New York's Museum of Modern Art in an exhibit called

*Art In Our Time*, alongside Frank Lloyd Wright's internationally renowned Fallingwater.

Yeon's Portland Oregon Visitors Center is a modest little aluminum-clad building that even the architect believed was not meant to stand the test of time. Yet it too attracted the Museum of Modern Art's attention, for a 1952 exhibit called *Built in USA: Post-War Architecture*, alongside the work of legendary architects like Wright, Charles and Ray Eames, Ludwig Mies van der Rohe, and Alvar Aalto. The Visitors Center would be his only public building, and Yeon, who was independently wealthy, eventually left architecture, instead designing museum exhibits and leading a campaign to create the Columbia River Gorge National Scenic Area. A 2017 Portland Art Museum retrospective curated by Randy Gragg celebrated the breadth of Yeon's life, as a talented architect and as a crusader for protecting Oregon's beautiful places.

The Rose Building comprises four pavilions surrounding a central courtyard. The façade alternates floor-to-ceiling glass and panes of plywood to frame views of the river and shield visitors from the then-adjacent Harbor Drive. Today there is not the same wide-open feel, for spaces are now divided by partitioning walls, but they stop short of the clerestory windows, so the rooms are still full of natural light. For a select few senior leaders of the organization, the glass-ensconced corner offices are an amenity unto themselves—and an opportunity for matchless people-watching.

"I can tell the weather in Portland without looking at the sky," said Clint. "I can tell because the park starts to fill up with people—on their bikes and skateboards, out running, or doing their exercise classes. It's amazing. I try not to look out the window all the time, but nobody can tell that I can see them, so they're being themselves, and it's almost like this glimpse into somebody's private life. You do kind of learn to look away from it to a certain extent, but then there are times when you can't look away. Sometimes it's stuff you absolutely don't want to see. And that happens every week. Sometimes the situation is unsavory or unsafe and you feel threatened by it. Other times it's just humbling."

For much of 2020 and 2021, while the building sat mostly empty during the pandemic, the Rose Building's windows were covered with plywood, as a preemptive measure because of the nearby social-justice protests and unrest. Yet Clint still came to work during that period instead of working from home. When the plywood coverings were taken down, she learned to appreciate Yeon's design all the more. "It's not just that there is light and views. It's all of the different *kinds* of light that comes into this building, whether it's the late afternoon light or the morning light," she told me. "It made me realize how much I crave that light."

That the Rose Festival Foundation occupies the former Visitors Center is appropriate, not just because each summer Waterfront Park is taken over by carnival rides and food vendors as a centerpiece of the two-week event. If Tom McCall Waterfront Park itself brings people together, so too does Rose Festival, which dates to 1904. Georgiana Pittock, wife of Oregon publisher Henry Pittock, founded the Portland Rose Society in 1888 as a flower show and fundraiser held in her back yard. As crowds grew for the annual event, it transitioned into a public exhibition and, beginning in 1907, included the Grand Floral Parade—Oregon's largest single-day spectator event. I remember attending the parade beginning in the 1970s as a young child, arriving before dawn with my mom to claim a spot by the curb and delighting as a succession of flower-festooned floats and marching bands went by; in 2016 I was invited to march in the parade, as part of the Friends of Memorial Coliseum.

The last stop, which will also begin my journey home, is the circa-1910 **Hawthorne Bridge** (SW Naito Parkway at Madison Street). I've traveled over it more than any other Portland bridge, and probably more than any other in the world. It's also perhaps the only bridge I've crossed more often by bicycle and on foot than by car. The Hawthorne Bridge is Portland's busiest span for pedestrians and cyclists, in addition to the approximately 30,000 cars and trucks and 800 buses it carries each day. That's certainly true this evening, as I see a stream of people moving in both directions.

Although the St. Johns Bridge is arguably Portland's most beautiful (the city's only suspension bridge), it's too far north to be considered part of the central city. The Fremont Bridge is handsome too, but because it's a freeway, you can only cross it in a car (save for the once-yearly Providence Bridge Pedal). Tilikum Crossing, our newest bridge, is relatively handsome, but

Hawthorne Bridge

its lack of automobile access and its location in the South Waterfront district mean it's not very busy. That leaves the Hawthorne, which is aesthetically rugged and industrial, with its 244-foot twin steel towers and rectangular cage of crisscrossing trusses, but I think the more historic these big, heavy, early twentieth-century spans (including downtown's Steel and Broadway) become, the more people appreciate them.

Then there's the Hawthorne's hypnotic sound, which I can hear while standing here. When any vehicle drives across the bridge's steel grating (which replaced the original wood deck in 1945), there is a sustained low-register vibrating sound, almost like a musical instrument. In fact, for the Portland Institute for Contemporary Art's Time-Based Art Festival in 2011, Portland musician Tim DuRoche and Brooklyn artist Ed Purver created a large-scale multimedia work, using several microphones to capture and mix this sound. "The Hawthorne has incredible resonance, and I wanted others to be able to, instead of just going from point A to point B, perhaps consider stopping or slowing to discover and appreciate the everyday music that the bridge manifests," DuRoche told me for a 2011 *Portland Architecture* blog post. "So we processed the sound of several cars together to create a choral effect. What's unique is that the faster one drives, or the heavier the vehicle's load (say, a TriMet bus), the more that pitch and its fundamental harmonic are accentuated."

Sitting lower on the river than any other downtown span, the Hawthorne also comes with the most drawbridge openings: about two hundred a month. In fact, the Hawthorne is regularly raised even when there's no river traffic; it must happen every eight hours to keep the cables and lift mechanism properly lubricated. There are lift moratoriums for two hours each morning and afternoon during rush hour, yet otherwise, river vessels have the right of way because Multnomah County follows the principle that the river was here before the bridges, meaning one person on a sailboat, or one industrial barge, can hold up scores of automobiles.

This is the third Hawthorne Bridge on this site. The first, opened in 1891, was a wooden swing-span called the Madison Street Bridge. It was replaced in 1900 by another swing-span of the same name (the city's last wooden bridge), and also lasted only about a decade, irrevocably damaged by a 1902 fire that claimed several blocks east of the river. Another five years went by before the city passed a bond funding a new steel-framed Hawthorne Bridge. In 1907, a delegation of local government and business leaders visited Chicago to see its many movable bridges and were impressed by the South Halsted Street bridge, the world's first vertical-lift span, which (though it had experienced many mechanical problems) opened and closed faster than any of Portland's bridges.

This bridge was named for Dr. James C. Hawthorne, who in 1861 co-founded the Pacific Northwest's first facility for the mentally ill, the Oregon Hospital for the Insane (also known as the Hawthorne Asylum), near present-day Southeast Twelfth Avenue and Salmon Street. A Pennsylvania native, Dr. Hawthorne had come to East Portland (then a separate city) in 1856 from California, where he had served two terms in the California State Senate. The asylum's 1863 patient population of 63 grew to 327 by 1881, receiving inmates from throughout the region. Hawthorne and his business partner, Dr. A. M. Loryea, were inspired by reformer Dorothea Dix, who visited the facility and gave it high marks. They were some of the first doctors in

Oregon to use surgical anesthesia. Mental health care was still a relatively young discipline, and while many patients suffered from serious cases, an 1880 audit showed that 43 percent of the asylum's patients were foreign-born, compared to just 17 percent of the general population, suggesting misdiagnoses. Dr. Hawthorne campaigned for the first bridge in this location, but died in 1881. The Hawthorne Asylum remained in operation until 1883, when the state opened its own facility in Salem. In 1888, the empty asylum was destroyed by fire.

When the present-day Hawthorne Bridge opened in 1910, its lift-span towers surpassed the height of any local building. The bridge's vertical-lift system elevates a middle portion of the grated roadway between the towers straight up, rather than the bascule style of the Morrison and Burnside. A system of counterweights and cables lifts the span up and down, including a pair of blocky 450-ton counterweights residing (in non-lifting mode) at the top of the towers.

In 1998, just a year after Valarie and I moved to Portland and only a few weeks after we relocated to an apartment near Southeast Hawthorne Boulevard, the Hawthorne Bridge was closed for a yearlong series of upgrades, including widened walkways. But we have since spent nearly three decades living near the bridge, which connects us to downtown like an umbilical cord. When stopped by one of its frequent drawbridge lifts, the enforced timeout, initially irritating, soon can feel meditative, prompting a gaze looking out at the moving water, toward the skyline, or even straight down. Once, while stopped, I remember getting out of my car, and shooting video through the Hawthorne's honeycomb-like steel grating of the river flowing below.

Now as I leave downtown at the blue hour just before sunset, I realize that even after one hundred stops, I've only begun to share the Portland I know. After all, there are so many more neighborhoods to see beyond the central city. Perhaps these can be my destinations in future books. In the meantime, I'd better get going, before the bridge's lift mechanism kicks into gear again. With one last glance out at the Willamette River, I'm heading east on Hawthorne Boulevard, to a little house near Mt. Tabor Park where Valarie and our cat Jenny await.

Acknowledgments

Gratitude begins and ends with my wife, Valarie Smith. Over the course of my entire career, but especially as I wrote and revised *In Search of Portland* during the past eight years, she has been my trusted editor, supporter, and confidante. Valarie brings out the best in me.

Thanks also to my parents, Don and Shirley Libby, for introducing me to Portland and many of its landmarks when I was a child, and for instilling in me a spirit of exploration.

I'm grateful to Tom Booth, the recently retired director of OSU Press, who was one of the first people to believe in my book; to Zach Dundas, a trusted writer-editor colleague who provided feedback as the manuscript initially took shape; and to friends Neil Griffiths, Becca Werlin, and Tim McCormick for editing assistance as I neared the finish line. I appreciate the illustrations that Nicolai Kruger created for this book, the maps by Lisa Holmes, and the cover design by Nora McKelvey.

Thank you to community radio station XRAY FM for producing my 2019–2021 podcast, also called In Search of Portland, where I road-tested parts of this manuscript and conducted more interviews. Additional thanks goes to readers of my Portland Architecture blog, where in 2017 I first began writing about revisiting places of architectural, cultural, and personal significance.

I am grateful to longtime friends like Paul Wolff and Chad Clark for encouraging me to trust my instincts and think like an artist. I also appreciate the support and encouragement of my sister Sara LaPietra, my sister-in-law Chris Guro, as well as my friends Joel Dunn, Reese Sterett, Nathan Cooprider, Ned Howard, Michael McHenry, Stuart Emmons, Avantika Bawa, Barb McClendon and Glenn Sanders.

Finally, sometimes nothing is better than having a purring cat on your lap. Thank you to Ruthie and Jenny for many years of unconditional love.

# Bibliography


Abbott, C. "Benjamin Stark (1820–1898)." *Oregon Encyclopedia*, August 8, 2024.

Abbott, C. *Portland in Three Centuries: The Place and the People*. Oregon State University Press, 2011.

Abbott, C. *Portland: Politics, Planning and Growth in a Twentieth-Century City*. University of Nebraska Press, 1983.

Baer, Adam. "The Wi-Fi Boom; Out and About, and Online." *The New York Times*, December 12, 2002.

Ballestrem, V. "In the Shadow of a Concrete Forest: Transportation Politics in Portland, Oregon, and the Revolt against the Mount Hood Freeway, 1955–1976." Master's thesis, Portland State University, 2009.

Ballestrem, V. *Lost Portland, Oregon*. The History Press, 2018.

Barbaro, M. "Ghosts in the Department Store." *The New York Times*, December 24, 2005.

Barnes, Tim. "C.E.S. Wood." *Oregon Encyclopedia*, May 31, 2023.

Bernstein, M. "Daughter of Mercy Corps Co-founder Seeks up to $54 Million in Punitive Damages against Global Charity." *The Oregonian*, March 7, 2024.

Bertram, N. "Tales from the Bill Walton Beat: Remembering a One-of-a-Kind Trail Blazers Great." *Oregonian*, May 31, 2024.

Bingham, E., and T. Barnes, eds. *Wood Works: The Life and Writings of Charles Erskine Scott Wood*. Oregon State University Press, 1997.

Blalock, B. *Portland's Lost Waterfront: Tall Ships, Steam Mills and Sailors' Boardinghouses*. The History Press, 2012.

Blanc, M., and P. Bashe. *That's Not All Folks*. Warner Books, 1988.

Bonner, E. "Major Events in Portland Planning History: Pioneer Courthouse Square." Portland State University, Ernie Bonner Collection, 2004.

Breslin, J. *Mark Rothko: A Biography*. University of Chicago Press, 1993.

Campbell, E. *Portland's Audacious Champion: How Bill Naito Overcame Anti-Japanese Hate and Became an Intrepid Civic Leader*. Oregon State University Press, 2024.

Casey, H. *Portland's Compromise: The Colored School—1867–1872*. Portland Public Schools Public Information Department, 1980.

Chamberlin, J. "Inside Indie Bookstores: Powell's Books in Portland, Oregon." *Poets & Writers*, March 1, 2010.

Chambers, J. *Abigail Scott Duniway and Susan B. Anthony in Oregon: Hesitate No Longer*. The History Press, 2018.

Clark, R. *Architecture, Oregon Style*. City of Albany, Oregon, 1983.

Clausen, M. *Pietro Belluschi: Modern American Architect*. Massachusetts Institute of Technology, 1994.

Comerford, J. *Sam Naito Interview*. Densho Digital Archive / Oregon Nikkei Endowment Collection, 2003.

Craghead, A. *Railway Palaces of Portland, Oregon: The Architectural Legacy of Henry Villard*. The History Press, 2016.

Crawford, A. "Is This the Dirtiest Song of the Sixties?" *New Yorker*, May 6, 2015.

DePaola, Amy-Xiaoshi. "Burnside Bridge Replacement Project Delays Construction Deadline to 2028." *KGW*, March 20, 2025.

Dietsche, R. *Jumptown: The Golden Years of Portland Jazz, 1942–1957*. Oregon State University Press, 2005.

Dundas, Z. "How Ace Changed the International Hotel Design Game." *Portland Monthly*, October 5, 2015.

Egan, T. "Threats and Responses: The Reaction in Portland; A Mixed Picture of Oregon Suspects." *The New York Times*, October 5, 2002.

Escamilla, M. "The Governor Hotel Building Marks 100 Years." *Oregonian*, April 23, 2009.

Gaston, J. *Portland, Oregon, Its History and Builders*. S.J. Clarke Publishing, 1911.

Gorsek, C. *Portland's Pearl District*. Arcadia Publishing, 2012.

Gragg, R. *John Yeon: Architecture*. University of Oregon John Yeon Center, 2017.

Gragg, R. *Where the Revolution Began: Lawrence and Anna Halprin and the Reinvention of Public Space*. Spacemaker Press, 2009.

Haneckow, D. "Mark Twain in Portland." *Café Unknown*, February 26, 2012.

Hawkins, K. "Abner Hunt 'A. H.' Francis (c. 1812–1872) and Isaac 'I. B.' Francis (1798–1856)." *Oregon Encyclopedia*, March 11, 2022.

Hawkins, W. *The Grand Era of Cast-Iron Architecture in Portland*. Binford & Mort, 1976.

Helphand, K. *Lawrence Halprin*. University of Georgia Press, 2017.

Hills, T. *The Many Lives of the Crystal Ballroom*. McMenamins Pubs & Breweries, 1997.

Hoeltje, H. "When Mark Twain Spoke in Portland." *Oregon Historical Quarterly*, March 1954.

Hood, J. "President Grant's Revealing Choice." *Carolina Journal*, October 2011.

Hutchinson, P. "So Good at Being Bad: Mayo Methot Was Far More Than Just the Third Mrs. Bogart." *Sight and Sound* 35, no. 1 (2024–2025).

Jahn, J. "Rothko's Portland." *PORT*, June 17, 2009.

John, F. *Wicked Portland: The Wild and Lusty Underworld of a Frontier Seaport Town*. The History Press, 2012.

Kelley, R. *Thelonious Monk: The Life and Times of an American Original*. Free Press, 2010.

King, B. *An Architectural Guidebook to Portland*. 2nd ed. Oregon State University Press, 2007.

Lacher, G., and S. Stone. *Theatres of Portland*. Arcadia Publishing, 2009.

Lansing, J. *Portland: People, Politics and Power, 1851–2001*. Oregon State University Press, 2005.

Levinson, J. "Newly Un-Redacted Report Shows How Feds Politicized Response to 2020 Portland Protests." Oregon Public Broadcasting, 2022.

Libby, B. "A First Glimpse Inside PNCA's Schnitzer Center for Art & Design." *Portland Architecture*, January 22, 2015.

Libby, B. "Allied Works' Renovated Oregonian Building Will Be a Showstopper." *Portland Architecture*, July 25, 2016.

Libby, B. "A Nation Challenged: Security; A Terrorism Comment in Oregon Prompts a Comedy of Errors." *The New York Times*, January 20, 2002.

Libby, B. "A Neo-Modernist Is Having His Moment." *The New York Times*, January 12, 2003.

Libby, B. "A Peek Inside the US Custom House as It Undergoes Renovation." *Portland Architecture*, February 21, 2013.

Libby, B. "A Postmodern Predicament." *Architect*, September 19, 2017.

Libby, B. "A Renovation Saves Michael Graves' Portland Building." *Metropolis*, October 13, 2020.

Libby, B. "A Return Visit to Lan Su, Portland's Classical Chinese Garden." *Portland Architecture*, October 18, 2012.

Libby, B. "Beyond the Bowtie: A Conversation with 'Shaping Portland' Author Paddy Tillett (Part Two)." *Portland Architecture*, January 8, 2018.

Libby, B. "Block 216." *In Search of Portland* podcast. XRAY FM, December 15, 2020.

Libby, B. "Can an Art Collector Save a Portland Ruin?" *CityLab*, December 22, 2014.

Libby, B. "Centennial Mills." *In Search of Portland* podcast. XRAY FM, January 27, 2021.

Libby, B. "Central Library." *In Search of Portland* podcast. XRAY FM, August 25, 2019.

Libby, B. "Creating Creative Class: Wieden + Kennedy's John C. Jay." *Oregon Business*, February 2007.

Libby, B. "Cultural Incubator: Visiting the Lumber Room." *Portland Architecture*, May 28, 2010.

Libby, B. "Dreamers + Builders: The Portland Architecture/Design Scene's Stars." *Oregonian*, February 26, 2008.

Libby, B. "Duke! Diz! Satchmo! Trane!" *Willamette Week*, December 11, 2001.

Libby, B. "Edith Green–Wendell Wyatt Federal Building, Designed by Cutler Anderson Architects." *Architect*, September 16, 2013.

Libby, B. "Experiment in the Desert." *Christian Science Monitor*, February 14, 2003.

Libby, B. "Far from New York and Loving It." *Christian Science Monitor*, November 1, 2002.

Libby, B. "Follow the LEEDer." *Metropolis*, July 14, 2008.

Libby, B. "Framing the Rothko Pavilion." *Oregon ArtsWatch*, August 27, 2023.

Libby, B. "Hawthorne and Morrison, Ready for Their Close-Up: Tim DuRoche on 'The Hidden Life of Bridges' at TBA Fest." *Portland Architecture*, September 8, 2011.

Libby, B. "In Portland, Ore., One Project with 2 Styles Reflects Its Neighborhood." *The New York Times*, June 12, 2018.

Libby, B. "Interview with an Emerging Architect." *Architecture Week*, January 2, 2002.

Libby, B. "John Montague's 'Willamette Greenway' at Nine Gallery: The Spirit of Place." *Oregon ArtsWatch*, October 26, 2024.

Libby, B. "Keller Auditorium: Renovate or Replace?" *Oregon ArtsWatch*, September 12, 2022.

Libby, B. "KOIN Center." *In Search of Portland* podcast. XRAY FM, October 7, 2019.

Libby, B. "Ladd Carriage House." *In Search of Portland* podcast. XRAY FM, December 29, 2020.

Libby, B. "Late Mid-Century Modern, New Century: The Portland Plaza after Its 10-Year, $10 Million Renovation." *Portland Architecture*, August 29, 2018.

Libby, B. "Lincoln Hall." *In Search of Portland* podcast. XRAY FM, July 29, 2019.

Libby, B. "Long Gone Blonde." *Portland Monthly*, October 14, 2011.

Libby, B. "Making It More: Holst Architecture's Dave Otte, John Holmes and Jeff Stuhr Discuss Bud Clark Commons." *Portland Architecture*, June 27, 2011.

Libby, B. "Mercy Corps Building." *In Search of Portland* podcast. XRAY FM, August 5, 2019.

Libby, B. "Notes from a Centennial Mills Forum." *Portland Architecture*, January 28, 2016.

Libby, B. "Pioneer Courthouse Square." *In Search of Portland* podcast. XRAY FM, June 23, 2021.

Libby, B. "Portland Art Museum." *In Search of Portland* podcast. XRAY FM, July 22, 2019.

Libby, B. "PSU's Sergio Palleroni on Creating the Nation's First Center for Public Interest Design." *Portland Architecture*, May 28, 2013.

Libby, B. "Requiem for the St. Francis Hotel." *Willamette Week*, December 5, 2001.

Libby, B. "Returning to Its Roots." *Metropolis*, March 1, 2006.

Libby, B. "Riverfront Revamp." *Portland Monthly*, Summer 2026.

Libby, B. "Shops and Sweets in Portland, Ore." *The New York Times*, March 9, 2014.

Libby, B. "Super-Sustainable Addition to Business School Quickly Becomes Center of Portland State Campus." *Metropolis*, August 31, 2018.

Libby, B. "St. Francis Hotel." *In Search of Portland* podcast. XRAY FM, September 2, 2019.

Libby, B. "The Architect's Questionnaire: Thomas Robinson." *Portland Architecture*, December 30, 2012.

Libby, B. "The Armory." *In Search of Portland* podcast. XRAY FM, August 20, 2019.

Libby, B. "The Art of Compromise." *Metropolis*, January 1, 2007.

Libby, B. "The Elk Statue." *In Search of Portland* podcast. XRAY FM, February 22, 2021.

Libby, B. "The Portland Building." *In Search of Portland* podcast. XRAY FM, August 12, 2019.

Libby, B. "Two Portland Art Museum Architects, Two Divergent Fates." *Portland Architecture*, August 10, 2010.

Libby, B. "Whitney and Gray Building." *In Search of Portland* podcast. XRAY FM, September 30, 2019.

Libby, B. "Wieden + Kennedy Agency World Headquarters." *In Search of Portland* podcast. XRAY FM, September 9, 2019.

McCann, I. "Louie Louie—Why the Influential Garage Classic Was Investigated by the FBI." *Financial Times*, October 8, 2018.

Monk, M. *The Portland Red Guide: Sites & Stories of Our Radical Past*. Ooligan Press, 2007.

Morris, C. "The People's Theater at Portland." *Motography*, November 1911.

Murphy, J. "Thomas Hacker, One of Oregon's Most Influential Architects, Died at 81." *Architect's Newspaper*, April 4, 2023.

Niles, P. *Beauty of the City: A.E. Doyle, Portland's Architect*. Oregon State University Press, 2008.

Norman, J. *Portland's Architectural Heritage: National Register Properties of the Portland Metropolitan Area*. Oregon Historical Society, 1986.

Olsen, P. *Stories from Jewish Portland*. The History Press, 2011.

Palahniuk, C. *Fugitives and Refugees: A Walk in Portland, Oregon*. Crown Journeys, 2003.

Paletta, A. "A Glass Addition by Vinci Hamp Architects and Hennebery Eddy Adds Contrast to the Portland Art Museum's Original Masonry." *Architect's Newspaper*, December 2, 2025.

Perry, D. "Battle of the Park Blocks at 50: How a Shocking Burst of Violence Defined Portland—and Panicked Nixon's White House." *Oregonian*, May 4, 2020.

Perry, D. "Martin Luther King Jr. Challenged Oregonians 60 Years Ago to Find a Way to Live Together—'or Perish as Fools.'" *Oregonian*, January 18, 2021.

Perry, D. "Rajneeshees Embraced Portland, Opening Wild Nightclub, Hotel That Became Bomber's Target." *Oregonian*, April 2, 2018.

Prichep, D. "'Louie Louie': The Story behind the Song Everyone Knows but No One Understands." *NPR*, October 31, 2023.

Radon, L. "27 Installations: Portland Center for the Visual Arts." Dill Pickle Club Publication Studio, 2011.

Ritz, R. *Architects of Oregon*. Lair Hill Publishing, 2002.

Russell, M. "The Red Coach Flips Its Last Burger after 55 Years in Downtown Portland." *Oregonian*, April 1, 2014.

Schults, Carol. "Jacqueline Schumacher (1920–2019)." *Oregon Encyclopedia*, August 23, 2023.

Slade, E., and J. Elkington. "Minor White Captures the Ornate Beauty of Portland's Past." *Oregon Public Broadcasting*, November 16, 2017.

Thompson, E. *Smashing Statues: The Rise and Fall of America's Public Monuments*. W.W. Norton, 2022.

Tillett, P. *Shaping Portland: Anatomy of a Healthy City*. Routledge, 2018.

Vaughn, T., and G. McMath. *A Century of Portland Architecture*. Oregon Historical Society, 1967.

Vigdor, N., and A. Traub. "Three Women Accuse Gordon Sondland of Sexual Misconduct, Report Says." *The New York Times*, November 27, 2019.

Williams, L. "Darcelle XV Turns 50 amid a Drag Scene It Helped Go Mainstream." *Oregonian*, September 18, 2017.

Wolfe, T. "The Copper Goddess." *Newsweek*, July 1986.

Woods, Jim. "Jap Leader Here Paid by Tokyo." *Oregon Journal*, March 30, 1942.

# Original Interviews

Beebe, Jane (owner of PDX Contemporary Art), October 2019.
Bernal, Tony (principal at Transition Projects), September 2020.
Bruder, Will (founder of Will Bruder Architects), November 2020.
Burmeister, Brett (food blogger), October 2019.
Chambers, Jennifer (author of *Abigail Scott Duniway and Susan B. Anthony in Oregon: Hesitate No Longer*), October 2019.
Clint, Marilyn (CEO of Rose Festival Foundation), December 2020.
Cloepfil, Brad (founder of Allied Works Architecture), October 2019.
Cohen, Jonathan (co-owner of Society Hotel), March 2021.
Cress, David (co-founder of Food Chain Films), November 2019.
Currier, Terry (owner of Music Millennium), January 2021.
Danadjieva, Angela (co-designer, Ira Keller Fountain), September 2019, November 2019, February 2020, March 2020.
Falsetto, Paul (founder of Paul M. Falsetto Architect LLC), April 2020.
Ferriso, Brian (director of Portland Art Museum), September 2025.
Gianola, Jeff (news anchor at KOIN), October 2019.
Graham, Sarah (co-founder of AGPS Architecture), January 2019.
Harrison, James (artist), January 2020.
Hawkins, William (architect and architectural historian), June 2020.
Hollins, Lionel (basketball player), January 2022.
Hubert, Sean (chief housing and strategy officer at Central City Concern), July 2020.
Hudson, Linda (program director of Imani Center), October 2020.
Jaquiss, Nigel (reporter at *Willamette Week*), July 2023.
Katz, Jesse (author/journalist, son of Vera Katz), April 2020.
Keltner, David (partner at Hacker Architects), November 2019.
Kook-Anderson, Grace (curator at Portland Art Museum), October 2019.
Kovel, Jeff (founder of Skylab Architecture), November 2019.
Lakeman, Mark (founder of Communitecture and City Repair Project), September 2020.
Leiken, David (owner of Roseland Theater, Double Tee Concerts), May 2021.
Lienhart, Nolan (principal at ZGF Architects), November 2020.
Liu, Rebecca (wife of Chinatown Gate founder Liu Chi), February 2021.
Margles, Judith (director of Oregon Jewish Museum), October 2020.
McConnell, Brian (manager of Jake's Famous Crawfish), October 2019.
Naito-Campbell, Erica (author of *Portland's Audacious Champion*), February 2019.
Nelson, John Allan (president of Mitchell Nelson Group LLC), August 2020.

Niles, Philip (author, *Beauty of the City: A. E. Doyle, Portland's Architect*), October 2019.

O'Neil, Dan (co-founder of Mercy Corps), November 2019.

Paley, Vitaly (chef), September 2020.

Pederson, William (partner at Kohn Pederson Fox), June 2020.

Penkin, Stanley (chair of Pearl District Neighborhood Association), October 2020.

Powell, Michael (co-founder of Powell's City of Books), February 2019.

Rauschenberg, Christopher (photographer, co-founder of Blue Sky Gallery), August 2020.

Robinson, Thomas (founder of Lever Architecture), November 2019.

Sandoval, Gene (partner at ZGF Architects), November 2019.

Scharf, Andrea (co-founder of Saturday Market), April 2019.

Schults, Carol (dance historian), July 2020.

Schultz, Kurt (principal at SERA Architects), October 2020.

Siegel, Matt (co-founder of Society Hotel), February 2021.

Signori, George (principal at Ankrom Moisan), December 2019.

Slappe, Stephen (associate professor at Pacific Northwest College of Art), October 2020.

Stuhr, Jeff (co-founder of HOLST Architecture), October 2019.

Thomas, Jeffrey (co-founder of Jamison/Thomas Gallery), April 2020.

Thomas, Maigen (senior UX designer at Syntellis Performance Solutions), October 2020.

Thompson, Robert (co-founder of TVA Architects), May 2020.

Tillett, Paddy (retired principal at ZGF Architects), October 2020.

Tingley, Michael (principal at Bora), October 2019.

Vaivoda, Ned (co-founder of TVA Architects), May 2020.

Van Sant, Gus (film director), September 2024.

Walker, David (partner at PWP Landscape Architecture), February 2020.

Walker, Peter (partner at PWP Landscape Architecture), February 2020.

Walton, Bill (basketball player and broadcaster), December 2021.

Weinheimer, Carla (retired principal, DLR Group), June 2021.

Weinstock, Bobby (housing placement specialist), October 2019.

Weyrens, Angela (librarian, Multnomah County Central Library), October 2019.